COMPLETE IDIOT'S GUIDE® TO

Managing People

Third Edition

by Arthur R. Pell, Ph.D.

ALPHA

A member of Penguin Group (USA) Inc.

This book is dedicated to my grandchildren: Benji, Caellan, and Duncan.

International Standard Book Number: 1-59257-145-X
Library of Congress Catalog Card Number: 2003111798

05   04   03   8   7   6   5   4   3   2   1

Interpretation of the printing code: The rightmost number of the first series of numbers is the year of the book's printing; the rightmost number of the second series of numbers is the number of the book's printing. For example, a printing code of 03-1 shows that the first printing occurred in 2003.

Printed in the United States of America

Note: This publication contains the opinions and ideas of its author. It is intended to provide helpful and informative material on the subject matter covered. It is sold with the understanding that the author and publisher are not engaged in rendering professional services in the book. If the reader requires personal assistance or advice, a competent professional should be consulted.

The author and publisher specifically disclaim any responsibility for any liability, loss, or risk, personal or otherwise, which is incurred as a consequence, directly or indirectly, of the use and application of any of the contents of this book.

Most Alpha books are available at special quantity discounts for bulk purchases for sales promotions, premiums, fund-raising, or educational use. Special books, or book excerpts, can also be created to fit specific needs.

For details, write: Special Markets, Alpha Books, 375 Hudson Street, New York, NY 10014.

Publisher: *Marie Butler-Knight*
Product Manager: *Phil Kitchel*
Senior Managing Editor: *Jennifer Chisholm*
Senior Acquisitions Editor: *Renee Wilmeth*
Development Editor: *Jennifer Moore*
Production Editor: *Billy Fields*
Copy Editor: *Tiffany Almond*
Illustrator: *Chris Eliopoulos*
Cover/Book Designer: *Trina Wurst*
Indexer: *Tonya Heard*
Layout/Proofreading: *Mary Hunt, Ayanna Lacey*

Contents at a Glance

Contents

Appendixes

Foreword

One of the things I like best about my job these days is the chance I have to interact with a wide range of interesting and very talented people from a variety of industries. Like many other consultants, it's not at all unusual to be working intensively with a group from, say, a manufacturing company one day, only to pack up and rush off for a meeting with a group from an aerospace company or a pharmaceutical company the next. Such is the life of a management consultant. And particularly those with specialties that tend to be generic and applicable to a broad audience.

Not long ago I was asked by a reporter to talk about the problems and challenges my clients seem to be concerned about the most these days. I've been asked similar questions many times before, but for some reason it suddenly dawned on me this time that my answer really hasn't changed very much in nearly 25 years! The simple fact is, despite the varied backgrounds of our best clients, and all of the wonderful training opportunities most of them have at their disposal, the one challenge that distresses them most still centers on the *managing of people*.

There's simply no doubt about it. It's not the economy, or the incredible pace of change, or the difficulties inherent in trying to stay a step ahead of the competition. It's *people* … and how best to *inspire* them, and *manage* them, and help them contribute even more to the major goals of the organization.

And as I say, it's a problem that's been around for as long as I can remember. It also respects no industry borders. Regardless of the kind of organization you work for, the story is the same. The day-to-day managing, motivating, and monitoring of people is a major and universal challenge, even for the very best and most seasoned of executives.

And that's why the new edition of *The Complete Idiot's Guide to Managing People* is such an important contribution to the business literature this year. Dr. Pell has provided a wonderfully rich and humorous "how-to" business guide, just *perfect* for every supervisor, manager, and senior executive struggling to lead a diverse workforce. Loaded with practical, easy-to-use advice and suggestions, he avoids all the usual temptations to get bogged down in theory, and instead delivers a smart, entertaining, no-holds-barred collection of principles and anecdotes of *real* and *lasting* value!

Managers and executives will learn all the latest techniques in effective team building, the motivating, and inspiring of employees, and how to deal positively and proactively with performance issues. They'll come to understand how to better organize their work and the work of others, and how to manage complex projects and solve complex organizational problems.

They'll also learn the latest in professional *coaching* techniques, and how these techniques are now being applied by skilled managers to build record levels of worker loyalty and stimulate even greater levels of innovation. Perhaps most importantly, they'll also discover how to build and sustain a truly positive and resilient *organizational culture*, based on high standards of performance, mutual trust, and a respect for others.

In my opinion, Dr. Pell's book belongs on every business bookshelf and in every business school library in the country. Why? Because it delivers something far too uncommon today in the business literature: a solid, no-nonsense look at how great managers and great organizations generate consistently terrific results through others … and how everyday people like you and me can do the very same thing.

If "people problems" are driving you a little wacky, look no further. You've found the cure!

Dr. Franklin C. Ashby is president of The Leadership Capital Group, LLC, a New York-based management consulting firm specializing in leadership, management development and executive coaching. Recognized as a leading authority on organizational effectiveness and improvement strategies, he was formerly an executive vice president of Manchester Partners International, the president of Manchester Training, and the vice president of instruction and chief educational officer of Dale Carnegie & Associates, Inc. Dr. Ashby is the author of *Revitalize Your Corporate Culture* (Butterworth Heinemann, 1999), and *Effective Leadership Programs* (ASTD Publishing, 1999), and the co-author of *Embracing Excellence* (Prentice Hall Press, 2001), recently named one of The 30 Best Business Books of the Year. He lives with his wife, Rita, and their son, Danny, in Smithtown, New York. His e-mail address is *FAshby1@optonline.net*

Introduction

Just as physicians must keep up with the state of the art in their specialties, lawyers with new laws and new interpretations of existing laws, and accountants with the changes in tax codes, so must managers at every level from the senior executives to the line supervisors or team leaders keep up with the art and science of effective management.

The world is changing, and management changes with it. Whether you're starting your first assignment as a supervisor or team leader or have years of experience, you have to keep up with these changes. Ideas that weren't even dreams a few years ago are now part and parcel of the corporate culture.

In this, the third edition of *The Complete Idiot's Guide to Managing People*, I'll talk about these concepts and much more. I'll not only describe them but also provide suggestions and examples of how you can apply them in the day-to-day situations you face on the job.

Your company may be organized in teams, in which you as the team leader are responsible for leading a group of collaborative associates in meeting the unit's goals. Or your organization may be structured in a more traditional format, where you, as a department manager and supervisor, may have a more authoritarian approach to accomplishing the mission. In either case, your goals can be achieved most successfully by understanding and applying the principles of managing people discussed in this book.

Here is a quick overview of what you will learn:

Part 1, "What It Takes to Be a Manager," explores how you can take advantage of the skills, brains, and creativity of every person on your staff. This part looks at the myths and misconceptions that have often dictated management style. Then it gets right into the pragmatic approaches to setting and implementing goals.

In **Part 2, "How to Talk the Talk,"** you'll learn how to develop channels of communication so that you can make sure that your ideas and instructions are understood and accepted by your staff members. You'll also learn how to delegate work and ensure that it actually gets done.

The ramifications of the equal employment opportunity (EEO) laws are discussed in **Part 3, "Following Labor and Equal Employment Laws."** This part of the book pays special attention to the latest developments in this area, including the Americans with Disabilities Act, how to avoid sexual harassment complaints, and the role of the team leader in affirmative action. It also presents a list of preemployment questions you can and cannot ask.

Part 4, "Staffing Your Organization," discusses the important issue of choosing team members who not only do the job but also fit in as part of your team. You'll also learn how to write realistic job specs, price the job, and locate hard-to-find personnel. In addition, you'll find out about 25 mistakes companies make in hiring and how you can avoid making them. You'll also pick up some practical tips on getting more valuable information from applicants at an interview.

In **Part 5, "Laying the Groundwork For Superior Perfomance,"** you'll learn about the practice of "on-boarding"—getting the new employee off on the right foot. In addition, you will pick up some training and development techniques and how to use top-level associates as mentors. This part also covers methods of motivating your people. Some of the issues discussed include money (does it really motivate?), incentive pay programs, recognition programs that work, and the special approaches, such as telecommuting and work/life programs, that companies use to retain good people.

No matter how good a leader you may be, there still will be people who don't make the grade, cause problems with you or other workers, or are always complaining and griping. In **Part 6, "Dealing with Employee Problems on the Job,"** you will learn how to deal with these situations and overcome the challenges of maintaining a top performing team.

Traditional and nontraditional disciplinary methods, up to and including termination, are explored in **Part 7, "The End of the Line."** This part also explores voluntary quits and reducing turnover. In addition, I pay special attention to layoffs and downsizing, including a discussion of the WARN law and the concept of "employment at will."

How to Make This Book Work for You

By using the following steps you will ensure that this book isn't just a reading exercise, but also a plan of action for you:

1. Create an action plan to implement what you've learned. After you read each chapter, indicate what action you will take, with whom you will take the action, and when you will begin.

2. Share your plan of action with your associates. Get them involved.

3. Set a follow-up date to check whether you did what you planned to do.

4. If not, reread the chapter, rethink what you did or didn't do, and make a new plan of action.

A Note on the Terminology

Because titles vary from company to company, in this book the titles *manager, supervisor,* and *team leader* are used interchangeably. Subordinates are referred to as *employees, associates, group members, staff members,* or *team members.*

Extras

The following boxed information will help you understand and implement the material in each chapter:

Words to Work By

Common and not-so-common management terms are defined in these boxes.

Stop! Look! Listen!

Learn from these common mistakes made by managers and save yourself time, money, energy, and embarrassment.

Now Hear This

These provide you with interesting tidbits about management and practical instructions for enhancing your management expertise.

Tactical Tools

These tips and techniques will help you implement some of the ideas you pick up in the book. Some of them come from the writings of management gurus, and others come from the experience of managers like you, who are happy to share them.

Special Thanks to the Technical Reviewer

The Complete Idiot's Guide to Managing People, Third Edition, was reviewed by an expert in the field who not only checked the technical accuracy of what you'll learn here but also provided insight and guidance to help us ensure that this book gives you everything you need to know to make the most of your management role. Special thanks are extended to Richard Beck.

Richard Beck has been a manager in the computer software industry for more than 20 years. Currently he is a senior executive for a large software development organization in New York City. He is a hands-on manager who has successfully dealt with the problems covered in this book on a day-to-basis. In addition, he has conducted seminars and workshops on both managerial and technical subjects in the United States and abroad.

Trademarks

All terms mentioned in this book that are known to be or are suspected of being trademarks or service marks have been appropriately capitalized. Alpha Books and Penguin Group (USA) Inc. cannot attest to the accuracy of this information. Use of a term in this book should not be regarded as affecting the validity of any trademark or service mark.

Part 1

What It Takes to Be a Manager

Managing people has become a lot more sophisticated over the past decades. Managers are dealing with a more sophisticated and better-educated staff. To get results, managers have to be leaders, who inspire and motivate employees to willingly cooperate and participate to achieve the goals of the team, the department, and the company.

Managing people isn't just using common sense. It takes planning, organizing, and directing a diverse group of human beings, each with his or her strengths and weaknesses. Good leaders learn to know the men and women they supervise and how to provide a climate in which staff members are encouraged to make their own analyses of problems, suggest solutions, and participate in decisions.

In this part of the book, we will lay the groundwork that will start you on the road to becoming a great leader.

Chapter 1

Don't Boss—Lead

In This Chapter

- ◆ The benefits of constructive discontent
- ◆ How to lead people
- ◆ Find out if you're a leader
- ◆ Thirteen traits of good leaders

The business world is changing at an unprecedented rate. Whole industries are born and extinguished—seemingly overnight. Companies that lead, anticipate, and benefit from these rapid changes succeed. Those who are unprepared, surprised, or overwhelmed by these changes, however, find themselves falling behind their competitors, and often fallen by the wayside.

Companies that fail to stay a step or two ahead of the competition do so in part because of complacency with the long established systems and procedures. Just as it is with companies, so it is with the people who manage those companies and the departments and teams within them. People tend to become slaves to the methods and techniques they have become accustomed to and are comfortable with.

To survive, however, managers and supervisors must overcome this complacency—get out of their rut, so to speak—by developing a habit of constructive discontent. They must continually examine the practices they are using, and if those practices are not achieving optimum results, they must change them. They, indeed, must become *leaders*—not *administrators*.

In this chapter we will look at what makes a great leader and how you can become one.

The True Leader

Let's start now by looking at what a leader really is.

There seems very little doubt anymore of the direct relationship between the leadership style exhibited most often within an organization and the effectiveness with which that same organization attracts and retains outstanding people.

According to a recent report by the Saratoga Institute, a management think tank, 50 percent of work-life satisfaction is determined by the relationship a worker has with his or her boss. Satisfaction with one's boss is a key factor in the department's success and the retention of good employees. Study after study has shown that a person-centered, visionary, value-based approach almost always works better than the often dictatorial, fear-based, heavy-handed strategies of the past.

Words to Work By

An **administrator** ensures that things are being done right. A **leader** ensures that the right things are being done.

Stop! Look! Listen!

By clinging to myths in the face of new realties, we close our minds to new ideas and viewpoints.

—Senator William Fulbright

This was reinforced by a Gallup poll that showed that most workers rate having a caring boss even higher than they value money or fringe benefits. In interviews with 2 million employees at 700 companies, Gallup found employee productivity and retention are strongly influenced by employees' relationships with their immediate supervisors. "People join companies and leave managers," said Marcus Buckingham, a senior managing consultant at Gallup and the primary analyst for the study.

Too often managers assume that their leadership style works well, when it doesn't work at all. Wondering whether your leadership style has any traction? Take the following leadership quiz to find out. It's a relatively easy way to help you focus on some of the key foundations of this very important topic.

The leadership quiz is based on more than 10 years of research and 50 years of combined training and consulting experience. Why not take out a pen and a piece of paper and jot down your answer to each question? My guess is you'll be surprised by at least a good part of what you learn.

The Leadership Quiz

Mark "True" or "False" next to each of the following statements:

True False

❑ ❑ 1. The most common characteristic among those recognized as outstanding leaders is an ability to inspire trust.

❑ ❑ 2. Good leaders most often emerge from the ranks of good followers.

❑ ❑ 3. Leadership ability is more often acquired than inborn.

❑ ❑ 4. The development and demonstration of leadership skills are most often inspired by a passion of some type.

❑ ❑ 5. The development of leadership skills is often inspired by some kind of misfortune, sacrifice, or injustice.

❑ ❑ 6. Most people with outstanding leadership ability consider themselves to be extroverted.

❑ ❑ 7. Companies are investing more money in training now than at any other time in U.S. history.

❑ ❑ 8. Working women, on average, tend to exhibit behaviors attributed to good leaders more frequently than working men.

❑ ❑ 9. More often than not, those acknowledged throughout history as great leaders had greatness thrust upon them (by some event).

❑ ❑ 10. The majority of people with outstanding leadership skills have above average IQs.

❑ ❑ 11. Outstanding leaders are often driven by a need to dominate.

❑ ❑ 12. Most great leaders in history emerged from humble beginnings.

Check Yourself Against These Answers

Question #1: **True.** People often get this one right. The literature has been filled with evidence of the need to restore faith and trust in management for a good long time now. In fact, one recent survey—a study involving 215 organizations—claimed that a shocking 75 percent of surveyed executives admitted that they felt that employees had less trust in management then they did when surveyed two years previously.

Question #2: **True.** Strong leaders *often* emerge from the ranks of loyal followers. According to organizational psychologists, such folks understand the importance of followership, and say they always felt that if they worked hard and remained loyal to their superiors that their day would come and they'd be suitably rewarded.

Question #3: **True.** While it's true that some people demonstrate an ability to lead at a very early age, most develop such skills over time and in response to leadership-related challenges and opportunities.

Question #4: **True.** According to research conducted for this book, 82 percent of surveyed executives who were identified as unusually strong leaders said they felt their leadership ability was inspired mostly by the *passion* they felt for a particular issue, cause, or objective. Among the items mentioned most frequently: a desire to excel, a strong desire to "right a wrong" or overcome some injustice, a competitive nature, sibling rivalry, or a deep-felt desire to please one or both parents.

Question #5: **True.** The answer to this question follows logically from question #4. The difference is the use of the words "misfortune," "sacrifice," and "injustice." Psychologists tell us that most people remain reasonably passive and content with their lives as long as the values and possessions they hold most dear aren't threatened. When something happens that disrupts or threatens one or more of these values, however, the response is often immediate and strong.

Now Hear This

Carolyn McCarthy is an excellent example of someone who overcame misfortune to become a leader. A homemaker and part-time nurse, Mrs. McCarthy had lived her entire life on Long Island with her family, when on December 7, 1993, her world was shattered. A crazed gunman shot and killed her husband and severely injured her son during an unprovoked rampage on a commuter train from Manhattan. After the horrendous experience, Carolyn discovered an inner strength that she never realized she had. She demonstrated tremendous courage during the ensuing police investigation, trial, and the ultimate conviction and sentencing of the killer. She became a passionate victim's rights advocate and lobbied for better gun control laws. In the fall of 1996, Carolyn McCarthy, the self-described quiet housewife from Mineola, was elected to Congress in one of the most thrilling and impressive shows of bilateral support in the history of the state.

Question #6: **False.** Nearly 65 percent of surveyed executives said that although they were aware others considered them outgoing and gregarious, they actually considered themselves to be introverted not extroverted. It's interesting to note that other informal studies I've conducted over the years have yielded similar results and may suggest that despite outward appearances, a high percentage of strong leaders are probably much more reserved and solitary—and less social—than we might suspect.

Question #7: **True.** A number of surveys have placed the estimates at between $60 billion and $100 billion a year, with expectations of continued growth in the range of 5 to 15 percent, per year, for the foreseeable future.

Question #8: **True.** In fact, a number of recent studies have suggested that working women, on average, demonstrate a far better command of key leadership skills than men, and that the gap may be widening. Among the abilities tested: listening skills, a values-based management style, consistency in decision-making, the ability to generate and sustain trust, and the ability to inspire and motivate.

Question #9: **True.** It does appear that the majority of people considered to be truly great leaders demonstrated their abilities during times of great crisis or uncertainty. Perhaps we all have vast quantities of untapped leadership potential that lies dormant until stimulated by some (often troubling) event or occurrence.

Question #10. **False.** Best-selling author, the psychologist Daniel Goleman, among others, has shown quite convincingly that although important, intelligence has much less to do with success in life, including success as a leader, than many of us previously thought. Dr. Goleman's findings suggest that emotional well-being and emotional maturity play the biggest role, followed by a number of other developmental considerations. The point here is that it's likely that many people, including trainers and educators, have placed too much emphasis on standard IQ testing as a predictor of success. Leaders can be found within a wide range of IQ scores, with some of the very best found toward the bottom of the "normal" ranges, and some of the worst toward the top.

Question #11. **False.** Research has consistently shown that truly great leaders are those most often driven by a desire to serve their fellow citizens, employees, or communities in some way, *not* to dominate.

Question #12. **True.** Sociologists and social psychologists have theorized that some measure of sacrifice growing up, and the discipline that sacrifice involved, may help stimulate creative abilities in children as well as greater resilience and a sustained ambition. According to researchers, these same qualities tend to be found less

Now Hear This

The superior leader is a cata-lyst and though things would not get done as well if he weren't there, when they succeed he takes no credit. And because he takes no credit, credit never leaves him.

—Lao Tzu, Chinese philosopher

Tactical Tools

To maintain high morale, improve productivity, and lower turnover, managers should encourage their staff members to express their ideas—even if they differ from company practices—without fear of reprisals.

frequently in people from extremely affluent and/or privileged families. Although there are many examples of leaders who came from prominent and wealthy families like the Kennedys, Rockefellers, and Bushes, a disproportionate number of today's outstanding business and political leaders still emerge from "blue collar" and "first generation" families. These leaders are noted for their strong family values and for their abilities to overcome challenging problems and other struggles.

The Changing Function of Leaders

As the dynamics of organizational culture have changed to keep up with the times and technology, so has the function of the leader. Leadership has been influenced by technological innovations, the ease and speed of communications, and, most important, the attitudes and psychology of the people who staff the organizations. A leader who once controlled by power now must coordinate and collaborate through persuasion and motivation.

The Thirteen Qualities of Truly Great Leaders

Although it's fair to say that most outstanding leaders have faced and overcome a multitude of diverse problems in their lives, they also exhibit many similar characteristics and behavior patterns. Let's take a look at them.

They Have Enthusiastic Followers

Of course, people in positions of authority can compel subordinates to follow orders. However, such people are not true leaders. Yes, the orders will be followed, but that is *all* that will happen. Instead, true leaders develop confidence and trust in their associates. Once trust is established, employees are usually happy to follow the lead of the manager, but they will also be more likely to initiate, innovate, and implement ideas of their own that fit into the company's goals.

Many business leaders have built up enthusiastic and loyal followers who put in extra hours,
sacrifice personal desires, and stretch their
thinking powers. When Steve Jobs was asked to
return to Apple Computer after the company

Tactical Tools
Consider the people on your staff as associates not subordinates.

had suffered a series of major setbacks, he agreed to do so with the understanding
that he wasn't interested in taking over the company but just to bring it back to profitability. He set an example by working day and night to turn the company around.
With a leader like that, managers at all levels pitched in and pushed the company
forward to achieve its goal—the development and marketing of the highly successful
iMac computer.

They Have Their Eyes and Ears Open for Ways to Improve

Good leaders aren't complacent. They're constantly on the alert for innovations that
will improve the way work is done, ensure continuing customer satisfaction, and
increase the profitability of the organization. Their minds are open to new ideas and
they welcome suggestions. Even after changes and improvements are made, they still
look for even better ways to accomplish their goals. Leaders like this are never fully
satisfied. They review practices and procedures on a regular basis to fine-tune them.
They don't fall in love with their own ideas. They are open to criticism and innovation.

They Consider Themselves a Work-in-Progress

Just as effective leaders are constructively discontent about their departments,
they are never entirely satisfied with themselves. They attend seminars and self-
improvement programs, purchase and listen to motivational tapes, read books and
periodicals to keep up their fields as well as areas outside their field.

Great leaders don't limit their talents to their jobs. They take active roles in professional and trade associations not only to keep in touch with new developments but to
share their ideas with colleagues from other organizations. They attend and participate in conventions and conferences and develop networks of people to whom they
can turn to obtain knowledge or ideas over the years.

They Excel When the Stakes Are High

We've all heard the old adage, "Leaders are made not born," and like most adages,
there is a great deal of truth in it. However, some people do seem to be born leaders.

From early childhood, they take the lead in playing games, are selected as team captains, are elected to student offices and take charge of everything in which they are involved. In some ways (at least according to their proud parents), they always seemed destined for big things in life. However, many of the greatest leaders were not born to greatness, but developed it when placed in leadership positions.

Now Hear This

History is replete with stories of ordinary men and women who rose to the heights when leadership was needed. Consider the story of Lech Walesa. In 1980, when the workers at the Lenin Shipyard in Gdansk, Poland, went on strike for better working conditions, the Communist government cracked down on them. Walesa was an electrician in the shipyard and one of the leaders of Solidarity, an independent trade union. He had little education and had never considered himself to be anything more than an artisan. But when his colleagues needed a leader, he spoke up for the striking workers. Despite several arrests and imprisonments, his leadership inspired the Polish people to work to overthrow the Communist regime. In 1983, he was awarded the Nobel Peace Price and in 1990 was elected president of Poland.

They Understand What Motivates People

Great leaders recognize the importance of being a motivating factor for people—appealing to the drives and the feelings of others. They take a genuine interest in the people with whom they interact. As Dale Carnegie once quipped, "You can make more friends in two months by becoming genuinely interested in others than you can in two years by trying to get others interested in you."

They Expect More from Themselves Than from Others

The best leaders set high standards for themselves and then work hard to exceed them. They know they are "visible," and take seriously their responsibilities as role models. They are also life-long learners. Like everyone, they make mistakes; and when they do, they view these mistakes as learning experiences and try to turn them into successes.

Now Hear This

If you've never made errors, you've never made decisions.

Coca Cola's late CEO, Roberto Goizueta, turned an infamous mistake into a profitable lesson. When he directed Coca Cola to change the long-time formula of their trademark soft drink to "the New Coke," the public's reaction shocked the company. Despite their market research, consumers did not like the New Coke and wanted their old Coca Cola back. A man with less integrity would have stuck to his decision and poured advertising dollars into saving his idea, but Goizueta swallowed his pride and brought back the old product under the new name, "Classic Coke." His decision was right. In a short time New Coke disappeared from the market as Classic Coke resumed its long established first-place position.

They Rely on a Set of Convictions to Guide Them

Sir John Templeton, the founder of the Templeton Fund, one of the most profitable mutual funds, adheres to the philosophy that the most successful people are often the most ethically motivated. He says that such people are likely to have the keenest understanding of the importance of morality in business, and can be trusted to give full measure and not cheat their customers. But the most ethical principles, Templeton insists, come from what goes on in the mind. "If you're filling your mind with kind, loving and helpful thoughts, then your decisions and actions will be ethical." Hard work combined with honesty and perseverance is key in the Templeton philosophy. "Individuals who have learned to invest themselves in their work are successful. They have earned what they have. More than simply knowing the value of money, they know their own value."

They Can Laugh at Themselves

Great leaders don't always take themselves seriously. Victor Kiam, owner and CEO of the Remington Shaver Company, likes to tell people a funny story about one of his first jobs. He sold Playtex girdles, and he came up with what he thought was a great marketing gimmick. Knowing that girdles were hard to clean, he offered a special promotion: Women who brought in their old, worn-out girdles could buy a new, Playtex model at a discount. The plan worked a little too well. So many dirty girdles were turned in at a New York department store that he was nearly arrested for violating health codes.

They Are Not Easily Deterred

Tom Monaghan didn't let failure get him down. He created and grew Domino Pizzas from a one-store pizza parlor to a chain of several thousand home-delivery outlets over a period of about 30 years. In 1989, he decided to sell his hugely successful company and concentrate on philanthropic work. His plan, however, didn't work out. After two and a half years, the company that purchased the chain failed to maintain the momentum that Monaghan had generated; in order to save the company, he returned to his former position as CEO.

The dogged determination that enabled Monaghan to rise from a childhood of deprivation, poverty, and abuse to become a great entrepreneur also enabled him to not only return Domino to its original prominence, but to expand it to 6,000 stores—of which 1,100 are in countries other than the United States.

They Are Positive Thinkers

Positive thinking increases one's effectiveness tremendously. It uncovers previously unrecognized abilities and personal resources; and it keeps the mind in harmony by killing fear, worry, and anxiety, which are the enemies of success and efficiency. It puts the mind in a condition to succeed. It sharpens the faculties, and makes them keener. Positive thinking allows you to concentrate on the goal rather than the obstacles between you and that goal.

> **Stop! Look! Listen!**
>
> Follow Franklin D. Roosevelt's words of encouragement to the American people in the depths of the depression: *The only thing we have to fear is fear itself.*

The leader who thinks positively will convey that attitude to the entire team. It will pay off with renewed enthusiasm and commitment to achieve the desired goals.

They Focus on Getting Things Done

We've all come across people in management positions who appear to have all the attributes of a good leader, but somehow never quite succeed. Somewhere along the line, they have missed the boat. Why does this happen?

Here's an example: One of my clients had hired a regional sales manager who they were extremely enthusiastic about. He had come to them highly recommended. During the selection process, he had impressed the interviewers with his thorough knowledge of their markets, his innovative ideas on how to increase business, and his charming personality. During the first several months on the job, he developed a creative and comprehensive marketing program. He spent weeks fine-tuning the program, writing materials, and creating graphics for it. This led to his making several impressive presentations to management and to the sales force. And that's where it ended. He never was able to actually get out and make the program work. When I was asked to investigate the problem, I discovered that in his previous job he was a staff marketer who had never had line responsibility. In that capacity he was excellent, but he did not have that key trait of leadership—*getting things done.*

They Understand the Power of the Informal Organization

Many people have developed a deep distrust of bosses or managers—often due to their experience with current or past managers. They turn to the informal leaders—fellow workers who have gained their respect and whose opinions and actions they admire and emulate. The effective leader recognizes the influence these men and women have in the acceptance of new ideas among their followers.

Barbara W., the supervisor of a department of 15 sewing machine operators, was commended by her boss for running a highly productive unit. At a staff meeting, her boss commented that her department was always the first to accept new ideas, adapt to changes in operation methods, and seemed to exhibit the highest morale. He asked Barbara to share with the other supervisors her "secret of success." Her response was one word: "Rachel." Rachel, she explained, was one of her best operators. She'd been with the company for 13 years and was a mother figure to the younger women in the department. They brought her all of their problems and accepted her advice whether the situation was job related or personal. When Barbara took over the supervisor's job a few years ago, she recognized the important role Rachel played and carefully moved to gain her support. Over the years she discussed with Rachel problems she had with any of the workers, changes that were to be made in the work, and together they determined how to deal with them. The result was a long-term, smooth, and successfully run department.

In most companies there is an informal structure parallel to the formal organization. Effective leaders work within that structure rather than trying to defy it. They identify and cultivate the informal leaders and together they work toward the achievement of their goals.

They Have Vision

Great leaders know what they want to accomplish and what steps they must take to achieve their goals. They look beyond meeting short-term objectives and keep the big picture clearly in their minds.

Now Hear This

The very essence of leadership is that you have to have vision. It's got to be a vision you articulate clearly and forcefully on every occasion. You can't blow an uncertain trumpet.

—Rev. Theodore Hesburgh, former president, Notre Dame University.

Make Your Commitment to Be a Leader

As you read the following chapters, decide what you must do to improve your leadership style. By the time you finish reading this book, you should be able to identify several new techniques for managing your department or team.

To help you put these new approaches into action, write them down, and include the following information:

What you want to do.

What tools or collaborators you will need to do it.

A time table: When you will start it and when results should be checked.

How you plan to measure results.

Make a point to review these weekly or monthly.

By doing this, you will turn this reference book into a tool to help you become a good—even a great—leader.

Now Hear This

Contrary to the opinion of many people, leaders are not born. Leaders are made, and they are made by effort and hard work.

The Least You Need to Know

♦ The job of the manager has changed. You can no longer be a "boss." You must become a leader.

♦ Too often managers think their management style is working well, when in fact, it isn't working at all.

♦ Evaluate how you are leading by taking the leadership quiz and identifying areas in which you must change.

♦ Study the traits of great leaders. Emulate them.

♦ Have a clear vision of what you wish to accomplish. Articulate it, communicate it, stick to it.

♦ Commit yourself to take whatever action is necessary to become not just an average, but a great leader.

Managing in the Twenty-First Century

In This Chapter

- ◆ What's happening here and now
- ◆ Evaluate your management style
- ◆ Learn to be a leader, not a boss
- ◆ What to do when business gets bad
- ◆ How to develop productive teams

Every day we read in the papers about major changes in the management of leading corporations. Ideas that seemed to have worked for years no longer work. Management, like all other aspects of life, is *always* in a state of flux. So why is keeping abreast of change so important now?

Speed! That's why. Things are changing so fast that it's easy to fall behind. This chapter looks at some of the changes that have taken place in the management of people and how they've affected the way leaders lead and the way people follow. You'll see how these changes affect you and how you can integrate them into your own management style.

Sound daunting? It really isn't. I've done it, I've helped my clients do it, and during the past few years, progressive managers in many companies have done it.

The first thing you have to do is examine your current management style (the quiz in this chapter will help you). Then I'll show you step-by-step how to make the changes that will enable you to excite and motivate your team more effectively.

What's Going On?

Companies are rapidly retooling the processes by which they operate. Old philosophies are being replaced with approaches that take advantage of new technologies and modern managerial thinking. I've outlined some of these approaches here:

- **Flatten the organizational structure.** Eliminating superfluous layers of management unclogs the channels through which orders and information flow.

> **Words to Work By**
>
> A **team** is a group of people who collaborate and interact synergistically to reach a common goal.

- **Encourage participatory decision making.** Employees at all levels now collaborate to plan the work—which includes scheduling production, ensuring quality, and establishing standards of performance—and get it done. When team members participate, they are more committed to its accomplishment.

- **Use *teams* to get the work done.** The team leader has replaced the "boss." The team is a collaborative group, not just people taking orders and carrying them out.

- **Implement total project management.** Under this concept, a manager supervises an entire project from start to finish. To do so, the manager coordinates with departments other than his own and over which he has no direct authority.

- **Outsource rather than employ.** To save money, a company will subcontract various phases of a job to other firms. This means that the company's own teams might have to coordinate their work with the work of several different outside firms.

- **Adopt just-in-time delivery.** Rather than store large inventories of supplies or finished products, companies today arrange to have them delivered as needed. A project manager or team leader coordinates with suppliers to schedule and ensure deliveries.

◆ **Re-engineer.** Re-engineering involves the radical restructuring of business processes, not just tinkering with isolated methods and procedures. When a company re-engineers, its managers have to rethink every aspect of their jobs in order to incorporate the changes.

Tactical Tools
Don't be afraid to try new approaches. The management climate is changing. To keep up and to make progress, you have to take risks. Go out on a limb. That's where the fruit is.

How Do These Organizational Changes Affect Me?

If you have management responsibilities or are preparing for a promotion to management, you have to meet the changing requirements of your job.

Now is the time to examine the way you currently manage people and the ways in which you'd like to be a better manager, and to learn what effective managers are doing to become even more effective.

As you read this book, you'll learn how to better deal with the day-to-day problems of managing people, and you'll learn that *you can't do it alone.* To succeed, you must utilize the talents of all members of your group. Beyond that, you must also take advantage of the brainpower and expertise of everyone involved—your own team members as well as the other people (within your company and from different firms) with whom you're collaborating.

Where Do You Fit In?

Maybe you've been managing people for years and you think you've got your department running like a well-oiled piece of machinery when, all of a sudden, your boss tells you that you aren't meeting the company's goals. "Get up-to-date or get out," he warns. You think, "I'm doing okay—the *boss* is being unreasonable."

On the other hand, you've just been promoted to your first supervisory job. The boss congratulates you, shakes your hand, and says "Take over." No training, no advice—just "take over." What about some training?

Perhaps the people who report directly to you are giving you a hard time. No matter how you try to get them to work harder, meet deadlines, or comply with quality standards, they continue to do just enough to keep from getting fired.

Stop blaming others. Look to yourself. Are you managing like a nineteenth-century autocrat or like a twenty-first-century leader?

Sure, you're entitled to your opinions, but you should keep an open mind. You want to do a better job—that's why you're reading this book. In the preceding chapter, you took a quiz on your leadership attitudes. Here's another quiz to help you take inventory of how you manage now. Once you take the quiz, we'll take a look at how your approach to management compares to what management gurus consider the "right way."

Test Your Managerial Skills

The following inventory will help you assess your managerial style. Read each statement, decide whether you agree or disagree with it, and check the appropriate box on the right. Then compare your responses to the answers that follow.

	Agree	**Disagree**
1. It's unnecessary for a manager to discuss long-range goals with team-member subordinates. As long as team members are aware of the immediate objective, they can do their work effectively.	❑	☑
2. The best way to make a reprimand effective is to belittle an offender in front of co-workers.	❑	☑
3. Managers appear ignorant and risk losing face if they answer a question with, "I don't know, but I'll find out and let you know."	❑	☑
4. It pays for managers to spend a great deal of time with a new employee to ensure that training has been effective.	☑	❑
5. Managers should ask their associates for ideas about work methods.	☑	❑
6. When disciplining is required, managers should avoid saying or doing anything that may cause resentment.	❑	☑
7. People work best for tough managers.	❑	☑
8. It's more important for a team to be composed of members who like their jobs than of people who do their jobs well.	❑	☑
9. Work gets done most efficiently if managers lay out plans in great detail.	❑	☑
10. To lead an effective team, managers should keep in mind the feelings, attitudes, and ideas of the team's members.	☑	❑

Okay, you've answered all the questions. Now look at the responses based on the advice of successful managers:

1. Disagree. People who know where they're going—who can see the big picture—are more committed and will work harder to reach those objectives than people who are aware only of immediate goals.

2. Disagree. Flaying a person doesn't solve the problem—it only makes the person feel small in front of co-workers. A good reprimand shouldn't be humiliating. It's best to reprimand in private—*never* in front of others.

3. Disagree. It's better to admit ignorance of a matter than to try to bluff. People respect leaders who accept that they don't know everything.

4. Agree. The most important step in developing the full capabilities of associates is good training on the part of managers. Managers who invest the time to lay a solid foundation in the beginning will reap huge returns: employees who are valuable assets to the organization.

5. Agree. People directly involved with the job can often contribute good ideas toward the solution of problems related to their work.

6. Agree. Resentment creates low morale and often leads to conscious or subconscious sabotage.

7. Disagree. Toughness is not as important as fairness or an inspiring attitude.

8. Disagree. The happiness and satisfaction of team members are important, but they are secondary to getting the job done.

9. Disagree. Psychologists have shown that most people work better when they are given broad project guidelines and can work out the details themselves. But there are some people who work better when tasks are given to them in detail. Good managers recognize the styles in which people work and then adapt to them.

10. Agree. Communication is a two-way street. To manage effectively, it's important to know what team members are thinking and how they feel about their jobs.

There is no passing or failing score for this inventory. Its purpose is to make you think about how you manage people. You may not agree with all the experts' answers, but do pay them some heed. Most of what you find here will be discussed in detail later in this book.

> ### Tactical Tools
> Most people work best with managers who treat them with respect, encourage them to make suggestions, and listen to their ideas even when those ideas may conflict with their own. Truly successful managers obtain the willing cooperation of all involved.

Teams: One Way to Encourage Participation

In recent years, more and more companies have changed from the traditional supervisor-subordinate structure to a team set-up in which the team leader is a facilitator, not a boss, and all team members participate in all aspects of the work including planning and decision making.

Team Members—Your Not-So-Secret Treasure

How do you get people to cooperate willingly? Use the team approach.

What is a team? Most people would define a team as a group of people working to achieve a common goal. But that's only half the answer. A key word must be added to this definition: A team is a group of people working *synergistically* to achieve a common goal. When people work together collaboratively, as a team, each team member benefits from the knowledge, work, and support of the others. A synergistic effort is much more productive than a mass of isolated individual efforts.

Words to Work By

When a team has **synergy,** its whole is greater than the sum of its parts. That is, two plus two may equal more than four.

Consider a surgical team. Each of the members of the team, the surgeon, assistant surgeon(s), anesthesiologist, surgical technicians, and nurses must be highly trained and expert in their jobs, but even if all of them are in tip top shape, the operation will not go smoothly unless all of them work interactively and synergistically.

You are the chief surgeon; your team members are the components. If you want your surgery to be a success, you must ensure that your team members work at optimum capacity individually and, then, that they all work together synergistically.

Molding Your Ragtag Group into a Team

Molding a group of people into a team involves more than changing each person's title from "employee" to "associate" or "team member." Your own attitude is the key to success. Act as a facilitator (as a coordinator or leader) rather than a boss and your staff members will begin to feel like—then act like—team members.

Teams don't happen by magic. Building your team requires careful planning. Start by clearly explaining the following factors to your team members:

- How they are expected to work.

- How this new method of operation differs from what they are used to.

- Where they can go for help.

- How the new team approach works.

Be wary of giving mere lip service to the team approach. You must "walk the talk." For example, change your way of dealing with problems. Rather than making decisions arbitrarily, encourage your team members to come up with their own solutions and implement them. You should guide and facilitate, not direct, the work of your team. The participation of all team members is the key to success.

> **Tactical Tools**
>
> Although you may be accustomed to handling many day-to-day details yourself, you should start delegating as many tasks as you can. You can't do it all by yourself, and you shouldn't have to. Help your team members develop their skills, then give them the ball and let them run with it.

When the Company Downsizes

Change isn't always for the better. Downturns in the economy, for example, may force management to institute a hiring freeze or even lay employees off. Managing is hard enough when the economy is robust; when things take a turn for the worse, you need to lead with extra finesse.

> **CAUTION**
>
> **Stop! Look! Listen!**
> Two-thirds of firms that cut jobs in a given year will do it again the next year.

Downsizing has become a way of life for many large corporations. This poses a big problem for managers who have to maintain the morale and productivity of the survivors.

How do these survivors feel?

Lucky that they still have a job? Sure, for the moment.

Guilty because their co-workers were cut and they weren't? Quite often.

Loyal to the company? Not a chance. Downsizing erodes any sense of loyalty.

How Survivors Fare

Downsizing is usually accompanied by salary freezes for the survivors (the company figures they're lucky enough to still have their jobs). Many people who survive the downsizing are forced to accept lower-ranking positions, which, of course, reduces their salaries, their status, and their power. For those who get to keep their positions, their opportunity for advancement is stifled.

That's just the beginning. After the downsizing, employees have to work harder and pick up the slack for those who were laid off. Not only that, the colleagues who once facilitated their work are no longer there to help. Worse, teams can fall apart—some of the team members, whose collaboration was key to success, are gone.

Challenges to Managers

What can you do as a manager when your company downsizes your department?

1. Once the downsized people have left the company, bring the rest of your team together and have an open discussion about the situation. Let them express their concerns. You may not be able to assure them that the worst is over or that their jobs are safe, but point out that everyone must work together to make the most of the situation.

2. Elicit ideas on how to restructure the work most effectively and have the team create a plan to redelegate duties.

3. Meet with team members individually to deal with personal concerns. For example, some people may be concerned about not having the necessary skills for the newly assigned work. Assure them that you will provide support to help them succeed in the new assignments.

Now Hear This

Companies that downsize through buyouts and attrition—that help the workers get new jobs—have a better chance of retaining the loyalty of the surviving workers.

—Robert Reich, former Secretary of Labor

4. Determine what additional training is needed to cover the work once done by the laid-off employees. Arrange for such training internally or with tuition-reimbursed outside programs.

5. Encourage team members to learn skills that might be needed in the future (e.g., computer skills, foreign languages, and so forth).

6. Once the dust has settled, boost morale by attending to each person's concerns, rebuilding team spirit, and recognizing accomplishments.

Get to Work

At the end of Chapter 1, I encouraged you to develop a follow-up plan for implementing what you have learned from this book. From this chapter, were you able to pinpoint aspects of your management style that may need improvement? If so, be sure to make note of them. In later chapters, I suggest specific solutions to many of these problems. As you read and absorb them, adapt them to your own situation and take steps to apply them.

The Least You Need to Know

◆ The job of the manager has changed. Bossing doesn't work. You have to lead.

◆ Team members respond better to participatory, rather than authoritarian, leadership.

◆ Give your associates the opportunity to use their talents, skills, and brainpower.

◆ A team is more than just a group of people—it's a synergistic, interactive, collaborative family.

◆ Think of yourself as a facilitator. Your job is to make it easy for team members to accomplish their jobs.

◆ If your company undergoes downsizing, work diligently with the survivors to restore morale and upgrade productivity.

Don't Believe Everything Your Old Boss Taught You

In This Chapter

- ◆ What's wrong with the way your old boss manages
- ◆ Common management misconceptions
- ◆ How employees *really* want to be treated
- ◆ Develop your team's potential
- ◆ The benefits of a long-term outlook

In the previous chapter, we explored the changing practice of management and the importance of adapting to new approaches. But managers' efforts to change are often frustrated by old-style bosses, colleagues, and associates who resist anything new.

What's the cause of this interference? Well, the field of management is rife with truisms that aren't true, "facts" that aren't factual, assumptions that are never challenged, and practices based on generations-old folklore.

Myths and stereotypes that have governed people's thinking for years (for lifetimes, in many cases) are tough to overcome. However, as a manager you must shatter them if you want to move ahead. This chapter examines some common misconceptions, tells you how they impede progress, and explains how you can put them in perspective.

Become a Modern Manager

Unlike professionals in other industries—physicians, lawyers, psychologists, engineers—who are required to complete advanced study and pass exams for certification, managers learn primarily on the job. Some managers may have special education (for instance, degrees in business administration), but *most are promoted from the ranks and have little or no training in management.*

More and more successful managers are making an effort to acquire skills through structured courses of study, but most managers still pick up their techniques by observing those of their bosses. The model they follow may be good. Too often, however, new managers are exposed to, and learn from, their bosses' outdated and invalid philosophies.

"It Ain't Necessarily So"

Some management ideas may have been valid in the past but are no longer; others were never true. Let's look at some of these myths and misconceptions about management.

Management Is Nothing More Than Common Sense

One manager said, "When I was promoted to my first management job, I asked a long-time manager for some tips about how to deal with people who report to me. He told me, 'Just use common sense, and you'll have no trouble.'"

Tactical Tools

Keep up with your field ...

- ◆ Attend seminars and read current books about management.
- ◆ Read trade and professional journals.
- ◆ Take an active role in business associations.
- ◆ Network with other managers.
- ◆ Benchmark the best companies in your field.

What is "common sense," exactly? What appears sensible to one person may be nonsense to another. Often the definition of common sense is culturally based. In Japan, for example, it's considered common sense to wait for a full consensus before making any decision; in the United States, this technique is often thought inefficient. Culture aside, different people also have their own ideas about what is good or bad, what is efficient or wasteful, what works and what doesn't.

We tend to use our own experiences to develop our particular brands of common sense. The problem is, a person's individual experience provides only limited perspective. To be a real leader, you must look beyond common sense. Books written by management experts abound. Make a practice of reading those books, subscribing to management periodicals, and learning from the experiences of men and women who have been successful leaders.

You can learn a lot about the art and science of management by reading industry-related books and periodicals, attending courses and seminars, and actively participating in trade associations in your field.

Managers Know Everything

Managers don't know everything. Nobody does. Accept that you don't have all the answers. However, know that you need the skills to get the answers. Get to know people in other companies who have faced similar situations, and you can learn a great deal. This *networking* process gives you access to new information and ideas, and provides you with a valuable source of assistance in solving problems.

Seeking organizations that have been successful in certain areas and learning their techniques is called *benchmarking*. Companies that participate in competitions such as the Malcolm Baldridge Awards (an annual recognition by the U.S. Department of Commerce of firms that demonstrate high quality in their work) must agree to share their techniques with any organization that requests them.

Words to Work By

Networking means making contacts in other companies to whom you can turn for suggestions, ideas, and problem-solving strategies. Organizations that have achieved success in a certain area are often willing to share their techniques and methods.

Words to Work By

Benchmarking is identifying those companies that have achieved excellence and making an effort to study what they have done and adapt it to your own situations.

Is Management by Fear an Effective Management Tool?

"Ya wanna keep your job?" is still heard from some managers. And it works—sometimes. People will work if they fear that they might lose their jobs, but how much work will they do? Just enough to keep from getting fired. That's why this technique isn't considered effective management. Successful management involves getting the *willing* cooperation of your associates.

Moreover, it's not that easy to fire people. Considering the implications of the civil rights laws (see Part 3) and labor unions and in many cases the difficulty and costs associated with hiring competent replacements, firing people may cause more problems than keeping employees with whom you're not satisfied.

You can't keep good workers for long when you manage by fear. When jobs are scarce in your community or industry, workers might tolerate high-handed arbitrary bosses. However, when the job market opens up, the best people will leave for companies with more pleasant working environments. Employee turnover can be expensive and often devastating.

In one of my consulting assignments, I was retained to help staff an entire office facility. As we reviewed the incoming resumés, we noticed loads of applications from one particular firm. My immediate assumption was that this other company was shaky and that its employees were seeking more stable employment. Nevertheless, the company was in excellent shape. Applicant after applicant told us that the company's arbitrary management style made their working environments unpleasant. Despite good pay and benefits, they wanted out. The moral of this story is that you should use positive rather than negative techniques to motivate people.

> **CAUTION**
>
> **Stop! Look! Listen!**
>
> Praise *can* be overdone. If people are repeatedly praised for every trivial accomplishment, the value of praise is diminished to the point of superficiality.

Give Them Some Praise and They'll Ask for a Raise

People need to be praised. Everyone wants to know that his or her good work is appreciated. Yet many managers are reluctant to praise their employees.

Why? Some managers fear that if they praise a team member's work, that person will become complacent and stop trying to improve (certainly, some people do react this way). The key is to phrase your praise in a way that encourages the team member to continue the good work. How to praise effectively will be discussed in Chapter 18.

Other managers are concerned that if team members are praised for good work, they will expect pay raises or bonuses. And some folks might. However, that's no reason to withhold praise when it's warranted.

Employees should already know how salary adjustments, bonuses, and other financial rewards are determined. If compensation is renegotiated at annual performance evaluations, team members should be assured that the good work for which they are praised would be considered in the evaluation.

Some managers simply don't believe in praise. One department head told me, "The people I supervise know that they're doing okay if I don't talk to them. If I have to speak to them, they know they're in trouble." Offering no feedback other than reprimands isn't effective either. You want to use positive, not negative, reinforcement.

> **Stop! Look! Listen!**
>
> Don't promise employees raises or bonuses based on the accomplishment of a specific task. Financial reward should be based on overall performance over time. Promise a raise only if it's part of a compensation or management-by-objective plan that has been formally approved by your superiors, the human resources department, or others in your organization who have the authority to approve compensation changes.

The Best Way to Get People to Work Is to Crack the Whip

As noted before, some managers manage by fear. Another variant of this is sometimes called "cracking the whip." When Tom P., a project manager at a large utility, gave an assignment to his staff, he often threatened them with dire consequences if the task wasn't accomplished on time. These threats ranged from denying privileges to even firing them. When I asked him why he did this, he responded that if he didn't crack the whip, his people would just dawdle along. He considered himself an effective manager and never realized how much more he could get from his people by more enlightened methods.

Every year, James Miller, management consultant and author of *The Corporate Coach*, holds a contest for Best and Worst Boss of the Year. The employees do the nominating. Miller reports that nominations for worst boss always outnumber those for best boss. Some of the chief reasons employees dislike their bosses, Miller found, is that the bosses use verbal whip snapping—continually finding fault with subordinates, expressing sarcasm, gloating over failures, and hollering and screaming at employees.

No one really knows why people behave this way. Some people have always been screamed at—by parents, teachers, former bosses—so they think it's an effective communication tool.

We all raise our voices occasionally, especially when we're under stress. Sometimes it takes great self-discipline *not* to yell. Effective leaders, however, control this tendency. An occasional lapse is okay, but when yelling becomes your normal manner of communication, you're admitting your failure to be a real leader. You cannot get the *willing* cooperation of your associates by screaming at them.

The Golden Rule? Try the Platinum Rule

When you manage people, the biblical rule "Do unto others as you would have others do unto you" is sound advice—to a point. Because people are *not* all alike, treating others as *you* want to be treated is not the same as treating them as *they* want to be treated.

> **Now Hear This**
>
> When you work with your associates, rather than follow the golden rule, remember the *platinum rule*: Do unto others as they would have you do unto them.

For example, Linda prefers to be given broad objectives and likes to work out the details of her job on her own. But her assistant, Jason, is not comfortable receiving an assignment unless all the details are spelled out for him. If Linda delegates work to her assistant the way she likes to have work assigned to her, she won't get the best results.

Sol needs continuous reinforcement. He's happy on the job only when his boss oversees his work and assures Sol that he's doing a good job. Tanya, however, gets upset if her boss checks her work too often. "Doesn't she trust me?" she complains. You can't do unto Tanya as you do unto Sol and get good results from each of them.

Each of us has our own style, our own approach, and our own eccentricities. To "do unto others" as we would have them do unto us may be the poorest way of managing people.

To be an effective manager, you must know each member of your team and tailor your method of management to each individual. Rather than follow the golden rule, follow the *platinum* rule: "Do unto others as they would have you do unto them."

Compromises must be made, of course. In some situations, work must be done in a manner that may not be ideal for some people. By knowing ahead of time what needs to be accomplished, you can anticipate problems and prepare team members to accept their tasks.

There's More to Management Than the Bottom Line

Production, performance, and profit are important aspects of your job as a manager, but are these all you have to consider? Certainly, if a business is to survive, it must produce results. Equally important, however, is the development of its employees' potential. If you ignore people's potential, you limit your team's ability to achieve results. Instead, you reap short-term benefits at the expense of long-term success and even survival.

When Lee founded his computer components company, he was a pioneer in what was then a new and growing industry. Determined to be a leader in his field, he drove his employees to maintain high levels of productivity, always keeping his eye trained on the profit picture. However, he paid no attention to the development of his staff. His technical and administrative staff members were given little opportunity to contribute ideas or to initiate their own projects.

Over the years, Lee's company saw reasonable profits but never grew to become an industry leader as Lee had hoped. Because he had stifled the potential and ambition of his employees, he lost much of his technical staff to other companies. And because he depended only on his own ideas, he missed out on all the innovative ideas his staff might have come up with.

> **Now Hear This**
>
> Most employees have an exaggerated idea about the profits most companies make. Surveys indicate that people think companies make 20 to 30 percent profits. Truth be told, most companies make closer to a 5 percent profit.

Consider the Long-Term Effects

In an economy where too many people analyze companies by their quarterly earnings, too much emphasis is placed on improving the short-term bottom line. With an eye on Wall Street, many CEOs encourage their line managers to do all they can to improve that critical figure.

The long-term objectives of a company and of each department or division must take into consideration developing the skills and solidifying the loyalty of employees. When people are given the opportunity to hone their skills, develop their own careers, and achieve desired results, they are encouraged to try harder and in the long run will contribute much more to increasing the long-term bottom line of the company.

The Least You Need to Know

- ◆ Leadership abilities aren't necessarily inborn. They can be acquired.
- ◆ Managers are often influenced by misconceptions and myths about management. Don't assume you have to follow in your old bosses' footsteps.

◆ You should always use common sense when dealing with people. But no individual's experience is broad enough to cover all the bases. Seek out advice on leadership from experts.

◆ Don't rule by fear. Earn the respect of your associates, and they'll knock themselves out to please you.

◆ Praise people for work that's well done. Unrecognized work is like an unwatered plant. Productivity will wither away.

◆ Practice the platinum rule: "Do unto others as *they* would have you do unto them."

◆ Don't get so caught up in tracking profits and losses that you forget to balance your team's potential and performance.

Chapter 4

Plotting the Course

In This Chapter

- ◆ How to set realistic and attainable goals
- ◆ Your long-term outlook
- ◆ Day-to-day activities
- ◆ Assemble resources to get the job done

Now that you've cleared away the management misconceptions that have been holding you back, you're ready to take the first steps toward becoming a modern manager. This process begins when you set goals. Like a good navigator, you set the course to reach those goals.

Some people like to set out on a journey without a map. They want to ride the currents and hope they'll find adventure and fortune—and sometimes they do—but managers can't afford to take those risks. Because managers must answer to their teams and their own supervisors, they need to know where they want to go, what they want to accomplish, what kinds of problems they may encounter along the way, and how to overcome them.

This chapter helps you to set short- and long-term goals and plan how to reach them.

Calibrating Your Compass

Unless you know exactly what you want to achieve, there's no way to measure how close you are to achieving it. Specific goals give you a standard against which to measure your progress.

The *goals* you set for your team must be in line with the larger goals that your company sets for you. If you don't coordinate the *objectives* of your job, department, or team with the objectives of your organization, you'll waste your time and energy.

Words to Work By

Goal and **objective** are interchangeable terms that describe the purpose, or long-term results, toward which an organization or individual's endeavors are directed.

Goals are the foundation of motivational programs. In striving to reach your goals, you become motivated. In knowing the goals of your team members and helping them reach those goals, you help motivate them.

In most organizations, big-picture goals are established by top management and filtered down to departments or teams, who use them as guides in establishing their own goals.

Setting Goals Is Serious Business

The process of setting goals takes time, energy, and effort. Goals aren't something you scribble on a napkin during your coffee break. You must plan what you truly want to accomplish, establish timetables, determine who will be responsible for which aspect of the job, and then anticipate and plan a resolution for any obstacle that may threaten to thwart the achievement of your goals.

The suggestions in this section provide a systematic approach to setting goals.

Realism vs. Wishful Thinking

Are you ready to set your goals? To prevent your goals from ending up mere pipe dreams of idealistic wishes, make sure they meet the following three conditions:

◆ **Clear and specific.** It's not enough to state that your goal is "to improve market share of our product." Be specific: "Market share of our product will increase from its current 12 percent to 20 percent in five years."

◆ **Attainable.** Pie-in-the-sky goals are self-defeating. If you can see your progress in reaching your goals, you'll have more incentive to continue working than if your goals seem completely unattainable.

◆ **Flexible.** Sometimes you just can't reach a goal. Circumstances may change: What once seemed viable may no longer be. Don't be frustrated.

Here's a lesson in flexibility: An assistant manager set a goal to become a store manager in two years, but it didn't happen. Rather than quit his job in frustration, he reviewed his situation. He had based his goal on the premise that his company would continue to open 6 to 10 new stores every year. During the preceding year, business had been slow, and only two new outlets were opened. However, business improved, and the company seemed likely to renew its expansion. He recognized that quitting would be the wrong solution and that he had to be flexible in the time limits he set for himself.

> ### Tactical Tools
> The way to achieve success is first to have a definite, clear, practical ideal—a goal, an objective. Second, have the necessary means to achieve your ends—wisdom, money, materials, methods. Third, adjust all your means to that end.
> —Aristotle

Build in Flexibility

All of us set goals based on certain circumstances we anticipate during the life of our project. Circumstances do change, however, and original goals may have to be adjusted. To that end, many companies use a goal-setting program that involves three levels:

> **A main, or standard, goal:** What you plan to accomplish if everything goes well.
>
> **Alternative 1:** A slightly lower goal. If circumstances change and it becomes obvious that your main goal cannot be achieved, rather than start from scratch in redefining your goal, you can shift to this alternative.
>
> **Alternative 2:** A higher-level goal. If you're making greater progress than you had originally thought you could, rather than be complacent about being ahead of target, shift to this alternative and accomplish even more.

Take, for example, CSC, a company in the metropolitan Philadelphia area that services and repairs computers. Its sales goal for one year was to open 10 new accounts. But when a national competitor opened a similar service in the same community, all of CSC's energies had to be redirected toward saving its current accounts. The goal for attracting new clients then had to be reduced.

Let's say CSC was having a good year. Its goals could have been accelerated. If CSC had gained eight new clients in the first half of the year, it could have automatically raised its goal to a higher level rather than using the next six months to open only two additional accounts.

Selling the Goals to Your Staff

At a recent goal-setting seminar, one participant complained, "I have trouble getting people to buy into the big picture concept. They're so absorbed in their individual jobs that they can't see beyond their own problems."

Here's how you can overcome this type of situation:

♦ Bring everyone in your department or team into the early stages of the planning process.

♦ Discuss the major points of the overall plan.

♦ Ask each person to describe how he or she will fit into the big picture plan.

♦ Give each person a chance to comment on each stage of the project.

Breaking a long-term goal into bite-size pieces helps people see how their role in a project fits in. It can also help them set overall team or project goals for the long run.

> **CAUTION**
>
> **Stop! Look! Listen!**
>
> Learn each of your team member's goals. If their goals aren't in line with those of your company, department, or project group, demonstrate to them that applying their skills to meeting the team's goals enhances the opportunity to fulfill their own expectations.

SOPs: The Company Bible

Your company may have a set of standard operating procedures (SOPs) or SPs (standard practices) that detail company plans and policies. Progressive companies usually restrict their SOPs to such matters as personnel policies, safety measures, and related matters. Many companies, however, incorporate specific job methods and procedures into their "bibles" or publish them in accompanying "instruction manuals." Providing policies and procedures for routine activities obviates the need to plan for them every time they occur. Because SOPs set standards that everyone must follow, they ensure consistent employee behavior in dealing with particular situations.

If you have to develop SOPs, keep them simple. Too often, managers draw up complicated SOPs in hopes of covering every possible contingency. *It can't be done.*

Managers will frequently have to make decisions based on unforeseeable factors. SOPs should cover common issues in detail, but leave room for managers (or non-managerial people, where appropriate) to make spontaneous decisions when circumstances warrant them.

Tactical Tools

To ensure that standard operating procedures are effective, follow these guidelines:

- ◆ Clearly state any expected actions.
- ◆ Provide guidelines for acceptable deviation from procedure.
- ◆ Be specific about areas in which no deviation may occur.
- ◆ Before setting any method as an SOP, test it on the job to ensure that it's the best way to accomplish the task.

SOPs should also be flexible. Don't make SOPs so rigid that they can't be changed with changing circumstances. Plans may become obsolete because of new technologies, competition, government regulations, or the development of more efficient methods. Build into SOPs a policy for periodic review and adjustment.

Also keep in mind that not all plans are SOPs. Plans can be developed for special purposes, sometimes to be used only once or for projects that last several months or years.

Planning, Planning, Who'll Do the Planning?

Standard operating procedures are just one phase of planning. As mentioned, SOPs should cover only broad policy matters so that specific plans can be designed for each new project.

Your entire team should be involved in developing the team's plans. As team leader, you should coordinate and lead the process: Delegate particular aspects of the planning to the team members who know the most about them.

Passing the Buck to Pros

Because many supervisors are so bogged down in the day-to-day details of the job, they don't have the time and energy for planning. Because planning is so important, many organizations have planning specialists work with the managers in the development and coordination of this function.

The people who are closest to the work—who will be responsible for implementing the plans—should also be directly involved. Planning experts can help facilitate the process, but only the people who will carry out the project's duties can create a realistic and workable plan.

The Art of Planning

To illustrate how planning works, let's look at how Louise, the owner and manager of Featherdusters (a janitorial service company in Rock Hill, South Carolina) developed a plan to clean a six-story office building. The following list shows you the steps Louise deemed necessary to implement her plan:

Step 1: List what needs to be done. After consulting with her client, Louise made the following list:

Must be done daily

Empty wastebaskets into dumpsters

Carry dumpsters to pick-up location

Dust furniture

Mop tile floors

Vacuum carpeted floors

Clean restrooms

Clean lounges

Must be done weekly

Sanitize telephones

Polish brass railings

Wax tile floors

Must be done monthly

Wash windows

Wash glass partitions

Step 2: Determine staffing. Louise hired two teams of three people. Each team was responsible for cleaning three floors. Each team was comprised of a trained floor waxer, a window washer, and a supervisor. The owner/manager oversaw the entire operation.

Step 3: Acquire supplies and equipment. Louise then acquired these supplies:

Vacuum cleaners

Dust cloths

Sponges

A waxing machine

Floor wax

Disinfectant

Window washing solvent

Step 4: Estimate timing. Louise calculated that the cleaning job would take five hours (from 5 P.M. to 10 P.M.) five days a week to complete. The following list serves as a guide to Louise and the supervisors to ensure that scheduled tasks get done at the scheduled time:

> **Daily tasks:** All tasks are performed daily.

> **Weekly tasks:** The supervisor assigns one floor every day to one or more workers to complete each of the weekly tasks.

> **Monthly tasks:** The owner/manager and window washer schedule these tasks every month. The schedule must be flexible enough to account for weather conditions.

Step 5: Methods. All work will be performed according to the company's SOP for cleaning methods. Supervisors are responsible for quality of work, and the owner/manager will inspect work on an ad hoc basis.

Step 6: Budget. Specific figures should be included to cover cost of materials, equipment amortization, labor, transportation to and from the site, and miscellaneous costs.

Step 7: Contingencies. Things don't always work out according to plan. Unforeseen circumstances can develop that impede the completion of scheduled tasks. Louise anticipated the types of contingencies most likely to be encountered:

> **Truck or van breakdown:** Make arrangements for renting replacement vehicles.

> **Equipment breakdown:** Additional waxing machines are stored in a warehouse.

> **Personnel:** Owner/manager and supervisors have lists of substitutes available on short notice.

Step 8: Follow-up. Owner/manager makes periodic visits to site to inspect work and meets at least once per quarter with client to ensure satisfaction with work.

The following planning worksheet will enable you to plan and schedule your projects. Feel free to photocopy it or adapt it to meet your special needs.

Planning Worksheet

Objective: _____

Specific actions to be taken: _____

_____

Staffing: _____

_____

Equipment and supplies: _____

_____

Timing (include deadlines where required): _____

_____

_____

Methods and techniques to be used: _____

_____

_____

Budget: _____

_____

_____

Contingencies: _____

_____

_____

Follow-up: _____

_____

_____

Converting Plans into Action

Plans similar to that of the Featherdusters are virtually self starting. Implementing an already developed and tested plan with a new client is relatively easy. The introduction of a brand new product, however, requires a much more complex plan, which may involve several phases spread out over several months or even years.

For example, when Procter & Gamble (P&G) introduced Crest toothpaste to the market, it set up separate year-long plans for each of the main aspects of the project: manufacturing, marketing, and distribution. The product manager who coordinated the entire operation then developed, in collaboration with the manufacturing, marketing, and distribution managers, month-by-month plans. Each of the involved parties knew just what it had to accomplish in the specified period and were kept informed of the other parties' progress. By following this plan, P&G was able to introduce Crest toothpaste on time: Simultaneously, P&G supplied its retailers, placed ads on TV and in magazines, and mailed samples and discount coupons to consumers.

Planning for Daily Activities

You've set your goals, and now you must apply them to your day-to-day work schedule. You'll achieve your goals only if you break down, day-by-day, how you plan to reach them.

Unless your work is primarily routine and already standardized in the SOPs, the next step for you and your team members is to determine when and what task each member will undertake.

The $25,000 Suggestion

In the early 1900s, Ivy Lee, a pioneer in management consulting, paid a visit to Charles Schwab, the president of U.S. Steel. Lee told Schwab that he could help U.S. Steel become more effective. When Schwab expressed skepticism, Lee said, "I'll give you one suggestion today, and I want you to put it into effect for one month. At the end of that time, we will meet again, and you can pay me whatever you think that idea was worth to you. If it was of no value, you owe me nothing."

Schwab accepted the challenge and implemented Lee's suggestion. When they met again, Schwab handed Lee a check for $25,000 and said, "That was the best advice I ever had. It worked so well for me that I passed it on to all my subordinate managers."

Words to Work By

When you **prioritize**, or put first things first, you determine the degree of importance a matter has in accomplishing your goals. Let your priorities dictate how you complete the tasks at hand.

Tactical Tools

Set priorities and stick to them. When you get interrupted, deal with the interruption and then immediately get back to what you were doing.

So, what was Lee's advice? *Prioritize.*

Every morning when you get to work (or every night before you go to bed), make a list of all the things you want to accomplish that day and put them in order of priority. Then work on the first item, and don't move on to the next one until you have done all you can. You'll be interrupted, of course—no job is free from interruption—so just handle the interruption, then return to what you were working on. Don't let any interruption make you forget what you were doing.

You probably won't have completed every item on your list at the end of the day. However, the important tasks will have been accomplished. Take the remaining tasks, add them to the new ones that have developed, and compile another prioritized list for the next day. At the end of the month, you might notice that certain items remain on your list day after day. That's a sign that they weren't important enough to do. You should either delegate them to someone else or perhaps not do them at all.

What Do I Do First?

In his book, *The Seven Habits of Highly Effective People*, Steven Covey cautions that many managers confuse what is urgent with what is truly important. Urgent matters must be attended to immediately or else serious consequences might ensue, but if you spend all your time putting out fires, your truly important goals won't be met.

Tactical Tools

Color code your calendar or planning chart so that you and your associates can tell at a glance the status of projects and assignments. This list suggests colors to use:

- **Red ink:** High-priority items for that day.
- **Blue ink:** Deadlines for projects (list in blue for two or three days before the actual deadline, then print in red on the day of the final deadline).
- **Green ink:** Follow-up of other people's work.
- **Black ink:** Routine work scheduled for that day.

Scheduling Projects

After your team has planned the actions it will take to complete a project, you must develop a schedule. Lay out what will be done, who will do it, and when each task should be started and completed. Your schedule can be as simple as notes on a wall calendar, or as complex as specially designed planning charts and computer-based schedules.

Enough of This Preparation—Let's Get It Done!

The first step in setting plans to action is assembling the necessary resources— obtaining and allocating funds, accumulating equipment and materials, and acquiring pertinent information. The major tasks of choosing, training, and assigning personnel to the project are discussed later in this book.

Where's the Dough?

Inadequate funding will doom any project to failure. The most common reason that start-up companies fold is lack of capital. Even large, well-established organizations must determine how much money they should spend to get a project started and to keep it going until it pays off.

When figuring out the budget for a project, be careful not to underestimate costs just to make the numbers impressive. You don't want to be like Mike: Mike wanted to impress his boss, Sheila. He knew that she watched every dollar her department spent and was always boasting that she could get work done less expensively than other managers. When Mike was assigned a new project, he cut corners and came up with an impossibly tight budget. Sheila praised him for his business acumen and gave his project the go-ahead.

Mike's lowball figures proved to be inadequate, and, shamefaced, he had to ask Sheila for additional funds. This mistake stalled not only the project but also Mike's career.

> **CAUTION**
>
> **Stop! Look! Listen!**
>
> If you're not sure how much money is necessary for a project, err on the high side. You'll look much better if you come in under budget than if you have to plead for more funds. Here's a safe rule: Underpromise and overdeliver!

Our Budget Is Too Low!

You may have no control over determining budgets for your department or team. If so, carefully study the budget you are given before starting a project. If the budget seems unrealistically small, discuss it with your manager. Whoever allotted the money for your work may not have been aware of certain factors. By presenting your case, you may persuade the company to provide a more realistic budget.

There are times you'll have to work with a less-than-ideal budget. That's when you have to sharpen your pencil and calculate how you can save money with minimal loss of productivity. Can some of the work you're farming out be done more cheaply in-house or vice versa? Can some of the work be re-engineered so that fewer costly hours are spent on it? Can deadlines be delayed to eliminate the need for overtime or additional temporary workers? Check all your costs. Saving small amounts of money in several areas can add up to your meeting the budget.

Lining Up Your Tools

Do you need any special equipment for the job? Most departments have easy access to the company's machinery, computers, and other hardware, but sometimes access is limited.

> **Tactical Tools**
>
> When you need special equipment or materials, make a list of them before you begin your assignment. Check availability. Arrange well in advance to obtain what you need when you need it.

In Angela's case, she was assigned to prepare a long-term market forecast for a new service proposed to her company. She created a software program especially for the project, but was stymied when the only computer sophisticated enough to deal with her program was tied up on a higher priority project. Angela was compelled to use an outside computer firm to run her program, which added cost and time to the project.

To avoid a glitch like Angela's, make sure all necessary equipment will be available to you as needed. Otherwise, consider your alternatives. Check to see whether another department has equipment you can use. Arrange to subcontract work you can't do in-house. Lease the equipment on a short-term basis. Budget for temporary personnel to augment your staff when necessary.

Information: The Golden Key to Accomplishment

Knowledge is the key to accomplishment. Having an accurate, balanced, and unbiased picture of what is happening in your company, in your industry, and in the economy is essential to sound decision making.

In the past, managers could wait for weekly or even monthly reports for the information necessary to run their companies or departments effectively. Today, *real time* is the magic formula for success.

Reports tell you what happened yesterday, last week, and last month—they are like snapshots, recording how things were at the time the picture was taken. They're helpful, of course, because it's useful to review the past, but to be an effective manager today, you have to know what's going on *now*.

Words to Work By

Real time refers to the actual time in which a process occurs (what's going on in the here and now).

You need better and faster information. Instead of a snapshot, you need a telecast—information that's reported as it happens. The tools are in place, but are you taking advantage of them? Take a look at what they can do for you:

If you're a sales manager, you can get up-to-the-minute information from field salespeople. Have them send reports about special accomplishments or unusual problems from their laptops directly to your home office.

In a branch facility, you can e-mail information about production, inventories, and special problems as often as necessary.

If you're a retail manager, you can continuously receive sales and stock information from the store's cash register computers.

If you're a general manager who needs specialized information, you can use the World Wide Web to obtain that information from anywhere anytime. You can subscribe to services that give you up-to-the-minute weather conditions worldwide, stock prices on foreign exchanges, transportation and shipping schedules, and virtually any other type of data you need.

The More You Learn About Planning, the Better the Plan

Information goes beyond simple facts and figures. Managers must have in-depth knowledge of the most effective and cutting edge work methods. Team leaders and team members alike must keep up with the latest technologies.

Tactical Tools
Start small
Think possibilities
Reach beyond your known abilities
Invest all you have in your dream
Visualize miracles
Expect to experience success.
—Rev. Robert H. Schuller

Maybe you've been in your field for many years, and you think you know your job and all the tricks of the trade. Do you really? The way you've been doing things works, of course, but are you sure it's the best way?

"If it ain't broke, don't fix it" doesn't apply anymore. A certain method may work, but that's no guarantee that it can't be done better. Equipment that didn't exist a few years ago may improve production or quality today. Techniques may have been refined or totally changed. This is a dynamic world, and you can never stop learning.

The Least You Need to Know

- Make sure you set clear, specific, and attainable goals.

- Prioritize your tasks: Do first things first.

- Your calendar is a scheduling tool. Plan your day and work your plan.

- Set budgets that will provide adequate funds for your job to be completed in the specified timeframe.

- Arrange in advance to have the necessary equipment, computer time, and materials at your disposal.

- Get data in real time so that you're always on top of every situation.

Part 2

How to Talk the Talk

Words, words, words. Yes, in order to get things done, we have to communicate with the people we work with. Without words, whether orally or in writing, no job could be accomplished.

However, it's not just what we say, but how we say it (or perhaps write it) that will determine whether our words lead to the actions we desire. We have to make sure that what we say, whether it be an order, a suggestion, or an idea, that the people we communicate with not only understand what we are conveying but accept it.

How can you do this? Read on and find out.

Communicating Made Easy

In This Chapter

- ◆ Get your ideas across to others
- ◆ Why people may not understand you
- ◆ Become a better listener

These days, *communication*—what you say and how you say it—can determine whether you succeed or fail. Take Ronald Reagan, for example. Many Americans believe that his chief attribute was his ability to communicate effectively with the public.

This skill, shared by the most successful professionals, business executives, and government leaders, is a skill you, too, can acquire. All you need is will and determination. Once you've improved your ability to communicate, you can more effectively present your ideas to your boss, your associates, your customers, your team, even your friends and family.

In this chapter, you'll learn some strategies to better your oral and written communication—a major step toward becoming a more successful team leader.

What You Say

Suppose you call a meeting to discuss a new project. Or you sit down with an associate for a serious discussion about performance. Or perhaps you're called upon to present a progress report to the executive committee. In all these situations, your choice of words and your delivery may determine your success or failure.

Whether you're addressing a group or having a one-to-one conversation, you should think out your message and how you plan to present it in advance. Sometimes you'll have to think on your feet with little or no time to prepare, but more often than not, when you're required to discuss something, you *can* prepare—even on short notice.

Know Your Subject

On the job, you'll usually communicate with others about subjects you're thoroughly familiar with: the work you're doing, matters in your own area of expertise, or company-related problems. Still, you should review the facts to be sure that you have a handle on all the available information and are prepared to answer any questions.

> **Words to Work By**
>
> **Communication** takes place when persons or groups exchange information, ideas, and concepts.

> **Stop! Look! Listen!**
>
> Unless your audience is familiar with it, don't use jargon—those special initials, acronyms, and words used in your field or company and nowhere else. A statement like, "We booked the perp on a 602A" probably won't mean anything to someone who's not a police officer.

From time to time, you may be asked to report on matters with which you are unfamiliar. Your company may want to purchase a new type of computer software, for example, and ask you to check it out. Here's how you should start tackling the assignment:

- Learn as much as possible about the subject.

- Know 10 times more than you think you ought to know for the presentation.

- Prepare notes about the pluses and minuses of the proposed purchase, solution, and so on.

- Whether you will make this report to one person (your boss, for example) or to a group of managers or technical specialists, be prepared to answer questions about any subject that might come up.

Know Your Audience

Even the most skilled orator will fail to communicate effectively if his audience can't understand him. Half of good communication is understanding your audience. Choose words that your listeners will easily comprehend. If the people you address come from a technical background, you can use technical terminology to communicate: Your listeners will clearly and readily understand these special terms. However, if you talk about technical subject matter to an audience unfamiliar with it, drop the technical language. If your listeners can't understand your vocabulary, your message will be lost.

For example, suppose you're an engineer whose work primarily involves dealing with other engineers. You're accustomed to using technical terms all the time. Now let's say you're called on to make a presentation to your company's finance department to arrange the funding for a new engineering project. It's *your* responsibility, not your audience's, to ensure that your message gets across. If you can explain the technical matter in layperson's terms, do so. If you have to use technical language, take the time to explain a term the first time you use it and at least once again if you feel that it needs reinforcement.

How You Say It

No matter how well thought out your message is, no one will understand it if you don't express it clearly and distinctly.

Following are the five most common problems people have with speaking clearly:

- **Mumbling.** Do you swallow word endings? Do you speak with your mouth almost closed? Practice in front of a mirror. Open up those lips.

- **Speaking too fast.** Whoa! Give people a chance to absorb what you're saying.

- **Speaking too slowly.** Speak too slowly, and you'll lose your audience. While you're plodding through your message, their minds wander to other matters.

- **Mispronouncing words.** Not sure how a word is pronounced? Look it up.

- **Speaking in a monotone.** Vary the inflection of the tone and pitch of your voice. Otherwise, you'll put your listeners to sleep.

> **CAUTION**
>
> ### Stop! Look! Listen!
>
> Do you use "word whiskers," those extra sounds, words, and phrases peppered throughout speech? You know what they are—"er," "uhhhh," and "y'know" are just a few. They distract you from your thoughts. Listen to yourself, and shave off those "whiskers."

Have You Ever Really Heard Your Own Voice?

You don't hear yourself as others hear you. Get a tape recorder and record your voice when you talk to others in person or on the phone. Listen to yourself on tape. The recording will tell you whether you mumble, or speak too fast, too slowly, or in a monotone.

All you need to do to correct most of these problems is to be aware. If you're aware that you mumble, you'll make an effort not to mumble. If you're aware that you speak too fast, you'll make an effort to slow down. If you're aware that you speak in a monotone, you'll work consciously to vary your tone.

Your Body Talks, Too

People communicate not only through words but also through their facial expressions and body movements. If there were only a dictionary of body language, we could easily interpret what those signs signify. Because body language isn't standardized like verbal language, no such dictionary can be written.

Our cultural or ethnic background, the way our parents expressed themselves nonverbally, and other individual experiences influence the way we use our body. Some gestures—a nod or a smile—may seem universal, but not everyone uses body language in the same way. When you're dealing with a specific person, you can't be sure that he or she is giving signals we have come to expect.

As you talk, your listener is nodding. Good, you assume that she's agreeing with you. Not necessarily so. There are some people who nod just to acknowledge that they're listening. When someone folds his arms as you speak you might think her action is a subconscious show of disagreement, but it could simply be that she's cold! There is danger in misreading nonverbal cues.

Take the time to learn people's body language. Study your colleagues' body language. You may notice that when John smiles in a certain way, it has one meaning; a different smile, a different meaning. On the other hand, maybe when Jane doesn't agree, she wrinkles her forehead. Make a conscious effort to study and remember people's individual body language.

Now Hear This

Body language is a lot more important than people think. Take a hint from top salespeople. They make a practice of carefully studying the body language of a prospect during the first few minutes of the interview. They note how the prospect's expressions often emphasize what is really important to him or her. They especially note the prospect's body language in reaction to the sales presentation, adapting their pitches accordingly. All of us can benefit from following this practice. It will enable us to become better communicators, whether we are the speaker or the listener.

Are You Really Listening?

Suppose one of your colleagues brings a problem to you and asks for help. You begin listening attentively, but before you know it, your mind is wandering. Instead of listening to the problem, you're thinking about the pile of work on your desk, the meeting you have scheduled with the company vice president, the scuffle your son got into at school. You hear your colleague's words, but you're not really listening.

Does this happen to you? Of course, it does. It happens to all of us. Why? Our minds can process ideas 10 times faster than we can talk. While someone is talking, your mind may race ahead. You complete the speaker's sentence in your mind—often incorrectly—long before he or she does. You "hear" what your mind dictates, not what's actually said.

This is human nature. But that's no excuse for being a bad listener. Read on to learn how to listen more effectively.

How to Pick Up the Pieces

Now suppose your mind was wandering and you didn't hear what the other person said. It's embarrassing to admit you weren't listening, so you fake it. You pick up on the last few words you heard and comment on them. If you make sense, you're lucky. But you may have missed the real gist of the discussion.

When you haven't been listening, you don't have to admit, "I'm sorry, I was day-dreaming." One way to get back on track is to ask a question or make a comment about the last item you did hear: "Can we go back a minute to such-and-such?"

Another method is to comment this way: "To make sure I can better understand your view on this, please elaborate."

Active Listening

One way of improving your listening skills is to take an *active* role. Instead of just sitting or standing with your ears open, follow these guidelines:

Tactical Tools

As soon as you realize you haven't been paying full attention to someone—when you start hearing a droning sound instead of words, when you hear only words but not ideas, or when you're anticipating what you *think* will be said—stop! Then start listening!

Words to Work By

An **active** listener not only pays close attention to what the other party says, but asks questions, makes comments, and reacts verbally and nonverbally to what is said.

- Look at the speaker. Eye contact is one way of showing interest, but don't overdo it. Look at the whole person, don't just stare into his or her eyes.

- Show interest by your facial expressions. Smile or show concern when appropriate.

- Indicate that you are following the conversation by nods or gestures.

- Ask questions about what's being said. You can paraphrase "So the way I understand it is …" or ask specific questions about specific points. This technique not only enables you to clarify points that may be unclear but also keeps you alert and paying full attention.

- Don't interrupt. A pause should not be a signal for you to start talking. Wait.

- Be an empathic listener. Listen with your heart as well as your head. Try to feel what other people are feeling when they speak. In other words, put yourself in the speaker's shoes.

Five Strategies to Make You a Better Listener

You can become a better listener. You can stop some of the main causes of ineffective listening before they begin. All you have to do is make a few changes in your work environment and in your approach to listening—a small effort with a big return:

- **Shut off the telephone.** It's probably your greatest distraction. If you know that you'll be having a lengthy discussion at your desk, arrange for someone else to handle your calls or set your voice mail to pick up all calls right away. If this isn't possible, get away from the telephone. Try an empty conference room: The phone there won't distract you, and no one knows that you're there—so it probably won't ring.

- **Turn off your computer's new mail message.** It's too tempting to check to see whom the e-mail message is from. You can wait to check your e-mail until after the meeting.

- **Hide the papers.** If your desk is strewn with paper, you'll probably sit there skimming them and, before you know it, you'll be reading a letter or memo instead of listening. If you go to a conference room, take only the papers that are related to the discussion. If you must stay at your desk, put the papers in a drawer so that you won't be tempted to read them.

- **Don't get too comfortable.** Some years ago I was discussing a situation with another manager. As was my custom, I sat in my comfortable executive chair with my hands behind my head. Maybe I rocked a little, but fortunately, I caught myself before I dozed off. Ever since then, rather than take a relaxing position when I engage in discussions, I've made a point of sitting on the edge of my chair and leaning forward rather than backward when engaged in discussions. This position not only brings me physically closer to the other person, but also enables me to be more attentive, and helps me to maintain eye contact. It also shows the other person that I'm truly interested in getting the full story he or she is relating and that I take seriously what is being said. And because I'm not quite so comfortable, there's less of a tendency to daydream.

- **Don't think about your rebuttal.** It's tempting to pick up one or two points that the speaker is making and plan how you will respond to them. Do this and you'll probably miss much of the balance of what is being said, often the really important matters. Concentrate on what is said through the entire process.

- **Take notes.** It's impossible to remember everything that's said in a lengthy discussion. Jot down key words or phrases. Write down figures or important facts, just enough to help you remember. Immediately after a meeting, while the information is still fresh in your mind, write a detailed summary. Dictate it into a recorder, enter it into your computer, or write it in your notebook, whichever is best for you.

Evaluate Your Listening Skills

Yes	No	
❏	❏	Do you keep interrupting when somebody is trying to tell you something?
❏	❏	Do you look at papers during the discussion?
❏	❏	Do you come to a conclusion before you hear the whole story?
❏	❏	Does your body language signal lack of interest?
❏	❏	Do you hear only what you want to hear and block out everything else?
❏	❏	Do you show impatience with the speaker?
❏	❏	Do you spend more time talking than listening?
❏	❏	Does your mind wander during the discussion?
❏	❏	Do you think about your rebuttal or response while the other person is speaking?
❏	❏	Do you ignore nonverbal signals from the speaker that will tell you the speaker wants you to respond?

If you answered "yes" to any of these questions, you should concentrate on improving your listening skills.

Barriers to Clear Communication

Some of the major barriers that impede communication are psychological, not physical. You may have perfect articulation and choose your words wisely, but the static develops in intangible areas: assumptions, attitudes, and the emotional baggage each of us has.

Check Out Your Assumptions

You've seen this situation repeatedly: You have a pretty good idea about what causes a particular problem and how to solve it. In discussing it with others, you assume that they know as much about it as you do, so what you say is based on the assumption that they have know-how, when they really don't. The result is that you don't give them adequate information.

Be Aware of Your Attitude

Another barrier to communication is the attitudes of the sender and the receiver. A manager might convey arrogance in the way he or she gives directions. He or she may appear to be talking down to staff members. This causes resentment, which blocks communication. In order for the message to be received, it must not only be understood but accepted by the receiver. When resentment develops, acceptance is unlikely.

> **Stop! Look! Listen!**
>
> An employee who is busy resenting the leader's attitude doesn't really "hear" what's being said. Good leaders avoid such indicators of arrogance as sarcasm and "pulling rank" when dealing with staff members.

Watch for Preconceptions

People tend to hear what they expect to hear. The message you receive is distorted by any information you have already heard about the subject. So if the new information is different from what's expected, you might reject it as being incorrect. Rather than actually hearing the new message, you may be hearing what your mind is telling you.

What does this mean to you? Keep your mind open. When someone tells you something, make an extra effort to listen and to evaluate the new information objectively, instead of blocking it out because it differs from your preconceptions.

In communicating with others, also try to learn their preconceptions. If they are people you work with regularly, you probably know how they view many of the matters you discuss. When you present your views to them, take into consideration what they already believe. If their beliefs differ from yours, be prepared to make the effort to jump over those hurdles.

> **Stop! Look! Listen!**
>
> Perception is reality in the minds of the perceiver. Unless your perception and team members' perception of a situation are congruent, you will be working at cross-purposes.

Prejudices and Biases—Yours and Theirs

Your biases for or against a person influence the way you receive his or her messages. We listen more attentively and are more likely to accept ideas from somebody we like and respect. We tend to blot out input from people we don't like, and reject their ideas.

Biases also affect the way subject matter is received. People turn a deaf ear to opposing viewpoints concerning matters about which they have strong feelings. Carol is a good example of such a person. As company controller, she is fixated on reducing costs. She won't even listen to any discussion that might increase costs no matter what the long-term benefits may be.

Be Aware of Your Emotional State

We all have bad days. On one of those bad days, one of your team members comes to you all excited about a new idea. How do you react? Probably, you think, "I have enough on my platter now, who needs this?" Your mind is closed and the message doesn't come through.

It works both ways. An important assignment comes up and you go over to two of your staff members, Dan and Joan, to discuss it. Joan is enthusiastic about the job; Dan is skeptical. Why? Dan is annoyed because he is busy working on another project and he wants to concentrate on it. He feels you are inconsiderate to assign him to this job.

Always get a sense of people's moods before launching into your discussion. A brief conversation with Dan and Joan about their current activities would have brought out how much time Dan was spending on his current project. That way, when you present the new assignment, you can make a point of saying that what he is doing now is important, and you are happy with his progress. Demonstrate that the reason you chose him for the new assignment is that it won't interfere with, but will complement, his current work.

Channels: The Distortion Between Sender and Receiver

In communication, one major source of interference and distortion is the path the message takes from sender to receiver. In many large organizations, communications must flow through set channels. The more extensive the channels, the more likely that distortion will occur. It is not unusual for a piece of information passed orally "through channels" to be distorted at each station, so that what the receiver receives is not at all what the sender sent.

One way to alleviate this difficulty is to use written communications. Writing is more difficult to distort, though interpretation of what is written may vary from station to station. Even so, writing has certain disadvantages: Many matters can't or shouldn't be communicated in writing. Writing is time consuming. For rush matters and matters of transient interest, writing is not appropriate.

A more effective way is to shorten channels and allow for bypassing where feasible. The fewer stations along the way, the less chance for distortion. The main reason for channels is to ensure that people who are responsible for a project are kept aware of everything that applies to it. This makes sense, but it is usually overdone. If a matter involves policy decisions or major areas of activity, channels are important. However, a great portion of the communications in companies concerns routine matters. Using channels for these not only may distort the message but also will slow down the work.

> **Tactical Tools**
>
> Often, when two groups are working on a project together, much time and trouble can be saved if, on routine matters, members bypass immediate supervisors and deal directly with their counterparts on the other team.

The Feedback Loop

The sender must always be sensitive to how the receiver receives and accepts the message. One way of checking on how messages have come across is the feedback loop.

Here's an example of the feedback loop in action: Mike sends a message to Amanda. Amanda responds stating her comments about Mike's message. If Amanda has misinterpreted all or parts of his message, Mike can now clarify it and send her a revised message. This continues until both parties are sure that the message has been understood.

One way feedback can be obtained is by asking questions. But you have to ask the right questions. The most commonly asked question is, "Do you understand?" However, that's not a good question because it's too vague. Most people will say "yes" even if they don't understand. He or she may be ashamed to say "no" for fear of being considered stupid, or may honestly believe he or she does understand, but actually only comprehends part of the message, or interprets it quite differently from how it was intended.

A better approach is to be more specific. Ask, "So that we both understand what you are going to do, let's go over it again" or, "Tell me how you view this?" Another approach is to ask questions about the key points, to ensure that they are fully understood.

Making Meetings More Meaningful

An effective way to exchange information is through meetings. But meetings can be a big waste of time—if they're not organized properly.

Stop! Look! Listen!

When people who are usually invited to meetings are not invited, they may worry: "Why wasn't I asked? Is the boss giving me a hidden message? Am I on the way out?" Avoid this concern by explaining before-hand why you're not inviting someone who usually attends. If it's a new policy, tell everyone involved why you instituted it.

Tactical Tools

In establishing the sequence of topics at a meeting, put the most complex ones at the beginning of the program. People come to meetings with clear minds and are able to approach deeper matters more effectively early on. If you schedule the important issues for later, participants are less likely to be attentive, and may be distracted by what has been discussed earlier.

Have you ever left a meeting thinking: "What a waste of time. I could have accomplished so much more if I had spent this past hour at my desk!" In a recent survey, more than 70 percent of the people interviewed felt they had wasted time in the meetings they had attended.

There is hope. Meetings can be made productive. In the following sections, I'll discuss a few ways to conduct your meetings more efficiently.

Limit Who Attends

Invite only appropriate participants. Some managers hold staff meetings on a regular basis—sometimes weekly or even daily. Quite often, many of the people who attend are not involved in the matters that are discussed. By inviting only those who can contribute to the meeting or will be affected by what is discussed, you can avoid wasting others' time and keep the meetings briefer.

Make an Agenda—and Stick to It

Prepare an agenda. An agenda is key to the success or failure of a meeting. Plan your agenda carefully, covering all matters that you want to discuss. By determining in advance not only what subjects will be addressed, but the order in which they will be covered, you'll make the meeting run more smoothly.

At least three days before the meeting, send the agenda to all people who will attend. This will allow them to study the topics of discussion and prepare their contribution.

Stick rigidly to the agenda. Don't allow people to bring up topics not on the agenda. If anyone tries, point out that unless it's an emergency, it cannot be discussed at this meeting. Suggest it be placed on the agenda for the next meeting.

Get Everyone into the Act

Attendees should be encouraged to study the agenda and be prepared to discuss each item. If you need specific data to make a point, organize it into easy-to-follow visuals (for example, charts or handouts) and bring them to the meeting. Encourage discussion and create an atmosphere in which people can disagree without fear of ridicule or retaliation.

Now Hear This

Provide "takeaway" photocopies of diagrams, flow charts, or whatever data you bring to the meeting. Distribute the copies to everyone at the meeting to ensure that they have a clear representation of the subjects you discuss. These copies also serve as permanent reminders of your message; participants can refer to them later if necessary.

If you have heftier handouts or other dense reading materials, distribute them far enough in advance of the meeting to enable team members to study them. The focus of a meeting should be on expanding, demonstrating, and clarifying information—not to introduce brand new concepts, particularly technical or complex material.

If you are the leader, ask questions that stimulate discussion. Be open to questions and dissension. It's better to have people butt heads during the meeting than let them stew over their problems over a long period of time.

Control Blabbermouths

Don't you hate it when one person tries to dominate a meeting? It's usually the same one or two people who always have something to say—usually not important, often a personal pet peeve, and always distracting. Here are some tips on how you, as a meeting leader, can attempt to keep them quiet:

◆ Take the blabbermouth aside before the meeting and tell him or her, "I know you like to contribute to our meetings and I appreciate it, but we have a limited amount of time and some of the other people want a chance to present their ideas. So let's give them a chance to talk, and you and I can discuss your issues after the meeting."

◆ If the blabbermouth still insists on dominating the meeting, wait until he or she pauses for breath—which they inevitably must do—and quickly say, "Thank you. Now let's hear what Sue has to say."

◆ Announce that each speaker has only three minutes to make his or her point. Be flexible with others, but be strict with the blabbermouths.

Close with a Bang

At the end of the meeting, after all the items on the agenda have been covered, the leader should summarize what has been accomplished. If any team members received assignments during the course of the meeting, have them indicate what they understand they will be expected to do and when they will do it.

Keep Minutes

Take notes so that there is no misunderstanding of what has been decided at a meeting. These need not be detailed transcripts of the entire discussion, but a summary of the decisions made on each issue. After the meeting, distribute copies of the minutes not only to the attendees, but also to all people who may be affected by what was determined. The minutes will serve as a reminder to the participants of what was decided and as a communication to those who didn't attend.

Conferences, Conventions, and Retreats

In addition to team or department level meetings, managers often participate in company-wide conferences or conventions. These are more elaborate than local meetings, and if you are asked to make a presentation at one of them, you should prepare it carefully. Companies also organize retreats to bring employees together at a facility away from the company offices—usually a resort hotel—to relax and informally discuss company problems. You'll play golf or tennis, take nature walks, go canoeing, build campfires, or splurge on buffets. The hope is that staff members will loosen up and be more creative in presenting ideas and more receptive to receiving them.

> **Tactical Tools**
>
> You can use a retreat to get to know your boss better or make contacts with people in other departments. This can be very valuable to your work and the advancement of your career.

If you are invited to any such gatherings you should accept—it's less an invitation than a command. Sure, have fun. Participate in the discussions. However, prepare what you will say and be businesslike in your demeanor. Dress informally, but not loudly. Drink moderately. Watch what you say.

Getting the Most out of Conventions or Conferences

Most managers who attend conferences often complain that they get little benefit from them. Here are 10 steps that will help make meetings more meaningful to you:

1. **Plan and prepare.** Most conferences and conventions are announced months in advance. Usually an agenda accompanies the announcement. Study it carefully. Does any subject listed require special preparation? You may want to read a book or an article on unfamiliar subjects to help you comprehend and contribute to the discussion. You may want to reexamine your company's experience in that area so you can relate what is being discussed to your own organization's problems.

2. **Don't sit with your colleagues.** You can speak to them anytime. Here is your chance to meet new people. At many meetings, participants are seated at tables either for the entire program or for parts of it. Make a point of sitting with different people at various stages of the meetings. Especially at luncheon or dinner discussions, you can pick up more ideas from your tablemates than from the speakers. In addition, you can make new contacts who may be valuable resources for information after the conference.

   Stop! Look! Listen!

   When attending a convention or retreat, don't relax completely. Don't think for a minute that your offhand remarks will be considered "off the record." The other participants are not necessarily your buddies. They may be your bosses, your rivals for advancement, or your competitors for company funds or recognition of power.

3. **Open your mind.** You go to conferences and conventions to learn. To get the most out of what a speaker says, keep your mind open to new suggestions. They may be different from what you honestly believe is best, but until you hear it all and think it through objectively, you won't really know. Progress comes through change. This does not mean that all new ideas are good ones, but they should be listened to, evaluated, and carefully and objectively considered.

4. **Be tolerant.** Have you ever listened to a speaker who turned you off immediately? You didn't like his or her appearance, clothes, voice, or accent, so you either stopped listening or rejected what he or she said. Prejudice against a speaker keeps many an attendee from really listening to what is discussed or from accepting the ideas presented.

5. **Take notes.** Note taking serves two important functions. It helps organize what you hear while you are at the conference, which leads to more systematic listening. It also becomes a source for future reference.

Stop! Look! Listen!

Once during a conference break, I overheard one participant tell another: "This meeting is a waste of time. How can a woman tell us men how to market machine tools? She ought to stick to housewares or cosmetics." Sexism prevented him from acquiring valuable information, which could have been important to his company.

Tactical Tools

Keep a record of the names and addresses of the speakers you hear at a conference or convention. You may want to contact some of them for additional information. Also list the names and addresses of people you meet at these events. They may be a source of information or guidance in the future.

6. **Ask questions.** Don't hesitate to query a speaker when the opportunity arises. But don't waste other people's time with trivial questions.

7. **Contribute ideas.** Some people will always contribute more than others; some just sit and listen. When asked why they didn't participate, they say: "Why should I give my ideas to these people? Some of them are my competitors and I won't give away my trade secrets."

Nobody expects you to say anything that would damage your firm or its competitive position, but most discussions are not of this nature. They're designed instead to promote the exchange of general ideas. The experience of one organization helps others. By contributing ideas, you provide richer experiences for everyone else, which in turn results in a more fulfilling experience for you.

8. **Summarize.** After the meeting, review your notes while the meeting is still fresh in mind. Write or dictate a report on the conference for your permanent files.

9. **Report.** Report on what you have learned to your boss or others in your organization who might find the information valuable. By sharing what you have learned, you add to the value your firm receives from sending you to the convention.

10. **Apply what you have learned.** If you don't do anything with what you learned at the conference, it's been a waste of time and money.

The Least You Need to Know

- Whether you're presenting your ideas to a group or to just one person, prepare what you're going to say before you say it.

- Speak clearly and distinctly so that you'll be easily understood. Speak with enthusiasm so that your audience doesn't fall asleep.

- Be aware of the body language of your listeners.

- Listen! Listen actively and fully and with an open mind.

- When you lead a meeting, have an agenda prepared, stick to it, and keep the meeting running smoothly and on time.

- When attending a conference or convention, remember the 10 steps for getting the most out of it.

Chapter 6

Get Your Staff into the Act

In This Chapter

◆ Overcome your fears of delegating

◆ The five elements of effective assigning

◆ How to schedule the workload

◆ Tips for managing multiple priorities

You and your department have lots of work to do. What will you do yourself, and what will you assign to other people? When you delegate, you assign to your staff members not only tasks but also the power and the authority to accomplish them.

Effective *delegation* means that a supervisor has enough confidence in his or her staff members to know that they'll carry out an assignment satisfactorily and expeditiously.

This chapter looks at some techniques and approaches to help you become a better delegator.

Don't Hesitate—Delegate!

Sure, you're responsible for everything that goes on in your department or team, but if you try to do everything yourself, you'll put in 12 or more hours a day. That can lead to burnout and ulcers, or even heart attacks and nervous breakdowns.

There are certain things, of course, that only you can do, decisions that only you can make, critical areas that only you can handle. That's where you earn your keep. Many of the activities you undertake, however, can and should be done by others. This list discusses some of the reasons you may hesitate to delegate and explains why you should reconsider:

- **You can do it better than your associates.** That may be the case, but you should spend your time and energy on more important things. Each of your staff members has talents and skills that contribute to your group's performance. By delegating assignments, you give them the opportunity to use those skills.

    How often have you thought, "By the time I tell a worker what to do, demonstrate how to do it, check the work, find it wrong, and have it done over, I could have it completed and go on to other things"? Showing someone how to perform a certain task will take time now, of course, but after your colleague masters the task, it will make your job easier later.

- **You get a great deal of satisfaction from a certain aspect of the work and hesitate to give it up.** You're not alone. All of us enjoy certain things about our work and are reluctant to assign them to others. Look at the tasks objectively. Even if you have a pet project, you must delegate it if your time can be spent handling other activities that are now your responsibility as a manager.

- **You're concerned that if you don't do it yourself, it won't get done right.** You have a right to be concerned. The following section explains how to minimize this risk. You won't have to be afraid of delegating work to others if you follow the principles I describe.

> **Words to Work By**
>
> **Delegation** enables you to position the right work at the right responsibility level, helping both you and your team members expand skills and contributions. You also ensure that all work gets done on time by the right person who has the right experience or interest.

Making Assignments

You know the capabilities of each of your associates. When you plan their assignments, consider which person can do which job most effectively. If you're under no time pressure, you can use the assignment to build up another person's skills. If no one on your staff can do the work, then of course you'll have to do it yourself. You should train one or more employees in several areas so you can delegate work in those areas when necessary. The more people who have the capabilities to take on a variety of assignments, the easier your job is for you.

Giving Workable Instructions

After you give detailed instructions to one of your staff members, make sure they understand them. Here's where those communication skills you learned in Chapter 5 will come in especially handy: Rather than ask "Do you understand?" ask "What are you going to do?" If the response indicates that one or more of your points isn't clear, you can correct it before the employee does something wrong.

When it's essential for an employee to rigidly conform to your instructions, you should make sure that he or she thoroughly understands them. Ask specific questions so that you both agree about what he or she will do. When it's not essential for a delegated activity to be performed in a specific manner, you can just get some general feedback.

Tailor the way you make assignments to the preferences of the person you're delegating to. Some people like to have responsibilities spelled out explicitly, perhaps in the form of a written list of items. Others prefer simple, concise instructions. Some people prefer e-mail, and others would rather have you delegate in person.

Make Sure They Understand—and Accept—Your Instructions

Your instructions must be both understood *and* accepted by your staff member. Suppose that on Tuesday morning, Janet, the office manager, gives an assignment to Jeremy with a deadline of 3:30 that afternoon. Jeremy looks at the amount of work involved and says to himself, "There's no way." It's unlikely that he will meet that *deadline*.

To gain acceptance, let your employee know just how important the work is. Janet might say, "Jeremy, this report must be on the director's desk when she comes in tomorrow morning. She needs it for an early morning meeting with the executive committee. When do you think I can have it?" Jeremy may think, "This is important. If I skip my break and don't call my girlfriend, I can have it by 5:00."

Why did Janet originally indicate that she wanted the report by 3:30 when she didn't even need it until the following morning? Maybe she thought that if she said 3:30, Jeremy would knock himself out and finish the report by the end of the day. However, most people don't react that way. Faced with what they consider to be an unreasonable deadline, most people won't even try. By letting people set their own schedules within reasonable limits, you get their full commitment to meeting or beating a deadline.

But suppose that Janet really did need that report by 3:30—so that it could be proofread, photocopied, collated, and bound. To get the report completed on time, she could have assigned someone to help Jeremy or allowed him to work overtime.

Be realistic when you assign deadlines. Don't make a practice of asking for projects to be completed earlier than you need them—people will stop taking your deadlines seriously.

Set Control Points

A control point is the point at which you stop a project, examine the work that has been completed, and correct any errors. Control points can help you catch errors before they blow up into catastrophes.

A control point is *not* a surprise inspection. Employees should know exactly when each control point is established and what should be accomplished by then.

Suppose Gary, a supervisor, gives a project to Kim on Monday morning. The deadline is the following Friday at 3 P.M. They agree that the first control point will be at 4 P.M. Tuesday, at which time Kim should have completed parts A and B. Notice that Kim knows exactly *what* and *when*. When Gary and Kim meet on Tuesday, they find several errors in part B. That's not good, but it's not terrible. The errors can be corrected before the work continues. If Gary and Kim had not scheduled a control point, the errors would have been perpetuated throughout the entire project.

Give Them the Authority to Get the Job Done

You can't do a job without the proper tools. Providing equipment, computer time, and access to resources is an obvious step, but giving away *authority* is another story.

Many managers are reluctant to give up any of their authority. If a job is to be done without your micro-management, you must give the people doing the job the power to make decisions.

For example, if they need supplies or materials, allot them a budget so that they can order what they need without having to ask your approval for every purchase. If a job might call for overtime, allow them to make the determination without having to ask your permission. If you have to be around to make every decision, the work will get bogged down.

When You Delegate, You Don't Abdicate

Team or workgroup members almost always have questions, seek advice, and need your help. Be there for them, but don't let them throw the entire project back at you. Let them know that you're available to help, advise, and support, but not to do their work.

> **Tactical Tools**
>
> When people bring you a problem, insist that they bring with it a suggested solution. At best, they will solve their own problems and not bother you. At the very least, they'll ask you, "Do you think this solution will work?" which is much easier to respond to than "What do I do now?"

Putting Delegation to Work

Now that you know the principles of delegation, you're ready to apply them on the job.

Delegating to Teams

When an organization is structured into teams, work should be delegated and assigned as a team activity. When people have some control over the assignments they get, they approach their work with enthusiasm and commitment.

When your boss gives you a complex project, present it in its entirety to your team. You should discuss with your team how to break the assignment into phases. Delegating each of the phases to individual team members will follow easily. Most members will choose to handle the areas in which they have the most expertise. If two members want the same area, let them iron it out with each other. However, if it gets sticky, you should step in and resolve the problem diplomatically: "Gustav did the research on our last project, so let's give Carol a chance to handle it this time."

Certain phases of the assignment are bound to be tough or unpleasant. No one's really going to volunteer to do them. Have your team set up an equitable system for assigning this type of work.

Now Hear This _____

If you have a difficult task, assign it to a capable, but lazy person. He or she will find an easy way to do it.

As team leader, be sure that every member of your team is aware of every team members' responsibilities. In this way, everyone will know what kind of support he or she can give or receive from others.

To keep everyone informed, create a chart listing each phase of the assignment, the person handling it, deadlines, and other pertinent information. Post the chart in the office for easy referral.

Multidepartmental Teams

Before companies began using the team concept, work was done interdepartmentally. For instance, the department manager would schedule production for his or her department with the assistance of support departments (for instance, production control, inventory control, and purchasing). The order department would process customers' orders and send the orders on to production scheduling. The production department would then determine priorities and assign various aspects of the job to the appropriate departments. Each department head would then assign specific phases of the task to individual employees.

As you can imagine, this process often resulted in bottlenecks. If one department fell behind, it caused delays in all the others.

The *multidepartmental team* can successfully handle projects that require coordination among many diverse workgroups within a company. An effective team has these characteristics:

♦ It is composed of representatives from all relevant internal departments. Team members are usually chosen by the team leader in conjunction with managers of the involved departments.

Words to Work By _____

In a **multidepartmental team,** also called a cross-functional team, representatives from different departments are temporarily assigned to work as a team. They combine their expertise to work collaboratively on a project.

♦ Outside representatives, such as customers, suppliers, and subcontractors, are invited to participate in team discussions when relevant. Although these people aren't members of the team, their input is important in helping the team accomplish its goal.

♦ One example of how this works is a project based on customers' needs. Team members are given detailed information about these needs and are encouraged to deal directly with customers to set schedules and keep up to date on necessary adjustments.

♦ Work assignments are planned collaboratively and control points are established. Some projects require teams to meet daily to coordinate and maintain attention to the assignment. Other projects require only occasional meetings to check on progress and deal with problems.

The key to the success of multidepartmental programs is communication. Team members are encouraged to communicate in person, on the telephone, or by writing, faxing, or e-mailing each other on a timely basis. Problems can then be addressed without delay.

The Least You Need to Know

♦ Overcome any reluctance to delegate. You can't do everything yourself.

♦ By getting good feedback when you discuss assignments, you can catch misunderstandings before they affect the work at hand.

♦ You and your team should set control points so that errors can be caught before causing real problems.

♦ Use multidepartmental teams to tackle assignments that cross departmental lines.

♦ Purchase computer software to assist you in scheduling complex work assignments.

♦ When you're faced with conflicting priorities, rethink the order of their importance. Diplomacy and open discussion with all parties involved can help you reach workable compromises.

Part 3

Following Labor and Equal Employment Laws

You're not a bigot. You believe in fair treatment of everybody regardless of their color, gender, ethnic background, or age. However, you are concerned that somewhere along the line you might inadvertently make a comment, ask a question, or do something in good faith, but still be accused of violating the law.

Like all laws, the laws governing equal employment opportunity are subject to interpretation. What appears clear and simple, therefore, easily becomes vague and complex.

This part of the book looks at these laws and some of the other labor laws. Included are suggestions and guidelines to help you cope with some common problems, such as questions you can and cannot ask an applicant, how to prevent sexual harassment, and making accommodations for people who have special challenges.

Chapter 7

What the Laws Require

In This Chapter

- ◆ What are these laws anyway
- ◆ Hiring under the civil rights laws
- ◆ What you need to know about EEO
- ◆ Avoiding age discrimination in hiring, firing, and retiring
- ◆ Adhering to the ADA: abilities not disabilities
- ◆ Penalties and punishments

The laws governing equal employment affect every aspect of your job as a manager. It begins even before your first contact with an applicant and governs all your relations with employees: how you screen candidates, what you pay employees, how you treat employees on the job—all the way to employees' separation from the company, and sometimes even after that.

This chapter looks at these laws and how you as a manager need to comply with them. It explores some of the problems that have plagued other employers, and suggests ways for you to avoid similar troubles. In addition to the federal laws, most states have related laws. In this book, we'll only deal with federal laws. Make it a point to check with your attorneys or local authorities on special state laws that may affect you.

The Civil Rights Act of 1964

The primary equal employment law is the Civil Rights Act of 1964, as amended, which prohibits discrimination in employment on the basis of race, color, sex, religion, or national origin. The section of the law that covers employment (Title VII) is usually referred to as the Equal Employment Opportunity (EEO) law and is administered by the Equal Employment Opportunity Commission (EEOC). The EEOC also administers the Age Discrimination in Employment Act (ADEA) and the Americans with Disabilities Act (ADA).

Race, Color, National Origin

Among the areas covered by Title VII of the federal Civil Rights Act of 1964 as amended is the prohibition of discriminating on the basis of race, color, or national origin. All companies or organizations with 15 or more employees must comply with this law. Although many states had passed fair employment laws—some as far back as the 1940s—the Civil Rights Act was the first all inclusive federal law in this area. Most companies recognize the importance of these laws and have made strong efforts to train and work with their staffs to comply with them. Many larger organizations have added equal employment officers to their human resources departments to ensure compliance with the laws. Smaller firms often assign this activity to a member of the management team.

The law made companies rethink many of the stereotypes that kept them from hiring minorities. However, the law did more than just change stereotypes. Many hiring practices and procedures had to be rethought as well.

Religion

Prior to the passage of this law, it wasn't uncommon for companies to refuse to hire people whose religious beliefs differed from theirs. Help Wanted ads often specified such requirements as "Protestants only," and application forms included questions on religion. The Civil Rights Act prohibited such requirements and questions.

In addition to prohibiting religious discrimination in hiring, the law requires companies to make reasonable accommodation for a person's *religious practices* unless doing so results in undue hardship on the company. This will be discussed in Chapter 9.

Words to Work By

According to the Equal Employment Opportunity Commission Guidelines, **religious practices** include not only traditional religious beliefs, but also moral and ethical beliefs, and beliefs individuals hold "with the strength of traditional religious view."

Gender

In addition to the prohibition of discrimination on the basis of race, religion, and national origin, the Civil Rights Act of 1964 also prohibits discrimination on the basis of gender.

Traditionally many jobs were associated with a particular gender. For the most part skilled artisans such as carpenters, machinists, and plumbers were considered jobs for men, as were positions in engineering, accounting, outside sales, and virtually all management positions. Women's jobs were usually lower paid positions such as nurses, typists, retail sales clerks, and low-skilled factory jobs. Although there always have been exceptions, until this law was passed, few men were hired as secretaries and receptionists, and few women were hired or promoted to supervisory or management jobs.

The Civil Rights Act changed the gender structure of most companies radically. You will now find women in most types of jobs and more men performing jobs that were formerly considered women's work.

Employers often claim that their policies on hiring women weren't based on prejudice, but had sound business reasons. Women often have children at home and can't travel, can't work overtime, and stay home every time a kid is sick. The law does *not* recognize these as legitimate reasons. Despite the laws, employers still ask women about these matters. Later in this chapter you'll find a list of what questions you may not ask as well as suggestions for how to get the information you need lawfully.

Now Hear This

When the Civil Rights Act of 1964 was introduced in Congress, it covered only race, color, religion and national origin. An opponent of the act added sex discrimination to it because he believed that such a radical provision would make the law unpassable. As they say, the rest is history.

Bona Fide Occupational Qualifications (BFOQs)

There are some positions for which a company is permitted to specify only a man or only a woman for the job. Clear-cut reasons must exist, however, for why a person of only that gender can perform the job. In the law, these reasons are referred to as *bona fide occupational qualifications*, or *BFOQs*.

If a job calls for heavy lifting, for example, is it a BFOQ for men only? Not necessarily. Certain strong women may be able to do the job, and certain weak men may not. It's legitimate to require that all applicants—both men and women—pass a weightlifting test.

Now Hear This ⎯⎯⎯⎯⎯

The only undisputed bona fide occupational qualifications are a wet nurse (for a woman) and a sperm donor (for a man).

And that's not all. Suppose that a job calls for driving a forklift truck and that the operator is occasionally required to do heavy lifting. A woman applicant may be able to drive the truck but not be able to do the lifting. If the lifting is only a small part of the job, you cannot reject her. She is capable of performing the major aspect of the work, and other people can be assigned to handle the lifting.

Suppose that you have always had an attractive woman as your receptionist and that the job is now open. Is this a BFOQ for a woman? Of course not. There's no reason that a man can't be just as effective.

Maternity and Pregnancy

The sex discrimination provisions of the Equal Employment laws also cover maternity and pregnancy. Although this was implied in the Civil Rights Act of 1964, it was clarified and strengthened by the Pregnancy Discrimination Act of 1978.

The basic principal of this law is that women who are pregnant must be treated the same as other applicants and employees. In screening a pregnant applicant, she must be judged on her ability to perform the job for which she applies without regard to her current condition.

You may be concerned that if you hire her, she will have to take time off for delivery and care of the infant, and perhaps will not even return to work. Under this law, you must assume that she will only be away from the job for a relatively short period of time. The law says that pregnancy should be considered the same as a "temporary disability." There's no question that it's temporary, and in most cases, it will be only a minor inconvenience to the company. The law also applies to current employees.

There are some jobs where working conditions such as exposure to certain chemicals might be dangerous to unborn children. Many companies had fetal protection policies that excluded pregnant women and sometimes all women of childbearing age from these jobs. The United States Supreme Court ruled that such policies were illegal and women could not be barred from these jobs.

Lawyers specializing in employment law strongly recommend that when a woman is hired or later assigned to work in such a position, she be carefully informed about the workplace risks and be asked to sign a release. Because recent studies show that certain workplace substances can affect the male reproductive system, men hired or assigned to such jobs should also be informed of the risk and releases obtained.

The Age Discrimination in Employment Act of 1967 (ADEA)

This act prohibits discrimination against individuals 40 years of age or older. Some state laws cover all persons over the age of 18.

Who Is Covered?

Unlike the Civil Rights Act of 1964, which covers all employers with 15 or more employees, the ADEA applies to organizations with 20 or more employees.

The original law only protected people between the ages of 40 and 65. Companies could legally refuse to hire people over 65. However, that was changed by later amendments. Now there is no maximum age. You may not refuse to hire an applicant so long as he or she is otherwise qualified even if that person is 100 years old. The law also prohibits mandatory retirement at any age with a few exceptions (e.g. companies may require senior executives to retire at a specified age).

Note that the law does not apply to people under 40. Theoretically, you can turn down a 35-year-old applicant as being too old for your "trainee" job—but don't try it. First, many states cover everybody over the age of 18. Nevertheless, even if your state has not reduced the age, you can get into trouble.

A few years ago a company rejected a 30-something applicant and told her they wanted a younger person for that position. She was advised that as she was under 40, she couldn't file a complaint of age discrimination under federal law or in that state. Here's what happened: The State Job Service sent a 43-year-old applicant for an interview, and when she was rejected, filed an age discrimination charge against the firm.

Even though most company application forms don't ask a person's age or date of birth and most people omit that information from their resumés, it's still easy to guess an applicant's age range within a few years. A team leader who prefers young people on his or her team may overlook potential members who could be of great value to the team just because of age.

Don't Fall for These Age-Old Stereotypes

When you interview older applicants, avoid the stereotypes that may keep you from hiring highly qualified people for the wrong reason:

- **"The applicant is overqualified."** The term "overqualified" is often a euphemism for "too old." Some people may have more know-how or experience than a job requires, but that doesn't necessarily mean that they won't be productive. Discuss the details of the work with the applicant. It may be an opportunity for the person to learn new things. On the other hand, he or she may be able to contribute to the job some expertise that makes it more challenging. Judge the person as an individual, not as a member of an age group.

- **"The applicant made more money in the last job."** People with many years of experience often have earned more money than those with less experience. If the amount of salary your company can offer is a factor in your hiring decision, discuss it with the applicant—he or she should be the one to determine whether the salary is satisfactory. You may worry that if a better-paying job comes along, the new member will jump to it. That may happen, of course, but a younger person would probably do the same.

- **"This person won't fit in with my team."** Being of different age levels isn't necessarily a barrier to cooperation and collaboration. Make that determination on the basis of the candidate's personality, not on his or her age.

Encouraging Retirement

One method companies use to cut costs when they downsize is to compel higher-paid workers (who are most often older men and women) to retire early. Under current law, employees cannot (with a few minor exceptions) be forced to retire, no matter how old they are, unless they're not capable of performing their work.

Although forcing out older workers is illegal, companies often persuade people to retire by offering them bonuses, benefits, or other rewards. You can use this strategy as long as you do it in good faith and according to the law. Because it's a legal matter, an attorney should prepare the appropriate documents.

The Americans with Disabilities Act (ADA)

The newest and probably least understood civil rights law is the Americans with Disabilities Act (ADA). Your company must adhere to this law if it has 15 or more employees.

What You Can Do—What You Don't Have to Do

The ADA makes it illegal to discriminate in hiring, in job assignments, and in the treatment of employees because of a disability. Employers must make *reasonable accommodation* so that these people can perform the essential duties of their jobs.

This accommodation can vary from building access ramps for wheelchair users to providing special equipment for people who are seeing- or hearing-challenged, unless this type of accommodation is an *undue hardship* for the company.

Undue hardship is usually defined in monetary terms. If an applicant who uses a wheelchair applies for a job with a small company, the cost of building an elevator or a ramp to give access to the floor on which the job is located may be a financial hardship. If it is not possible to provide a less expensive accommodation, the company could reject the applicant. If the same applicant applied for a job in a more affluent company, however, it may not be considered undue hardship to do the necessary construction.

Accommodation doesn't always require expensive construction. The hypothetical examples in this list examine some other ways to meet this requirement:

- ◆ The small company you work for wants to hire Neil, an accountant who uses a wheelchair, but the accounting department is on the second floor of your building. The building has no elevator or ramp, and providing one would cost more than the company can afford. Must you do it? No. That would be an undue hardship for your company. There may be other ways to accommodate Neil, however. Use your imagination. You could let him work on the ground floor. His work could be brought to him. It may be an inconvenience, but it would qualify as reasonable accommodation, and it would enable you to hire a particularly competent accountant.

◆ Tiffany, a highly skilled word processor operator is legally blind and walks with the aid of a white cane. She can transcribe from dictated material faster and more accurately than many sighted people can. You want to hire her, but you're concerned that in case of a fire or other emergency she would be a danger to herself and others. The accommodation you can make is to assign someone to escort Tiffany in case of an emergency.

◆ LeRoy, an applicant for an assembler in a factory had been badly injured in an automobile accident. The job requires him to stand at a workbench all day. LeRoy is unable to stand for long periods. Is this a legitimate reason to reject him? Accommodations can be made. Perhaps a high stool could be provided so that LeRoy could reach the workbench without having to stand. If that option wasn't feasible, the job structure could be changed so that he could work part time on that job and do other work that didn't require standing for long portions of the day.

Stop! Look! Listen!

If you suspect that an employee cannot perform a job because of alcohol or drug abuse, have the person tested. Employees should be made aware that this policy will be followed, and it should be clearly stated in the company's policy manual.

What About Alcoholics and Drug Users?

Alcohol and drug users are considered disabled under the ADA. If a person can perform a job satisfactorily, a previous record of alcoholism or drug addiction is not reason enough to refuse hiring. If an applicant is still addicted, however, and it resulted in poor attendance or poor performance in his or her previous job, you can reject the person—not because of the addiction, but because of poor work habits.

Utilizing the Talents of Physically and Mentally Challenged People

Even in this day of computers and technological sophistication, many types of work are still routine and repetitive, resulting in high turnover among workers who are assigned to that work.

Many companies have found that people who are mentally challenged can do this work and are not bored by it. It takes more patience, and some tasks may have to be simplified, but trainees who master these tasks retain the skills and often improve on them. Coaches who are specially trained to work with people who are mentally challenged people are available in many communities. Your local mental health association can tell you whether this type of help is available in your area.

Tactical Tools
When you interview a candidate for a new job or consider someone for a promotion, don't focus on disabilities. Concentrate on that person's *abilities*.

Things I'd Like to Know, but Can't Ask

To make sure that the person you hire will, in your judgment, be effective, you believe that there are certain questions you *must* ask. Although civil rights laws vary somewhat from state to state, federal law governs all organizations doing business in the United States. The "lawful and unlawful" questions in the following table are presented as general guidelines that apply under federal laws and the laws of the strictest states. To ensure that you're in compliance with legal requirements and interpretations in any specific state, however, check with local authorities and an attorney specializing in this field.

(Note that questions that would otherwise be deemed lawful may in certain circumstances be deemed as evidence of unlawful discrimination when the question seeks to elicit information about a selection criterion that isn't job related and that has a disproportionate effect on the members of a minority group and cannot be justified by business necessity.)

Legal and Illegal Preemployment Questions

Subject	Lawful	Unlawful
Age	"Are you 18 years or older? If not, state age."	
Arrest record	"Have you ever been convicted of a crime? (Give details.)"	
Birth control	None.	

continues

Legal and Illegal Preemployment Questions (continued)

Subject	Lawful	Unlawful
Birthdate	None. (After person is employed, proof of age for insurance or other purposes may be requested.)	
Birthplace	None.	
Citizenship	"Are you a citizen of the United States? If not a citizen of the United States, do you intend to become a citizen of the United States? If not a citizen of the United States, have you the legal right to remain permanently in the United States?" (See Chapter 8.) "Do you intend to remain permanently in the United States?"	
Disability	"Do you have any impairments (physical, mental, or medical) that would interfere with your ability to perform the job for which you have applied?"	
Driver's license	"Do you possess a valid driver's license?"	
Education	Inquiry into applicant's academic, vocational, or professional education and schools attended.	None.
Experience	Inquiry into work experience.	None.
Gender	None.	Any inquiry about gender on application form or interview. "Do you wish to be addressed as Mr., Miss, Mrs., or Ms.?"

Subject	Lawful	Unlawful
Language	Inquiry into languages applicant speaks and writes fluently.	"What is your native language?" or any inquiry into how applicant acquired ability to read, write, or speak a foreign language.
Marital status	None.	"Are you married, single, divorced, or separated?"
		Name or other information about spouse.
		Where spouse works.
		"How many children do you have?"
		"How old are your children?"
		"What arrangements have you made for child care when you're at work?"
Military experience	Inquiry into applicant's military experience in the Armed Forces of the United States or in a state militia.	Inquiry into applicant's general military experience (for example, a military unit of another country).
	Inquiry into applicant's service in specific branch of United States Armed Forces.	
Name	"Have you ever worked for this company under a different name?"	Original name of applicant whose name has been changed by court order or otherwise. Maiden name of married woman.
	"Is any additional information (a change of name or use of assumed name or nickname) necessary to enable a check of your work record? If yes, explain."	"Have you ever worked under a different name? State name and dates."

continues

Legal and Illegal Preemployment Questions (continued)

Subject	Lawful	Unlawful
National origin	None.	Inquiry into applicant's lineage, ancestry, national origin, descent, parentage, or nationality. Spouse's nationality. "What is your native tongue?"
Notify in case	None.	Name and address of person be notified in case of an emergency. (This information may be asked only after an applicant is employed.)
Organizations	Inquiry into applicant's memberships in organizations that the applicant considers relevant to ability to perform job.	"List all clubs, societies, and lodges to which you belong."
Photograph	None.	Requirement or option that applicant affix a photograph to employment form at any time before being hired.
Race or color	None.	Complexion, color of skin, coloring.
Relatives	Names of applicant's relatives other than spouse already employed by company.	Names, addresses, number, or other information concerning applicant's spouse, children, or other relatives not employed by company.
Religion or creed	None.	Inquiry into applicant's religious denomination, religious affiliations, church, parish, pastor, or religious holidays observed. Applicants may not be told "This is a Catholic (or Protestant or Jewish) organization."

Marriage and Children

In your desire to obtain as much information as you can about an applicant so that you'll make the right hiring decision, you may ask questions that seem to be important but that violate equal employment opportunity laws. The most frequently asked illegal questions relate to marriage and child care. "But this stuff is important," you might say. "I *need* to know."

Suppose your team puts in a great deal of overtime—often on short notice. One applicant is a married woman (you noticed the ring on her finger), and you think that you have to know whether she has children at home. You reason that everyone knows that women with children have to pick them up at day care and can't work overtime. Another applicant isn't wearing a ring. Maybe she's divorced. Maybe she has children. You have to find out in order to know her availability, right?

Wrong, in both cases. Of course it's important to know whether applicants can work overtime on short notice, but you cannot assume their availability to work based on their responsibility for child care. In many families the father picks up a couple's children from a day care facility. The inability to work overtime isn't limited to child care matters. Anyone—single or married, man or woman—may not be able to work overtime for many reasons.

> **Tactical Tools**
>
> In choosing interview questions, ask yourself whether knowing the answers to those questions are necessary to determine an applicant's suitability to the position. Steer clear of questions that even hint at relating to a person's race, religion, national origin, gender, age, or disabilities.

How do you deal with this issue? You tell both men and women applicants about the overtime and then ask whether that will be a problem.

Here's a good rule of thumb: Don't ask questions of one gender that you wouldn't ask of the other. "Okay," you think, "I'll ask both men and women about their children, and then I'll be safe." Nope, even this method can be interpreted as discrimination.

If you ask a male applicant how many children he has and he says that he has four, your reaction may be, "Good, here's a stable family man. He'll work hard to support his family."

If you ask a woman applicant the same question and she gives the same answer, do you have the same reaction? Usually not. Managers often think that a woman will stay home from work every time one of her children gets sick, but such assumptions are unfair. In many families, both spouses share child care responsibilities or make arrangements for it.

Here's another good rule of thumb: Don't ask applicants any questions about marriage or family. Period. These types of questions elicit information that may be used to discriminate against women.

Criminal Records

You cannot ask applicants whether they have ever been arrested. Surprised? You shouldn't be. In our judicial system, after all, a person is innocent until proven guilty. Because police are often tougher and more likely to make arrests in minority neighborhoods, asking about arrests has an adverse effect on some minority groups.

You can ask about *convictions* for a felony; however, you cannot refuse to hire a person solely on the basis of a conviction—unless it's job related. You might, for example, disqualify an applicant from a cashier's position if he was convicted for theft, but not if he was convicted for disorderly conduct.

Ouch! What Happens When You Violate the EEO Laws?

If, after hearings before state or federal agencies responsible for enforcing civil rights laws, a company is found to be in violation of these laws, any or a combination of the following penalties may be invoked:

- If the complainant is an applicant, you may be required to hire that person with back pay to the date of the interview. If no job is available, a financial settlement will be negotiated.

- If the complainant is a discharged employee, you may have to reinstate that person with back pay from the date of termination.

- If the complainant has been denied a promotion, raise, or other benefit, you will be required to make that person "whole" (promote or give him or her the raise or benefit retroactively).

- If it's a class action, in which a pattern of discrimination is found, all parties to the class action may be awarded a financial settlement (frequently hundreds of thousands of dollars).

- In addition to financial penalties, companies have been required to institute an affirmative action plan to correct imbalances of minorities or women in the organization.

- Government contractors who violate the law or executive orders may lose their contracts or be banned from receiving future contracts.

◆ Companies that don't comply with orders from administrative agencies can be prosecuted in the courts and fined. Executives who defy the orders can be jailed.

◆ Companies can be sued by persons whose rights have been violated under these laws. Damages may be awarded for lost pay. In addition, companies can incur punitive damages, which can amount to tens or even hundreds of thousand dollars.

The Least You Need to Know

◆ Equal employment opportunity laws prohibit discrimination in employment based on color, race, religion, national origin, gender, age, and disability.

◆ Job specifications should be determined by what's necessary for success on the job, not by preconceived stereotypes.

◆ Study carefully what is lawful and unlawful and make it an integral part of your managerial behavior.

◆ Don't ask any applicants—male or female—questions relating to their marital status or family.

◆ You cannot refuse to hire or force to retire anyone over the age of 40 just because of age.

◆ In screening people for hiring, transfer, training programs, or promotion, focus on their abilities, not on their disabilities.

Sexual Harassment on the Job

In This Chapter

- ◆ What exactly is sexual harassment?
- ◆ Defining "an intimidating and hostile environment"
- ◆ Dating and romance on the job
- ◆ Ten steps to preventing sexual harassment charges

Articles about sexual harassment appear over and over again in the newspapers and on television. In one case, the president of a famous cosmetics company was accused of sexually harassing 15 female employees, and the company paid the women $1.2 million in an out-of-court settlement. In another, a U.S. senator was forced to resign because he was accused of sexually harassing at least 26 women who worked for him.

It's not only company presidents and senators who are accused of sexual harassment. Organizations of all sizes and types have faced charges brought against them by both female and male employees claiming sexual harassment by managers at all levels and even by nonmanagerial employees.

Sex Harassment Is a Big Buck Offense

In 1998, the Mitsubishi Company settled a sexual harassment suit by agreeing to pay $34 million to 360 women who had been harassed in their plant in Normal, Illinois.

The women reported that they had been fondled by male workers, propositioned by supervisors, called crude, sexually explicit names, subjected to viewing pornographic graffiti on the walls, and generally mistreated. Complaints to management were ignored.

> **Now Hear This**
>
> Although sexual harassment on the job has been illegal since 1965, relatively few cases were filed until Anita Hill brought sexual harassment charges against Clarence Thomas during his confirmation hearings. In the three years preceding these hearings, 18,300 sexual-harassment complaints were filed with the EEOC. In the three years following the hearings, 40,800 cases were filed.

In Long Island, New York, several female employees of Salomon Smith Barney, one of the top stock brokerage firms, accused their managers of creating a hostile and offensive working environment. They reported that the employee lounge was nicknamed the "boom-boom" room and that male employees made passes at the women there and considered it "good fun" to make sexually oriented remarks.

Women in other Salomon Smith Barney offices joined the class action. A federal court ordered the firm to submit the claims to an arbitration board to determine how much each individual claimant should be paid. In addition, the company was ordered to institute a diversity-training program to recruit, train, and promote women to jobs within the company where they were under-represented. The total cost was estimated to be more than $15 million.

What the Supreme Court Ruled

In 1998, the Supreme Court handed down two major decisions related to sexual harassment. In one case, they ruled that a company can be forced to pay damages to their workers who are sexually harassed by a low-level supervisor, even if they company knew nothing of the harassment and the victim failed to complain.

The Court said the general rule is that companies and public employers are automatically liable for a supervisor's sexual harassment. However, the rulings did contain some good news for employers. If sued, companies can sometimes successfully defend themselves by proving that they have a strong policy against sexual harassment and that they respond quickly to complaints. They must also show that the victim failed to take advantage of this policy by failing to file a complaint. But the burden of proof remains on the employers. The Court said, in effect, that companies must prove their innocence if a worker claims sexual harassment on the job. When in doubt, the company is liable.

In another case, a Chicago woman claimed that her boss made repeated comments to her with sexual innuendos. He urged her to wear shorter skirts, and told her that she was not "loose enough" to suit him. He commented he could make her life very hard or very easy.

After a year the woman quit and sued the company, Burlington Industries. A lower court judge threw out her claim, however, because she had not suffered a "tangible job consequence," such as a demotion, for refusing her supervisor's advances.

The United States Court of Appeals in Chicago overturned the lower court's decision, holding Burlington liable for the supervisor's harassment even though no specific job consequence had been involved.

The Supreme Court agreed. Although the woman had not suffered a tangible job action at the hands of her employer, Burlington was still subject to liability for her manager's action. To defend itself, the company would have had to prove that it "exercised reasonable care" to prevent harassment in the workplace.

What Exactly Is Sexual Harassment?

What one might assume is sexual harassment isn't always the same as what the courts have defined it to be. The legal definition of sexual harassment covers much more than just demanding sexual favors for favorable treatment on the job (naturally, these types of demands are included).

Here's the way the courts and the EEOC define sexual harassment. Any unwelcome sexual advances or requests for sexual favors or any conduct of a sexual nature when

◆ Submission is made explicitly or implicitly a term or condition of initial or continued employment.

◆ Submission or rejection is used as a basis of working conditions including promotion, salary adjustment, assignment of work, or termination.

◆ Such conduct has the purpose or effect of substantially interfering with an individual's work environment or creates an intimidating, hostile, or offensive work environment.

But what does this mean in plain English? Let's see how this concept works on the job.

> **Words to Work By**
>
> **Sexual harassment** is defined as any unwelcome sexual advances or requests for sexual favors, or any conduct of a sexual nature when an employer makes submission to sexual advances a condition of employment, or when submission or rejection is used as a basis of working conditions including promotion, salary adjustment, assignment of work, or termination, or has the effect of interfering with an individual's work or creating a hostile or intimidating work environment.

Subtlety Is No Excuse

You would think that corporate presidents and senators would have common sense enough to refrain from making *explicit* sexual demands, and most do. That's why people in positions of authority who sexually harass their subordinates use much more subtle tactics. Some men (and women) in positions of authority make it clear to subordinates that if they want to get favorable treatment or even keep their jobs, they must submit to these demands. But harassment is often much more subtle. The harasser doesn't make any actual demands; instead, it's implied. References are made to other employees who have benefited by being "more friendly." Comments about a person's physical attributes and similar remarks are made. These can be interpreted as harassment.

"Wait a minute! If I tell a woman that she's attractive, *that's* harassment?" It depends on what you say and how you say it. A comment such as, "That's an attractive dress" is much different from the comment "That dress is sexy." The statement "I like your new hairdo" is also acceptable, but the statement "Wearing your hair like that excites me" is not.

Take Randy, for example. He's is a "toucher." When he greets people, he grasps their hands, pats them on the back, and gives them hugs. That's his way of expressing himself, and he's been doing it for years. He also is a kisser. He doesn't kiss his male associates, but when he greets his female colleagues, he often pecks them on the cheek. Randy was shocked when he was called into the human resources office and told that some of the women in his department had complained about his hugging and kissing. In Randy's eyes, these acts were acts of friendship with no sexual connotation, but to the women who complained, they were unwelcome.

> **Stop! Look! Listen!**
>
> Unless you know someone well, other than the traditional handshake, don't hug, don't pat, and certainly don't kiss.

Creating an "Intimidating, Hostile, Work Environment"

As noted earlier, according to its legal definition, sexual harassment isn't limited to demands for sexual favors. It also includes conduct that creates an "intimidating and hostile work environment."

Ken's team had always been all male, and now two women have been added to his group. Some of the men resent this "intrusion" on their masculine camaraderie, and as a result, make life unpleasant for the female team members. The men make snide remarks and even stoop so low to give the women incorrect information that causes them to make errors in their work. They exclude them from work-related discussions. No actions are taken that can be interpreted as "sexual" in nature, but it still qualifies as sexual harassment. The men have created a hostile work environment for the women.

Tina works in a warehouse. The street language some of the men continually use offends her. When she complains, she is told, "That's the way these guys talk. They talked this way before women worked here, and they're not going to change now. Get used to it."

Because people may find that this dirty language creates "an offensive work environment," it can be legal grounds for a complaint.

If one or more of your employees is creating similar situations, talk to the people (or person) using the inappropriate language. Point out diplomatically that this behavior is unprofessional and offensive to both women and men and that it isn't appropriate to use it in a business environment. Inform them that such behavior can cause legal problems for the company and for them as individuals. Tell them that if they continue to use street language they will be subject to the same type of disciplinary action as what is given for violating other company work rules.

Dating, Romance, and Marriage on the Job

A company's responsibility to preventing sexual harassment extends beyond the workplace as long as all parties involved work for the company.

Cathy, a department manager, was perplexed. Dennis, one of the men in her department, had gone out a few times with Diane, who worked in another department. It never developed into a romance, but Diane kept bugging Dennis to go out with her again. Diane came into Dennis' office several times a day to talk with him, even though Dennis didn't welcome her visits. Diane's constant attention interfered with his work, and he wasn't interested in seeing her. The next time Diane visited Dennis,

Cathy called her aside and told her that social visits were not permissible. Diane never returned, but continued to harass Dennis by telephoning him and bombarding him with e-mails to his home.

Is the company off the hook? Not yet. Even though the harassment has ceased on the job, because both Dennis and Diane are employed by the same company, the company has an obligation to stop Diane from bothering Dennis. Cathy should discuss the situation with Diane's manager and, if necessary, with the human resources department. If Diane continues her harassment, appropriate disciplinary action should be taken.

Stop! Look! Listen!

It's not good business to restrict married couples from working in the same company. Why lose productive workers because of an archaic rule? Most married couples work well together and have enough control over their own lives not to bring their personal problems into the workplace.

Tactical Tools

Companies can protect themselves from charges of sexual harassment by clearly notifying all employees that such behavior will not be tolerated and by establishing and publicizing a procedure for dealing with complaints. A senior executive should administer this policy, and all complaints should be quickly investigated and, if verified, promptly corrected.

Intra-Marriage

Many romances that start on the job develop into marriages. So, what effect does it have on your group when two associates become romantically involved? This situation can be a delicate one. Some companies, fearing that closely related people working together will cause problems, prohibit parents, children, siblings, and spouses from working on the same department or even in positions in which they must interrelate.

If a company prohibits married couples from working together and two team members marry, which one should leave the team? Some companies base their policy on rank (the lower-ranking spouse leaves) or salary (the lower-paid spouse leaves). Because it may be more likely for the man to be the higher-ranked or higher-paid employee, this policy discriminates against women. The best way to deal with it is to let the couple make the determination about which one will leave.

Federal law doesn't expressly prohibit discrimination based on marital status, but it is barred by interpretations of the sex-discrimination clauses by the EEOC. Some states do have specific laws prohibiting discrimination based on marital status.

Sex Harassment by Others

Suppose that a salesman who comes into your office makes a point of telling off-color jokes to the women who work there. Some of them think that he's hilarious, but you notice the look of disgust on the faces of others. Although no complaints have been made, you see that the behavior is creating an offensive work environment. The salesperson doesn't work for your company, but you still have an obligation to do something about it.

The courts have ruled that an employer is responsible for the offensive behavior of all its employees (regardless of whether they're in management) and even nonemployees when the employer or its agents (that's you, in this case) know about it *or should have known* about it.

Speak to the person on whom that sales rep calls. Tell him or her to discuss the matter with the sales rep. If the undesirable behavior continues, the company has an obligation to tell the salesperson that it cannot continue doing business with him.

Note that your company is responsible not only when it knows about the offensive behavior but also *when it should have known* about it. This point is a delicate one. How are you supposed to know about everything that might happen? You can't, of course, but if you're observant, you should know a great deal about what transpires.

Ten Steps to Preventing Sexual Harassment Charges

◆ Establish a formal policy prohibiting sexual harassment. Clearly indicate all actions that could be construed as harassment and specify what steps employees should take if they are harassed. Appoint a senior executive to administer the policy.

◆ Publicize the policy through bulletins, articles in the company newspaper, regularly scheduled meetings, and training programs.

◆ Make it easy for complainants to bring matters to the attention of management. Post notices throughout your offices detailing who to go to and how to do it. Make sure that all employees know that there will be no retaliation against persons bringing complaints against anybody in the organization, regardless of rank or position.

◆ Investigate all complaints—no matter how trivial or unjustified they appear to you. Keep written records of all findings (including memos, reports of interviews, and statements from the complainant, the person accused, and witnesses).

- Never terminate or threaten complainants or potential complainants.

- Don't make rash decisions. Analyze all the facts. Consult your attorney (remember that the matter may wind up in court).

- Take action. If the complaint is justified, correct the situation. Depending on the case, this may include requiring the harasser to apologize, ordering a cessation of the acts that led to the complaint, adjusting the salary, promoting or changing the working conditions of the persons who have suffered, or, in flagrant or repeated offenses, firing the harasser.

- If the investigation finds the complaint was not justified, explain the decision carefully and diplomatically to the complainant. Keep in mind that if he or she is not satisfied, a charge can still be filed with appropriate government agencies or brought to court.

- Don't look for easy ways out. Transferring the harasser to another department may solve the immediate problem, but if the harasser repeats the offense in the new assignment, the situation is compounded.

- If a formal complaint is made to the EEOC or a state equivalent, even if you feel the complaint is groundless, treat it seriously.

By following these 10 guidelines, not only will you will reduce your chances of having sexual harassment charges filed against your company, but also you will improve the morale in the company because employees will see that you take this situation seriously.

The Least You Need to Know

- Sexual harassment is not limited to demands for sexual favors. It also includes permitting a work environment that is hostile or offensive to employees because of their gender.

- Make all employees aware of your policy prohibiting sexual harassment and specify steps to be taken to bring it to management's attention.

- Managers can be held liable for sexual harassment in their departments not only if they knew about it and fail to take action, but even if they didn't know about it, if they reasonably should have known.

- Be vigilant. Follow the 10 steps to prevent sexual harassment charges that are listed in this chapter.

Chapter 9

More on Labor Laws

In This Chapter

- ◆ Working with people from diverse cultures
- ◆ Making accommodations for religious requirements
- ◆ Complying with affirmative action laws

Although a good number of the cases that have been filed since the inception of equal opportunity laws have concerned race, sex, and age, in recent years, more and more attention has been given to other areas, such as national origin and religion. As the number of immigrants coming to this country from Latin America and Asia has proliferated over the past 10 years, the employee make-up of most companies has become diverse. In this chapter, we will examine what employers need to do to comply with these laws. We'll also look at the Family Leave law, which requires many companies to give time off to employees to deal with personal problems, and at the sensitive area of Affirmative Action.

Working with a Multicultural Workforce

If your staff consists of men and women who come from different cultures, it may lead to misunderstandings and conflicts. As a manager, you cannot ignore these situations if they come up. Your job is to make your team a smooth-running, collaborative group.

Coping with the Language Barrier

"How can I supervise these people when they don't speak English and I don't know their language?" You've heard this complaint over and over again. It's not a new phenomenon. A hundred or more years ago when immigrants from Europe flooded this country, their supervisors were faced with the same problem. The usual approach then—and it still works—was to find employees who did speak the language and use them as interpreters. If the non-English speakers in your company are all from the same country, you can make an effort to learn enough of their language for basic communication. Of course, many companies today offer English as a Second Language programs for their employees.

If you're worried about your non-English speaking employees' abilities to understand instruction manuals, just have the manuals translated. On the other hand, think about using nonverbal tools, such as demonstrations, training films, and graphics, to train people to perform manual operations.

Other Types of Cultural Diversity

Diversity is not limited to integrating persons from other countries into the work force, but recognizing that there are other cultures within the American population that must be accommodated.

I've previously noted that to discriminate against the physically and mentally challenged is illegal, and that such employees often bring valuable talents and skills to the company. However, because accommodations must sometimes be made to assist this group, other workers may be resentful. This is another challenge of the diverse work force.

Integrating women into positions traditionally held by men (or vice versa) is another challenge of diversity.

How should organizations cope with these issues?

Decision-makers must learn to accept the reality of diversity. This calls for abandonment of traditional stereotypes about workers—who they are, what they look like, and why they work. Rather than argue over whether to support diversity, direct your energy toward designing work systems that anticipate the varying and unique qualities of a diverse work force.

Second, develop more objective methods of personnel selection and appraisal. Instead of depending on traditional interviews—which often perpetuate biases—use methods that sample the applicant's ability to do the necessary work. Such tests can serve two purposes. First, they would increase your chances of hiring talented individuals who might otherwise be rejected under the subjective approach. In addition, they can protect your organization from legal challenges in instances when a member of some protected group has been rejected.

> **CAUTION**
>
> **Stop! Look! Listen!**
>
> Unless the need to speak English is job related, you cannot require employees to speak only English in the workplace. Employees who normally speak a different language and are more comfortable conversing in their native tongue cannot be compelled to speak English among themselves.

Establishing Diversity Programs in Your Company

Formal diversity programs have been developed in a number of companies, but they tend to be concentrated in larger organizations. According to a survey by the Society for Human Resources Management, 75 percent of Fortune 500 companies have diversity programs that were developed more than five years ago. In comparison, only 36 percent of companies at-large have diversity programs.

The American Banker's Association has published a guidebook for banks that want to develop diversity programs. Although written expressly for banks, the principles can be applied to any industry.

The first step in a sound hiring and selection process, the guidebook recommends, is writing a thorough job description that identifies the knowledge, skills, and abilities needed. Only job functions viewed as essential to the job should be used to screen applicants. A thorough and accurate job description that is well communicated to the hiring managers and the HR department will help ensure diverse hiring and prevent legal troubles later.

Determining salaries is another crucial step in promoting a diverse workforce. It is important that a documented method of comparing internal job worth exists in order to support salary practices and policies.

The guidebook advises that a diverse applicant pool should be developed, focusing on both outreach as well as equal and consistent treatment of applicants. All incoming candidates should receive the same information. Employment agencies and temporary agencies used by the company should be instructed to provide applicants from all cultures.

The ABA guidebook also includes the following helpful items:

- A comprehensive guide to managing the application process and making selections. The guidebook recommends structured interview forms so that all applicants are asked the same series of questions.

- Samples of permissible interview questions, interview evaluation forms, and telephone reference-checking forms.

- An overview of equal employment laws.

- The mailing addresses of outreach sources with large minority populations and publications aimed at minorities.

- Instructions for conducting adverse impact analysis on tests and selection procedures.

With a little imagination and sensitivity, any team leader can adopt a similar program.

Tactical Tools

Some companies have created programs to open the lines of communication among colleagues of different cultures. Small groups of employees meet regularly to explore people's assumptions and stereotypes about their own culture and those they have of others. Such programs are intended to achieve some of the following goals:

- To identify and eliminate preconceptions and myths about new ethnic groups in the company.

- To overcome the tendency of people to fraternize with people of only their own ethnic group. All employees—Americans and new immigrants—are encouraged to make friends with people from other backgrounds.

- To become aware of assumptions that cause differences in the perception of other cultures and to take steps to correct them.

Maintaining Diversity When Downsizing

In the expansion of companies in the 1980s and 1990s, diversity was easy. They reached out to all ethnic communities and the numbers of people from minority groups increased significantly. When the boom burst and companies were faced with downsizing, layoffs often hit minority groups the hardest. If management followed the traditional (and, when bound by a union contract, mandated) principle of "last in, first out, those members of minority groups most likely would be at the head of the list of terminated personnel devastating the diversity population.

Human resources directors had to work out a program that would meet the downsizing needs of the organization and still keep their commitment to maintaining a heterogeneous workforce.

As one HR executive reported, "Business considerations and skills came first, but it was also important to us that we maintain the diversity we worked so hard to build." There is no easy way to do this and it is a challenge that must be met as layoffs continue.

The Immigration Reform and Control Act of 1986

Immigrant workers can be divided into general categories.

First, there are the immigrants who come into this country—many legally; many more illegally—looking for work. The great percentage of these people seeks lower level positions as farm hands, factory workers, hospital and nursing home attendants, taxi drivers, and similar positions. Your main concern here is to make sure that the applicant has the proper documentation. You cannot discriminate against a person because he or she isn't an American. However, you must ensure that an applicant is legally allowed to work in this country.

Now Hear This

You're worried. You continually read about companies that get into trouble for hiring undocumented aliens (no, not Martians—people from foreign countries). You're almost afraid to hire anyone who has a foreign accent. Uh, Uh! Not hiring someone because of this fear is illegal.

Second, there are situations in which an employer actively recruits men and women from foreign countries for hard-to-fill jobs. Most of these people are professional or highly skilled workers. Hospitals need physicians and nurses, who are in short supply in many communities. Technical organizations need engineers and technicians to staff their teams.

Failure to obtain the documentation when hiring noncitizens, such as their "green card" or other authorization to work, can lead at the minimum to loss of production due to deportation of the undocumented workers, and at the most to fines or imprisonment. I'll explain what is required in order to ensure that you have the proper documentation for both types of immigrant workers in the following sections.

Examine the Documentation

Noncitizens who work in the United States must have proper documentation. To ensure that you comply with these regulations, follow these steps:

- ◆ Have all new employees (not just those that you suspect are foreign) fill out an I-9 form required by the Bureau of Citizen and Immigration Services (BCIS), part of the Department of Homeland Security. You can obtain copies from BCIS. This form should not be completed until after a person is hired. When a starting date is agreed on, the employee should be advised that he or she must submit proper documentation before being put on the payroll.

- ◆ Have new employees provide documents to prove their identity. You have to be sure that a new employee isn't using someone else's papers. Acceptable documents include a driver's license with photo, a school ID with photo, and similar documents.

- ◆ Have new employees who are citizens provide documents to prove citizenship. These documents can include a current U.S. passport, certificate of naturalization, birth certificate, or voter-registration card. Note: You may not ask for these forms until after an employee is hired.

- ◆ Noncitizens must have documents that authorize employment. The most commonly used authorization is Form I-551, usually called the "green card" (it originally was green, but now it's white). The employee's photograph is laminated to the card. Other forms are acceptable for students who may work while in school and some other exceptional cases.

> **Tactical Tools**
>
> Make photocopies of all documents. If some documents are not provided, get proof they have been applied for. If not presented within 21 days of starting job, employee must be terminated.

If the Employee Doesn't Have the Required Documents ...

If the person you hire can't show you the required documents, advise him or her to do everything possible to locate them.

If they can't be located, the person should apply for them at once. When this is done, the employee must give proof to the employer that shows that an application for the document has been made. This can be in the form of a receipt from the appropriate agency or of certified mail sent to the agency.

These receipts should be photocopied and kept until the immigrant receives the documents and shows them to you. The law states that the employee must present the documents to the employer within 21 days of starting the job, or that person's employment *must* be terminated.

When the documents have been examined, notations should be made on the I-9 form indicating type of document and identification number (if any). Make photocopies of the documents. The originals should be returned to the employee.

Employers who hire undocumented aliens are subject to fines, and in cases of repeated offenses, imprisonment. If you have any doubts about a document or any questions concerning the law, contact the customer service office of the Bureau of Citizen and Immigration Services at 1-800-375-5282.

Stop! Look! Listen!

The Immigration laws don't prohibit you from hiring noncitizens. As a matter of fact, refusal to hire a person who is legally permitted to work in this country because of his or her nationality is unlawful under the Civil Rights laws.

Hiring Foreign Students and Specialists

Other situations in which you may put foreign nationals on your payroll include the following:

♦ Foreign students who come to the United States to study in a field in which practical training is desirable. The student's university can apply for a practical training (F1) visa. This will allow the student to work for one year in his or her field of study. If the person you want to hire has this visa, you can hire that person immediately and you need not take any further action. But remember, the visa expires one year after it's issued and that person can no longer be allowed to work in the United States unless some other visa is attained. If you are interested in hiring such students, contact universities who train them for referrals.

♦ Exchange students from foreign universities who come here to continue their studies and pick up practical experience in their fields of expertise. To obtain such students, contact an exchange student organization. They arrange for the necessary documentation (J-1 visa).

◆ People who quality for nonpermanent work authorization (H-1 visa). (There are several different types of visas depending on the kind of work the individual engages in, for example, registered nurses require form H-1A; technical workers, form H-1B.) If you can prove to the Immigration and Naturalization (INS) Service that the skills needed to fill a job cannot be found among American citizens or permanent residents, you may obtain permission to recruit the needed employee from a foreign country.

Stop! Look! Listen!

The rules on bringing employees into your company are so complex that you should retain a consultant specializing in this field to guide you through the paper work.

Once you locate a suitable candidate, you must apply for the H-1 visa. The process is very complicated and an attorney or consultant specializing in immigration should be retained. Even if you find a qualified candidate who is already in the United States and has an H-1 visa to work in another company, you will need to apply to the INS to transfer it. This takes from four to eight weeks.

Dress Codes—Yes or No?

Suppose you're upset that some of the young people on your staff come to work dressed in clothes that are more appropriate for leisure activities. The women wear shorts and tank tops; the men, shirts open to their navels. What can you do about it?

It's not illegal to require people to obey a *dress code*, as long as the dress code isn't discriminatory. If women are prohibited from wearing shorts, for example, but nothing is done about the men's open shirts, it would not be considered equal treatment under the law. Prohibiting a Muslim woman from dressing as prescribed by her religion or an Orthodox Jew from wearing a yarmulke would also violate the law's religious provisions.

Dress codes may vary within a company depending on the type of work that's done. Dress codes for factory and warehouse workers will be different from those of office employees and employees who deal with the public.

Don't overdo it. Even IBM has dropped its requirement that male employees wear dark suits, white shirts, and blue ties and that women wear dark dresses or suits. As long as what an employee wears is in good taste, it should be acceptable.

Thank You for Not Smoking

Today if you enter many buildings, you're likely to see several people standing in front—rain or shine, winter or summer—puffing away. They have been prohibited from smoking within the building.

Despite the surgeon general's warning and increasing evidence of the dangers of secondhand smoke, no federal law prohibits smoking on the job. Several states and local communities have laws, however, that restrict smoking in commercial buildings.

Even in areas in which no local laws apply to this situation, many companies have either prohibited smoking or restricted it to specific areas.

Some companies that have no company-wide policy allow employees to determine the smoking policy for their work area. These policies vary from total prohibition to restricted smoking places and times, or no restrictions at all.

Now Hear This _____

Stereotypes are hard to break. San Diego State University has been ordering classroom furniture for more than 100 years. Only recently has it awakened to the reality that not all students are right-handed!

Religion in the Workplace

The law requires you to make reasonable accommodation for a person's religious practices unless doing so results in undue hardship on your company.

Sometimes accommodation is easy. Suppose your company is open seven days a week and that members of your team take turns working on Saturdays and Sundays. One of your employees, David, who is Jewish, can never work on Saturdays. Just schedule him for Sunday work. Say you're not open on Sunday but you have other employees who can work Saturdays; then you're still required to excuse David from Saturday assignments. The other employees may resent having to work on Saturday, but the unhappiness of other employees doesn't qualify as "undue hardship." If your business is small and there aren't enough people qualified to cover the Saturday shift, it may be considered an undue hardship, and you would not have to hire David.

Here are three other religious considerations in the workplace:

Religious holidays: Employees must be given time off to observe their religious holidays, though you're not required to pay them for these days. These holidays are usually considered excused absences and are charged against personal or vacation days.

Prayer time: With the increase in the number of Muslims in this country, particularly in those areas where people from the near-east, Pakistan, and other Muslim countries tend to settle, employers often set aside a site for Muslims to pray at the times required by their religion.

Now Hear This

Here we go again. What is "reasonable accommodation"? And what is "undue hardship"? These same words were mentioned in discussing the implementation of the Americans with Disabilities Act (see Chapter 7). You must make an honest effort to accommodate the affected employee as long as it can be done without having a negative effect on your company.

Proselytizing on company premises: Margaret, a devout member of her denomination, believed that it was her mission to convert people to her religion. She continually pressed her religious beliefs on her co-workers and distributed tracts and other religious literature. At the request of the staff, her supervisor asked her to refrain from this behavior. She refused, claiming that the religious accommodation law and the First Amendment gave her the right to proselytize. Margaret was wrong. Just as a company can prohibit political campaigning on company premises and during working hours, it can restrict religious behavior that disturbs other people in the workplace.

Affirmative Action

Under current civil rights laws, you're not required to give women or minorities any preferential treatment in hiring or promotion. Companies with government contracts or organizations that receive federal funds, however, fall under an executive order requiring them to establish formal *affirmative action plans* (AAP).

If your firm has an AAP, it was probably drawn up by a specialist in the legal or human resources department. You don't have to worry about the technical aspects of this plan. All you have to know is the company's goals for staffing your department with various minority groups and women, so you can make every effort to comply with them.

Words to Work By

Companies that have government contracts in excess of $50,000 and more than 50 employees must have a written **affirmative action plan** committed to hiring women and minorities in proportion to their representation in the community in which the firm is located.

If your department isn't in line with the affirmative action goals of your company, you should make an effort to hire or promote a person from the group in which the deficiency exists. This advice doesn't mean that you must hire unqualified people just because of their minority status. If you have two candidates with relatively equal qualifications, you're expected to give preference to the minority candidate even if he or she needs more support or training to become productive.

Recent Developments in Affirmative Action

California, Texas, and a few other states have passed laws to loosen their affirmative action practices. For example, colleges and universities are no longer required to engage in affirmative action in admission of students. In addition, these laws repeal affirmative action requirements for state and municipal positions and eliminate pref-erential treatment of minorities in awarding contracts. Acts have been introduced in Congress to change federal affirmative action policies, but have not passed as of this writing. Note that none of the state laws affect the private sector. The federal laws and executive orders discussed throughout this chapter do apply to private companies, however, and are strictly enforced. Any changes that are made will be widely publicized.

> **Tactical Tools**
>
> Affirmative action is not required for every minority group. It only applies to African-Americans, Hispanics, Asians and Pacific Islanders, Native Americans, and women.

The Wage and Hour Laws

The first comprehensive federal law regulating wages and hours was the Fair Labor Standards Act of 1938. Over the years, it has been amended many times and is still the basic law in this area.

The Least You Can Pay

The minimum wage is established periodi-cally by Congress and has become something of a political football. Every few years it is raised to be at least congruent with the cost of living, but the exact amount of the increase is always a battle between the "pro-labor" group who wants it to be high and the "pro-employer" group that fights to keep it down.

The one area that has been consistent since the beginning has been the 40-hour week. Non-exempt employees must be paid at the rate of one and one half their hourly pay for each hour in excess of 40 hours worked in any week. *Exempt employees* need not be paid for overtime.

> **Words to Work By**
>
> An **exempt employee** is someone who is engaged in management, administration, pro-fessional work or who uses "inde-pendent judgment" in his or her work. In addition, outside sales persons are considered as exempt. Person falling into this category can be required to work overtime with no extra com-pensation.

If you're not certain whether an employee is exempt, contact the local office of the U.S. Department of Labor (listed in the phone book under U.S. Government) for specific rulings.

Most states have similar labor laws. Check the state departments of labor in each of the states in which your company has facilities.

Special Laws Related to Government Contractors

Even before the Fair Labor Standards Act was passed in 1938, there were two laws on the books governing companies that had public works contracts:

- **The Davis Bacon Act (1931).** The minimum rate paid by companies engaged in public works projects must be at least equal to the prevailing rate in the community in which the work is being done. The "prevailing rate" has been defined as that paid to 30 percent of the workers in that area. As this law primarily applies to the construction industry and usually at least 30 percent of these workers are in labor unions, the rate paid is often really higher than the average rate in the area. Attempts to repeal the act or at least the 30 percent rule have consistently been defeated in Congress.

- **The Walsh-Healy Act (1936).** This act also only covers companies engaged in public works projects. It reiterates the prevailing wage rule of the Davis Bacon Act and adds the provision that time and one half (overtime) pay be paid for all hours worked over eight hours in any one day or 40 hours in one week, depending on which is higher.

> **Tactical Tools**
>
> If your company is engaged in a federally contracted public works project, nonexempt employees must be paid at the rate of time and a half for all hours worked over eight any day even if they don't work a full 40-hour week. Some union contracts also have such a provision.

Equal Pay Act

The Equal Pay Act of 1963 requires that an employee's gender not be considered in determining salary (equal pay for equal work).

As this act is an amendment to the Fair Labor Standards Act, all employers engaged in interstate commerce are covered no matter how many employees they have. The law was passed to counter a common practice of paying women less than men who were doing similar work. For example, a male "porter" on the cleaning crew was paid more than a female "maid." Often this was justified by claiming the porter had heavier work such as climbing ladders and lifting heavy loads. However, often this represented a minuscule part of his work. Most was the same as that of his female counterpart.

In the "olden days" it was assumed men should be paid more because they supported a family and women only worked if they were single and had to support just themselves. If a married woman worked, it was to earn "pin money," to supplement her husband's income. Now, of course, we don't accept these notions, but the practice of paying less to women persists. According to the latest figures, in 2002 women in the workplace earned about 77.5 percent of what men earned.

The National Labor Relations Act

Long before the Civil Rights Acts were passed, Congress enacted the Wagner Act in 1935, which prohibited employers from discriminating against workers on the basis of union membership or activity. This law, as amended in 1947 by the Taft Hartley Act, is still in effect.

Don't Discriminate Against Union Members

The Wagner and Taft Hartley acts cover a variety of matters related to employer-union relations. One section of the law applies to the hiring process. For instance, it is illegal to discriminate against a person because he or she is a member of a union. You may not even inquire if an applicant is a union member.

The basic provisions of these acts are as follows:

◆ Employers may not interfere with, restrain from, or coerce employees to organize or participate in unions.

◆ Employers may not contribute to the financial support of a union. (This was to restrict formation of phony, company-dominated unions.)

◆ Employers may not discriminate in hiring applicants or retaining employees because of their union membership or activities.

◆ Employers may not refuse to bargain collectively with unions that have been certified to represent their employees.

The Taft Hartley Act (1947) added these restrictions on unions:

◆ Unions may not restrain or coerce employees in the exercise of their rights.

◆ Unions may not restrain or coerce employees in their selection of a bargaining unit.

◆ Unions may not require employers to discriminate against any of their employees who may not join the union.

◆ Unions may not refuse to bargain with an employer.

◆ Unions may not charge excessive initiation fees or dues.

In addition, the National Labor Relations Board, which enforces these laws, has added a variety of interpretations and administrative rulings.

Before the passage of the Taft Hartley Act, many management-union contracts called for a *closed shop*. The company was required to hire people who were members of the union—often through the union's hiring halls. This was outlawed by Taft Hartley. However, contracts may call for a *union shop* in which nonunion members may be hired, but they must join the union within a specified period of time after employment.

What About "Right to Work" Laws?

One of the major areas of contention in the debates in Congress when the Taft Hartley Act was proposed was the right of workers to decide if they wanted to join a union. If the contract called for a union shop, employees of that company would be compelled to join the union whether they liked it or not. A compromise was reached on this point. Instead of outlawing union shops nationally, the decision was delegated to the states.

Several states passed "right to work" laws, which prohibit a company or union to require employees to join a union as a condition of employment.

If your company has a union, or is facing union organization, it's best to obtain the services of an attorney who specializes in labor relations.

Laws on Safety and Health

In 1970, Congress passed the Occupational Safety and Health Act (OSHA). The act was designed to "assure so far as possible every working man and woman in the nation safe and healthy working conditions and to preserve our human resources."

Enforcement of this law is in the jurisdiction of Occupational Safety and Health Administration (also referred to as OSHA) of the U.S. Department of Labor. In addition, many states have enacted similar legislation.

Regulations on health and safety are promulgated by OSHA and must be adhered to by all companies engaged in interstate commerce. These regulations are published in the Federal Register. However, it's in the best interest of all companies to study and implement these rules.

 **Stop! Look! Listen!**

Companies must ensure that all managers, supervisors, and team leaders are thoroughly familiar with the OSHA regulations and, when pertinent, state safety and health rules related to the works and facilities that they supervise. Failure to comply can be very costly.

Time Off for Personal Needs

Congress passed the Family and Medical Leave Act (FMLA) in 1993, requiring companies with 50 or more employees to provide eligible employees with as much as 12 weeks of unpaid leave in any 12-month period for the following reasons:

- The birth or adoption of a child or the placement of a child for foster care.

- To care for a spouse, child, or parent with a serious health condition.

- The employee's own serious health condition.

To be eligible, the employee must have been employed by the company for at least 12 months and must request this leave at least 30 days before the expected birth or adoption of the child. When this notification isn't possible, such as the onset of a serious illness of a family member, employees are required to provide as much notice as possible.

Both men and women are eligible for leave under this law. If both husband and wife work for the same employer, however, the total amount of leave is limited to 12 weeks for the couple.

The key provisions of the law make these requirements:

- The company must provide the employee, after returning from the leave, with the same position or with a position with equivalent pay, benefits, and other conditions of employment.

- Health insurance must be continued during the leave period and paid for in the same manner as though the employee were still on the payroll.

As with most laws, variations apply in special circumstances. For example, Dick's mother receives outpatient chemotherapy every Tuesday, and he brings her to the hospital on Tuesday and stays with her on Wednesday while she regains her strength. Although the law primarily calls for continuing periods of leave, special arrangements can be made so that Dick can take off the time he needs. If the type of work Dick does makes this arrangement unfeasible, however, the company has the right to transfer him temporarily to another job with the same pay and benefits that enable him to take the days off.

To obtain the details about how this law may affect you or someone on your staff, check with your human resources department, legal department, or local office of the Wage and Hour Division of the U.S. Department of Labor (listed in the U.S. government pages of most local telephone directories).

Now Hear This

The emergence of mandated family leave is largely a result of unprecedented changes in the composition of the workforce and the nature of workers' family responsibilities, dramatically altering the traditional relationship between employees' work and personal lives.

Conflict between work and family obligations has become an inevitable aspect of modern work life, often resulting in absenteeism, work interference, job turnover, and other deleterious impacts. While conflict between work and family responsibilities cannot be eliminated, family leave and other work/family policies can make it easier for America's workers to fulfill their responsibilities as parents, family members, and workers.

The Least You Need to Know

◆ Encourage employees from different cultural backgrounds to get to know each other as people—not as members of an ethnic group.

◆ Know the immigration laws. Failure to obtain the documentation when hiring noncitizens can lead at the minimum to loss of production due to deportation of the undocumented workers, but can also involve fines or imprisonment

◆ Companies must make provisions for employees to observe their personal religious practices.

◆ If your company has an affirmative action plan, you're required to seek out members of protected minority groups and women for hire and promotion.

◆ The Fair Labor Standards Act requires that all nonexempt employees be paid time and one-half overtime for all hours worked over 40 hours in any week.

◆ The Equal Pay Act of 1963 requires that an employee's gender not be considered in determining salary (equal pay for equal work).

◆ You cannot refuse to hire or discriminate against a person on the job because he or she is a member of a labor union.

◆ All managers and supervisors must be prepared to implement the OSHA regulations concerning their company and workplace.

◆ In companies with more than 50 employees, an employee may take up to 12 weeks off without pay to deal with certain personal needs.

Part 4

Staffing Your Organization

Hiring people is time consuming, expensive, and—to many managers—a side issue that takes them away from their real duties: getting their employees to produce.

Even if you have a human resources department that does much of the work in seeking new employees, the manager must be actively involved in the process. You have to determine just what qualifications the new employee must have to succeed in the job. You have to participate in the interviewing process, and you almost always have to make the final decision to hire or reject.

Even the best supervisors can use help in this function. In the following chapters, I'll show you how to avoid the major hiring mistakes and then steer you through the steps that will enable you to make better hiring decisions.

Chapter 10

Twenty-Five Hiring Mistakes That Managers Make

In This Chapter

- ◆ Starting off on the wrong foot
- ◆ Not using all available resources
- ◆ Improperly prescreening applicants
- ◆ Making unwise decisions
- ◆ Losing applicants you want to hire

What do you do when a vacancy develops in your department? Most managers hate the time, energy, and emotional drain of hiring new employees. It takes them away from their regular duties, adds extra hours to their day, and worst of all, they fear that they will make the wrong choice and have to go through the whole process over again in a few months.

In most large companies and in many smaller firms, the human resources departments recruit and select new employees. However, supervisors and team leaders usually still participate in the process, and they almost always interview prospects. After all, they are the people to whom the person hired will report and they are responsible for the new employee's success or failure.

In some companies, there may not be an HR department or, if there is one, it is situated at the home office, so managers at branch facilities are required to do the hiring themselves. Unfortunately, these managers usually don't have the training and experience required for successful hiring. I have observed the hiring process in hundreds of companies and I've witnessed countless errors that have resulted in wasted time and effort in hiring people who were doomed to fail.

In this chapter, I identify 25 of the most frequently made hiring mistakes and suggest how to avoid them.

Let's look at some of the major errors companies make in hiring.

Getting Started All Wrong

The hiring process, like all effective processes, must be carefully planned. You cannot wait until a vacancy occurs. You need to develop a job analysis and continually update all of the jobs in your organization.

1. Not Updating the Specs

It may seem that the "logical" way to begin to fill a vacancy is to pull out the current job description and specifications and advertise the position based on those documents. However, is this really logical?

Jobs change over time. The job description may have been written several years ago. The skills required of the person in the position may be quite different than what is called for in the description. For instance, Lisa, a customer service representative, just notified her supervisor that she's decided to go back to school and will leave the job in two weeks.

> **Now Hear This**
>
> According to the Society for Human Resources Management (SHRM), the cost of hiring an employee costs 1.5 times the annual salary. This includes recruiting costs, training time, and lost productivity as co-workers and supervisors pitch in during the time the job is left unfilled.

When Lisa was hired, customer service reps wrote out customer complaints on a form, checked them out, and then telephoned or wrote to the customer with the results and suggested solutions. During her tenure the customer service department got all new computer systems, making it possible for many of the problems to be checked and adjusted during the first telephone call. Although Lisa was very good in her dealings with customers, her computer skills were poor and she was much slower at resolving problems than other reps. Consequently, the job description and job specs should be rewritten with more emphasis placed on computer skills.

To make sure you hire the most appropriate person for the job, it's a good idea to review every job description before starting the search to fill it. I discuss job analysis and writing job descriptions and specifications in Chapter 11.

2. Inflexible Specs

Job specs can be so rigid that you're unable to find anyone who meets all your requirements. If you can't find the right candidate, you'll have to make compromises. Reexamine the job specs and set priorities. Which of the specs are nonnegotiable? These requirements are the ones a new employee absolutely must bring to a job or else there is no way the job can be done—a candidate must have a jet pilot's license to fly the company plane, a candidate must be able to do machine work to precise tolerances or the work will not pass inspection.

Other specs are not essential but preferable. If the job calls for using spreadsheets, it would be preferable if the applicant was experienced with Excel, but having worked with other spreadsheets or similar programs could be acceptable as the new employee will be able to learn to use Excel on the job.

Suppose that your specs call for sales experience. One of the applicants has no job experience in selling, but, as a volunteer, was a top fund-raiser for the local community theater. That person may well be able to do the job. In seeking to fill a job, the manager or supervisor should make every effort to abide by the job specs but should also have the authority to use his or her judgment to determine when deviation from the job specs is acceptable.

3. Seeking the Ideal Candidate

You may have a dream candidate—the man or woman you imagine is ideal for the job. This can lead to unrealistic specifications that are not really needed to do the job. By including them, the best candidates may be eliminated for the wrong reason.

When the Property Development Corp. expanded its Minneapolis division, one of the jobs they created was Divisional Controller. The job included managing their accounting department, dealing with banks and other financial institutions, and coordinating financial matters with the home office. In determining the specifications for the job, in addition to comprehensive experience in performing similar work, the company required that candidates have a degree in accounting and be certified as a CPA and have an MBA.

Are these educational requirements truly needed for success in the job? Because the job calls for extensive knowledge of accounting, the degree in accounting is most likely an essential factor. But why an MBA? Graduate degrees in business may provide a good deal of knowledge and analytical skills that may not be acquired by experience. However, the specific skills needed for being a successful controller can also be acquired through work experience. If an MBA is a requirement, men and women who have the necessary skills, but not the degree will be eliminated. To avoid this, the MBA may be considered as *one* of the means of acquiring the skills needed to do the job, but the lack of the degree should not eliminate an otherwise viable candidate.

Tactical Tools

Develop an ongoing recruiting policy. Even if there is no vacancy in your department, accept applications from good prospects, keep an active resource file, so when an opening does occur, you have a head start in the recruiting process.

---

4. Waiting for Vacancies

Sometimes you know when a person plans to leave. He may be reaching retirement age; she may be expecting a child and has decided that she will quit her job so that she can remain at home with the baby. This gives you weeks or months to find a replacement—lucky you! Unfortunately, employees usually don't give much notice, and unless you have a plan for hiring new people, positions might remain unfilled for a long time. Having an ongoing hiring program can minimize such problems.

5. Settling for a "Warm Body"

The job is open and the right candidate just hasn't come along. So you hire a marginally qualified person to "do the work." Big mistake. This is how companies often wind up with a glut of marginal workers. You figure you can train them to become at least "satisfactory," but the time, energy, and money spent will rarely pay off. Better to get the work done by having other team members put in extra time to meet work schedules or to employ temps or outsource the work than put marginal workers on the payroll. Take your time and aim for well-qualified people.

6. Cloning the Incumbents

In seeking to replace an effective employee who has moved on, companies often seek that person's mirror image. Or, if he or she was not effective, they search for the exact opposite.

Say, for instance, that you loved Diane. You wished you had 10 employees like her. When she left because her husband was transferred to another city, you were devastated. Your goal: hire another Diane. So you used her background as the specs for her replacement. Diane graduated from an Ivy League college. Therefore her replacement must come from an Ivy League school. Diane always dressed in bright colors—really made the place more cheerful, therefore applicants with bright clothes will be preferred. Before she worked here, Diane worked in a bank. Bank experience is important, and so on.

You fired Alfred. Alfred was from New York. His successor should come from a smaller community. Alfred was an avid sports fan—always talked about sports. People like that don't really concentrate on their work. No sports fans. Alfred had background in Macintosh computers. Although he did learn our PCs, he always complained that Macs were better. No Mac users, and on and on.

Such trivial factors often enter into the unofficial job specs. Using the incumbent or a predecessor's personal characteristics as significant factors in determining the qualifications for a job might keep you from hiring the most qualified person or influence you to hire an unqualified person just because he or she is like (or unlike) the previous holder of that job.

Using Regrettable Recruiting Resources

To get the best possible candidates for a job, it's a good idea to use as many sources as possible. Just because the last administrative assistant you hired came from an ad in the local paper doesn't mean you can depend exclusively on running an ad. Open your mind, open your Rolodex, and use your imagination. Broaden the market.

7. Up from the Ranks

Promoting or transferring a current employee to a new position is commendable and should be encouraged. Internal candidates are known factors. The company has seen them in action. They know their strengths and weaknesses, their personality quirks, their work habits, their attendance and punctuality patterns, and all the little things that months or years of observation uncover. It also is good for employee morale and motivation. The problem, however, is *limiting* the candidates for a position to current employees only. In this highly competitive world, a company should attempt to find the very best candidate for open positions—and that person may not be currently on your payroll.

CAUTION

Stop! Look! Listen!

When companies primarily fill advanced positions with current employees, they tend to perpetuate the racial, ethnic, and gender makeup of the staff. To achieve a diverse workforce, expand the resources from which you choose candidates for all positions.

There was a time when companies boasted that when the chairman retired, they hired a junior clerk. Everybody moved up a notch. It is likely that in a large organization there are many highly competent people who are available for filling the new openings and of course, they should be given serious consideration. However, a search for outside candidates may bring to the company skills and expertise that are now lacking and new ideas that often elude people in-bred within the organization.

8. Relying on a Friend of a Friend

Personal contacts are excellent sources for referrals. People you know from your business and social worlds often may be ideal candidates themselves or may recommend highly qualified people from their networks. Indeed, networking can be a prime source of potential applicants.

However, using personal contacts has its downside. First, the people you contact may not know anybody at this time who is qualified. Or worse, they may palm off a friend or relative who needs a job, but has limited abilities for your opening. Turning down a friend of a friend may jeopardize your relationship with that person.

On the other hand, you might be overly impressed with the personality or sociability of a person you know and not consider his or her true capability for the open position. A good example of this is Harry L., the sales manager of Amalgamated Products. Harry was always looking for good salespeople. He knew Jim D. for years. They belonged to the same golf club and occasionally played together or socialized in the restaurant or bar. When Harry learned that Jim was looking for a job, he offered him a position on his sales force. It didn't take long for Harry to realize that Jim needed considerable training and supervision if he were to succeed. It was only after months of wasted effort and frustration that Harry finally let him go. Had Harry used even minimum screening, he would have learned that Jim had a pattern of failures in his previous jobs.

Many companies encourage their current employees to recommend friends and acquaintances for open jobs. This can be a valuable source and should be used. But it should be made clear that the referral by another employee is not a guarantee of a job and the applicant will be treated as any other applicant.

9. Ads That Don't Pull

Help wanted advertising is expensive. Whether you are running a classified ad in the local paper to fill a clerical or blue-collar position or a display ad in a national publication for a technical expert or an executive, the results can range from just a few replies or a deluge of resumés.

No matter how many responses you receive, the key is whether the respondents actually fit the job. Too many companies place ads that either do not pull at all or bring in a plethora of responses from unqualified people.

Too many managers write help wanted ads without giving them adequate thought. They scribble the ad on a scratch pad while waiting for a phone call to go through or on a paper napkin while eating lunch. It's worth the time to learn how to write and place effective ads. You can get help in writing ads from your own advertising department or an ad agency.

Now Hear This

Studies show that when screening responses received from an ad, employment specialists spend an average of 30 seconds to read each resumé and decide whether the applicant should be given further consideration.

10. Failure to Take Proactive Steps in Seeking Candidates

Are your recruiters surfing the Internet on a 24/7 basis? Are they visiting websites of competitors to identify their top producers and attempt to entice them away? Are they reviewing the constant flow of listings on the Internet referral services such as Monster.com? According to a poll of 400 employers taken by Recruiters Network of Milwaukee, Wisconsin, in August 2000, 59 percent of the respondents reported that Internet recruiting reduced the cost per hire significantly.

Screening Fiascos

It takes time—lots of time—to screen out unqualified candidates and to select the ones you think are worth interviewing.

How much time do you have to devote to interviewing? Even if you are a full-time interviewer in the human resources department, there are only so many hours each day you can schedule. In addition, if you are a team leader, department head, or senior executive, your day is probably already full, and interviewing means putting in extra hours. You must prescreen candidates so those you do interview are viable prospects for the open position.

11. Resumé Fantasies

The resumé is the most common prescreening device. Most employers ask prospective employees to provide a resumé either before they meet with them or at the interview. Because resumés are written to impress prospective employers, you must learn how to separate the facts from the fluff. Here are some pointers:

Beware of the functional style resumé. In this format, the writer describes the functions performed in previous jobs. This is very helpful in learning about the applicant's background, but often it is used to play up functions in which the applicant has only superficial knowledge—and it may not indicate the duration of the experience or the name or type of company in which it was attained.

For example, a candidate for a position in your human resources department might list four functions on her resumé: Administration, Data Processing, Human Resources, and Secretarial. You have no way of knowing what percentage of her job was devoted to these functions—it could very well be that she spent 80 percent of her time in data processing and only a few hours a month doing HR work.

This doesn't mean you should not consider the candidate for the job, but it does mean that you must be prepared to ask very pointed questions about the specific details on her experience in each of the functions listed.

When seeking an Information technology position, Ted L. used the more traditional chronological resumé—but instead of listing the dates of his employment, he just noted the number of years in each position, as follows, and included a description of the duties performed:

Systems Specialist, ABC Co. (5 years)

Programmer, XYZ Co. (3 years)

Sales Representative, Apex Insurance Co. (8 years)

CAUTION

Stop! Look! Listen!

Remember a resumé is written to promote the applicant. Don't take it at face value. In studying it, read between the lines and try to determine what the applicant has really accomplished.

This gives the impression that the past eight years were in computer work, but in reality, the most recent job was the last one listed—selling insurance. He has been away from computer work for some time—and the field has changed significantly during those years.

12. Asking Candidates to Apply in Person or over the Phone

Sometimes when companies are in a rush to fill a job, they may ask applicants to telephone for appointments or come right to the office. Despite all the problems of reading and evaluating resumés, they serve the purpose of helping eliminate unqualified people and saving interviewing time. When no resumé is used, it is more difficult to weed out time-wasting candidates. One way to overcome this is by a carefully structured telephone interview. Asking good questions will help determine whether or not to invite the candidate in for an interview.

13. The Casual Interview

An interview should be more than a polite conversation. Yet, many interviewers sit down with the applicant and expect by asking a few questions and conversing about the applicant's background and the job requirements, they will get enough information to make a decision to hire or reject the candidate.

To ensure that you obtain significant information about a candidate, you must ask very specific questions that will bring out whether that person can perform the job and what he or she offers in comparison with other applicants for the same position. This may or may not develop in a pleasant conversation. A definite structure must be designed to elicit the key points, give the candidate the opportunity to expound on his or her credentials and accomplishments, and enable the interviewer to size up the applicant's personal characteristics.

14. Overly Structuring the Interview

Some interviewers, in their efforts to cover all the bases, overly structure their interview plan. They make a list of questions and read them to each candidate. In this way they will get responses that enable them to determine basic qualifications and, because they ask each candidate the same questions, they can easily compare the candidates' responses.

Sounds good? Maybe. The problem is that quite often an answer requires a follow-up question. If you stick to the structure—with no flexibility—you may miss an important point. For example:

> Interviewer: What was your greatest accomplishment on that job?

> Applicant: I saved the company a lot of money.

> Interviewer: What was your greatest disappointment on that job?

Tactical Tools
Make every question count. If the answer is vague or not clear, ask appropriate follow-up questions.

Note that the interviewer asked the next question on the list instead of finding out what the applicant did that saved the company money. The answer to that might have opened the door to even more questions that would give considerable insight into the prospect's qualifications.

As noted, there will be many more suggestions for improving your interviewing in Chapter 13.

15. You Can't Ask That!

It's been almost 40 years since the federal equal employment opportunity law went into effect. You would think that by now companies would no longer ask applicants questions that are considered unlawful. Yet, every day some interviewer in some company—maybe yours—will ask an illegal question.

Why? Sometimes it's ignorance of the laws. Although most HR professionals know the laws, team leaders, managers and, often, team members participate in the interviewing process, and many of these people have little knowledge of the laws. Making matters worse, it's not always clear just what the law allows and prohibits.

Make it your business to learn what the laws require and how you can get the information you need to make a hiring decision without violating any laws. See Chapter 7 for a list of unlawful questions.

16. Telling Too Much Too Soon

One of the major errors interviewers make is to tell the applicant all about the job early in the interview. Often they may give the applicant a copy of the job description before the interview begins. What's wrong with that? It enables the smart applicant to tailor his or her background to fit the job description. For example, the open job calls for somebody who has extensive experience in administering employee benefits. In her last job, Shirley had some exposure to benefits. Knowing that this is an important aspect of the open position, Shirley might play up—perhaps exaggerate—her background in this field.

Of course, the applicant should have some concept of what job he or she is being interviewed for. The best way to do this is to first ask questions about the applicant's background in the area under discussion. Then, after the response, tell the candidate more about the job.

17. Verify, Verify, Verify!

The applicant has presented you with a slick resumé and has come across well in the interview. Promise me that before you offer him or her the job, you will verify that what the applicant claims to be is true.

By calling references, you'll go a long way to verifying the applicant's statements and perhaps catch an "artful liar." Unfortunately, this essential part of the employment process is often disregarded or treated much too casually.

Often the background check is assigned to a junior employee who may send reference letters to previous employers or telephone them—with little training or know-how in asking probing questions and interpreting the responses.

In recent years, many companies have been advised by their attorneys not to give references for fear of defamation suits. They limit responses to reference inquiries to the dates of employment and some generalized information about job duties.

Because of this, some organizations don't bother to check out potential employees. This can be a costly mistake. It's important that you make every effort to get as much information about an applicant as you can before you make the hiring decision.

Stop! Look! Listen!

Automatically rejecting an applicant if you get a poor reference can be a mistake, too. You may lose a good applicant for the wrong reason. Arrange for another interview. Don't mention the poor reference, but ask questions that may uncover the reason for it. Hold your judgment until you know the entire story.

Decision-Making Goofs

The bottom line in the hiring procedure is selecting the best candidate for the open position. There are times when there are very few qualified people and you may be tempted to lower your standards and take a marginally qualified applicant to fill the vacancy. This can be a costly mistake. It's far better to keep looking. On the other hand, you may be blessed with a choice of several good candidates. You want to pick the best. So watch out for some of the following mistakes in making that important decision.

18. The Applicant's So Charming

There's an old saying that the decision to hire or not to hire is often made in the first 30 seconds of the interview. There is some truth to this. One of the major factors in

Words to Work By

Lookism: Overemphasizing appearance in making decisions about a person.

hiring is the first impression made by the applicant—and that is primarily physical appearance. This has been categorized as *lookism*—overemphasis on appearance.

It's a well-known fact that good-looking people are far more likely to be hired than equally qualified but less attractive people. In an informal exercise I administered at a series of seminars conducted a few years ago, a job description and several resumés of more or less equally qualified prospective candidates were distributed to the participants. Half the class received resumés with photos of the applicant attached; the other half had no photos. In virtually every instance, the participants who received photos selected the more attractive candidate, while the choices of the nonphoto group were about equally divided among all the candidates.

Common sense tells us that just because a person's attractive it's no assurance of competence, yet both men and women may decide in favor of the better-looking applicant. Perhaps we just like to have nice-looking people around us.

Some first impressions create a *halo effect*. Because you are so impressed by some superficial facet, it is assumed all other aspects of his or her background are outstanding. He's so charming, he must be a good salesman. She speaks so well, she'll make a great supervisor. Halo effects are not limited to appearance. Sometimes because an applicant is highly competent in one aspect of a job, it is assumed he or she is equally competent in others. Charles could type on the word processor at 90 words per minute. With that speed, the supervisor figured he had hired a winner. However, it wasn't until after Charles started work that they realized that speed was his only asset. He was a poor organizer, he was temperamental, he didn't work well with others, and he had other unsatisfactory work habits.

Words to Work By

The assumption that because of one outstanding characteristic, all of the applicant's characteristics are outstanding is called the **halo effect**. The opposite, one poor characteristic, you assume that the person is not satisfactory in every aspect of background is called the **pitchfork effect**.

It works the other way, too. Poor first impressions may cause you to reject an otherwise well-qualified candidate—this is called the *pitchfork effect*. An applicant may be downgraded in your mind because he or she does not speak well—important if the job calls for oral communication, but should not be a factor in jobs where that isn't required. One of my clients wouldn't even consider an applicant who had a straggly beard and long, unkempt hair. Only after the person who referred the applicant persuaded him that the man was a computer whiz did he hire him.

This man has since solved countless problems for the company and has saved them tens of thousands of dollars.

Smart employers don't make hiring decisions based on one or two factors. No matter how impressed you may be by an applicant, learn as much as you can about him or her before choosing the new employee.

19. Watch Your Biases

We all have biases, and they aren't limited to prejudice against people because of their race, religion, or sex. Biases may be based on long-held beliefs or stereotypes—true or false—in any aspect of life. They may be influenced by our personal tastes or idiosyncrasies.

I once asked seminar participants to share with the group some of their hiring mistakes. Most attendees told about people that they hired who didn't make the grade. But one of the participants told about a salesman he had rejected. He said, "At a luncheon meeting of our trade association, the sales manager of one of our competitors was bragging about his top sales rep. He said that in his first year, he broke all records for bringing in new accounts. When he mentioned his name, it rang a bell. I recalled having interviewed him some time ago. When I returned to my office, I checked my files. Sure enough, I had interviewed and rejected him. Why? My notes on his application just said: 'not suitable.' Then I remembered. I turned him down because he was wearing a bow tie. My stupid bias against bow ties had kept me from hiring a potential winner."

Many people have biases in favor of people like themselves. One manager reported that his boss preferred to hire people who graduated from the University of Michigan and would never— no matter now qualified he or she may be—hire a Michigan State grad. If you want to succeed as a manager, then save college rivalries for game day.

Tactical Tools
To get the best people, you have to identify your own biases and compensate for them in making the decision.

20. Is It a Good Match?

The importance of having realistic job specs was noted earlier in this chapter. The whole purpose of developing a list of specifications is to make sure that the person you hire can do all (or most of) the facets of the job.

Sometimes, though, it's difficult—if not impossible—to find somebody who meets every criteria. In such cases, you must determine which of the specs are absolutely essential and in which areas a new employee can be trained after employment. There are certain aspects of most jobs in which experience or technical know-how is essential and cannot be taught on the job. The big mistake organizations make is to hire a candidate who may qualify in several of the specs but is weak in the essential areas.

21. Don't Overlook the Intangibles

When making a hiring decision, it's just as important to evaluate the intangibles as the ability to perform the job. Too often, employers limit the selection procedure to applicants' technical skills. They overlook such factors as whether the person can work in a team, can communicate ideas, can work under pressure, has the capacity to be flexible, and the countless other personality factors that affect how well we do our jobs.

The intangibles that make for success on a job are just as important as education, skills, and experience. In making your job analysis, be as diligent in determining the intangible factors as you do the tangible factors.

Losing Good Applicants

You have screened hundreds of resumés, interviewed dozens of applicants, tested or sent many of them for evaluation, and checked their references. You finally make up your mind and make an offer, only to have the candidate turn you down. This is the most frustrating experience one can have in the hiring process. Why does this happen, and what can you do to prevent it?

22. Making Unrealistic Job Offers

You should think long and hard about the terms of employment before you make an offer. Too many companies have a preconceived idea of the offer before they even interview applicants. This makes for sound business, but unless the offer is shaped to fit the needs of the applicant, there's a good chance it will be rejected.

Obviously, the salary is a key component of the job offer. We'll talk about it in the following section. You'll also want to think about the amount of travel required, the hours of work (including the likelihood of extensive overtime), whether the job will call for relocation now or in the future, and any other special aspects of the position. Discuss all of these issues with the candidate during the interview to make sure you know how he or she feels about them. Whatever you do, don't surprise the applicant at the time of the offer with something like "By the way, you will have to go to our plant in California for three months' training."

23. The Compensation Package Is Too Low

With lower level employees, salary is nonnegotiable. It's "take it or leave it." However, when the position is hard to fill, you must be more flexible or you'll lose the best applicants.

It's not necessary or even advisable to commit to a salary too early in the interviewing process. But, it makes sense to have an approximation of the salary range clearly established early on. If you and the applicant have wildly different ideas about an acceptable salary, there's no point in considering the applicant seriously.

Most benefits plans are standardized. However, more and more organizations are constructing individual benefit programs for each employee. The amount paid into the package may vary with the position and pay scale. The specifics of what is covered within the package can be tailored to fit the desires of the employee.

Now Hear This

The benefits package for each employee of most large organizations costs from 30 to 50 percent of that person's salary.

24. The Spouse Is Unwilling to Relocate

Everything seemed to go OK. You brought the applicant to your facility on three separate occasions. You agree on the terms of the job. He appears to be enthusiastic about joining your company.

And then, surprise! He phones and tells you that his wife doesn't want to move to your city.

How could you have avoided this? When a job calls for relocation, it's imperative that you spend considerable time with both husband and wife to ensure that both of them are amenable to the relocation.

Let's look at Tom and Geri. Tom is being considered for a senior position in your IT department. Early in the interviewing process—as soon as you recognize that Tom is a viable candidate, you should point out that inasmuch as the job calls for relocating, you would like to invite his wife to the facility so she can observe the new community for herself.

When Tom and Geri come to town, have one of your staff give Geri a tour of the town, and uncover any special concerns she may have. Be prepared to discuss schools (if there are school-age children), cultural and entertainment activities, religious facilities, and housing. If Geri is interested in finding a job in her own field, give her information about that field, and offer to help her locate a suitable job. Try to bring any reservations out into the open, and discuss them with both Tom and Geri, preferably over lunch or dinner.

Tactical Tools
If job calls for relocation, you must determine as early in the process as feasible that the applicant's spouse is amenable to making the move.

If Geri isn't happy about the move, and you cannot persuade her to change her mind, it is far better to have Tom withdraw from consideration in the early stages of the interviewing process than after you've already decided to hire him.

25. A Counteroffer Is Made

Talk about frustration! After all the time, energy, thought, and emotion you've expended in finding the right candidate and determining an appropriate salary package, you offer the job to Tom. Bingo—he accepts! You think your troubles are over and you can get back to work. But a week later, Tom calls and sheepishly tells you that he gave notice to his boss, his boss made a counteroffer, and so he decided to stay. You have to start all over.

You must expect that counteroffers will be made to good workers. You probably have done the same when one of your best people gave notice. To beat this, you have to be proactive. You must prepare the person to whom you make a job offer to expect and reject a counteroffer. I'll talk you through this process in Chapter 14.

The Least You Need to Know

- ◆ Plan the hiring process before you even look for applicants. Stick to the plan.

- ◆ Develop job specs that are realistic and have direct bearing on job success.

- ◆ To get the best possible candidates for your job openings, it's smart to use as many sources as possible.

- ◆ Prescreen candidates so those whom you do interview are viable prospects for the open position.

- ◆ Don't tell the applicant too much about the job too early in the interviewing process.

◆ Verify the applicant's background by a well-planned check of education and experience.

◆ When making a hiring decision, it's just as important to evaluate the intangibles as the ability to perform the job.

◆ In addition to salary and benefits, discuss with the candidate the amount of travel required, hours of work including the likelihood of extensive overtime, whether the job will call for relocation now or in the future, and any other special aspects of the position.

◆ Expect that counteroffers will be made to good workers. Be proactive. Prepare the person to whom you make a job offer to expect and reject a counteroffer.

Chapter 11

Writing Realistic Job Specs

In This Chapter

◆ Creating a meaningful job description

◆ Reevaluating existing jobs you create a new job

◆ Matching job specs to a job description

◆ How much is the job worth?

Suppose you have an opening in your department. You want to fill that position with a person who has the necessary skills to perform the required duties of the job and who can contribute to your department's success. Before you can even begin searching for this person, however, you had better have a clear and realistic concept of what you need.

Maybe you're seeking to fill the position of a person who has left your staff, and you already have a job description for that job. I already stressed the importance of evaluating the description in light of changes that may have developed since it was originally written. If necessary, you can then write a new job description before advertising the position. That's what you'll learn to do in this chapter.

Creating a Good Job Description

Job descriptions are important. Even if you know the job requirements as well as you know the back of your hand, you still need a written job description to begin the hiring process. This description serves many useful purposes:

◆ **Hiring.** Develop realistic specifications that enable you to seek out candidates who can do the job.

◆ **Training.** Determine what knowledge has to be acquired and which skills have to be developed in your training program.

◆ **Reference.** Devise a permanent job duty reference for supervisors or team leaders and the staff members.

◆ **Performance.** Create a list of standards against which performance can be measured so that everyone knows just what is expected in a job. Each person can measure his or her own performance against those standards.

◆ **Appraisal.** When a formal performance appraisal is made, the job description becomes a touchstone against which performance can be evaluated.

Keep It Flexible

Critics of job descriptions are concerned that they stifle creativity and innovation. They fear many people will take these descriptions too literally and be unwilling to do anything not specifically listed.

How often have you asked someone to do something other than his or her routine work and heard the response, "It's not in my job description"? All job descriptions should include the phrase "and any other duties that are assigned." The inclusion of this phrase doesn't mean that you have a servant who can be ordered to do any job that pops up. It means that you can assign duties that are at least job related.

> **Tactical Tools**
>
> A job description isn't a rigid circumscription of functions, and it consists of more than just suggested guidelines. You should make provisions so that deviations, additions, and variations are always open for discussion.

Suppose Don finishes typing a document and you ask him to please take it to the purchasing department. He refuses and says, "I'm an executive assistant, not a messenger. Delivering papers isn't in my job description." That's true: It's not specified, but it is a related duty.

On the other hand, if you say, "Don, you're not busy now; please wash the windows," you're out of line. Your request falls under the phrase "other duties," but it isn't a reasonable extension of his regular work.

When Refilling a Position

When refilling a position, don't make the mistake (Hiring Mistake #6 from Chapter 10) of trying to clone cherished employees or searching for the exact opposite of staff whom you disliked.

Certainly, the backgrounds of people who have been successful (or unsuccessful) in performing particular jobs should be a factor, but not the primary factor, in determining which qualities you should seek in the new person you employ.

To learn the key requirements, make a thorough job analysis.

When It's a Brand New Position

Suppose you have finally persuaded your boss to authorize the hiring of an additional member of your team. This position is a new one, so what exactly do you want it to cover?

If the new position is for another person who will perform exactly the same duties as other team members, you can use the same job description and specifications used by team members. In our ever-changing business world, however, a team's functions constantly expand, and new functions and responsibilities require different talents and abilities. If you're hiring someone to perform new duties, do a *job analysis*.

> **Words to Work By**
>
> When you perform a **job analysis,** you determine the duties, functions, and responsibilities of a job (the **job description**) and the requirements for the successful performance of that job (the **job specifications**).

In some companies job analyses are performed by specialists. They may be industrial engineers, systems analysts, or members of your human resources staff. If your company employs these people, use them as a resource. The best people to make an analysis, however, are those closest to a job—you and other members of your staff.

There are several ways of developing information for the job description.

Observing the Action

For jobs that are primarily physical in nature, watching a person perform the job will give you most of the material you need in order to write the description. If several people are engaged in the same type of work, observe more than one performer.

Stop! Look! Listen!

When several people perform the same type job, don't select the most or least experienced or skilled workers to observe. Studying a few mid-level performers will give you a more realistic concept of what is actually done on that job.

Even a good observer, however, may not understand what he or she is observing. Sometimes it involves much more than meets the eye. Additional steps must be taken to get the full picture. In jobs that are not primarily manual, however, there is little that you can learn from observation alone. Just watching someone sitting at a computer terminal, for example, isn't enough to learn what's being done.

Interviewing the Worker

Ask the people who perform a job to describe the activities they perform. This technique fleshes out what you're observing. You must know enough about the work, of course, to be able to understand what's being said and to be able to ask appropriate questions. It's a good idea to prepare a series of questions in advance. Ask only those questions that are pertinent to the job. Questions like the following will elicit good information:

- Tell me about how you spend a typical day.

- Tell me about some of the other work you occasionally do. How often and when do you do this work?

- What positions do you supervise (if any) and how much of your time is spent in supervising others?

- What responsibilities do you have for financial matters such as budgeting, purchasing, authorizing expenditures, and similar decisions?

- What equipment do you operate?

- What performance standards are you expected to meet on this job?

- What education and experience did you have prior to taking this job that prepared you for it?

- What training did you get on this job to help you do it effectively?

Interviewing the Supervisor or Team Leader

If you're analyzing a job other than the ones you supervise, speak to the team leader or supervisor of that group to obtain that person's perspective of the position. Ask the supervisor or team leader questions about his or her perception of the job similar to those you asked the worker. Note variations in their answers. Probe to determine which is the more accurate description.

If you are evaluating a job that you personally supervise, try to take an objective view of the position and review it as if you were looking at in the same way a stranger might. Not easy to do, but you'll be amazed at the results. You'll see things you never noticed before and interpret some of the aspects of what is being performed and how it is done in a different light.

Now Hear This

Companies have found that when the performance standards are developed collaboratively by managers and the people who perform the work, they are more realistic and more likely to be accepted and achieved.

Indicate Performance Expectations

Some companies prefer to call the job description a "position results description" or a "job results description." They feel that the true objective of this document is to determine what is expected of the people performing the job. Each description should include the major goal (why the job exists), the *key results areas* (KRAs)—aspects of the job on which the performer should focus attention, and the standards on which performance will be measured.

By indicating results expected and performance standards by which they are measured, both managers and performers are not only given a standard against which they can continually measure their performance, but a motivational instrument impelling action that will lead to desired results.

The following job description worksheet is a helpful tool. Tailor the form you use to the type of job you're analyzing.

Words to Work By

The major aspects of a job that must be accomplished by the employee are referred to as **key results areas (KRAs)**.

Job Description Worksheet

Job title: _____

Reports to: _____

Duties performed: _____

_____

_____

Equipment used: _____

_____

_____

Skills used: _____

_____

Leadership responsibility: _____

_____

_____

Responsibility for equipment: _____

_____

_____

Responsibility for money: _____

_____

_____

Other aspects of job: _____

_____

Special working conditions: _____

_____

Performance standards: _____

_____

Analysis made by: _____   Date: _____

What You Seek in a Candidate

After you know just what a job entails, you can determine which qualities you seek for the person who will be assigned to do the job.

The job specifications in some situations must be rigidly followed; others may allow for some flexibility. In civil service jobs or in cases in which job specs are part of a union contract, for example, even a slight variation from job specs can have legal implications. In some technical jobs, a specific degree or certification may be mandated by company standards or to meet professional requirements. For example, an accountant making formal audits must be a certified public account (CPA); an engineer who approves structural plans must be licensed as a professional engineer (PE). On the other hand, if there's no compelling reason for the candidate to have a specific qualification, you may deviate from the specs and accept an equivalent type of background.

> **Tactical Tools**
>
> The intangibles that make for success on a job are just as important as education, skills, and experience. In making your job analysis, be as diligent in determining the intangible factors as you do the tangible factors.

Components of a Job Spec

Most job specifications include the following elements:

- **Education.** Does a job call for college? Advanced education? Schooling in a special skill?

- **Skills.** Must the candidate be skilled in computers? Machinery? Drafting? Statistics? Technical work? Any of the skills necessary to perform a job?

- **Work experience.** What are the type and duration of previous experience in related job functions?

- **Physical strength or stamina.** Does the job require heavy lifting or hard physical labor? If so, is it a significant part of the job or does it only occur occasionally?

- **Intelligence.** Some jobs call for a high level of intelligence. Decisions must be made that require deep thinking, solving complex problems, or being able to think on one's feet.

- **Communication skills.** The job spec should specify exactly which communication skills you need: for example, one-to-one communication, the ability to speak to large groups, innovative telephone sales methods, or creative writing skills.

♦ **Accuracy of work.** If a job calls for "attention to detail," specify what type of detail work. In some jobs there is no room for margins of error. Work must be done right the first time or serious problems may result. For example, working on a nuclear reactor or piloting a jet plane.

♦ **Dealing with stress.** If a job calls for "the ability to work under pressure," indicate what type of pressure (for example, daily deadlines, occasional deadlines, round-the-clock sessions, difficult working conditions, or a demanding boss).

> **Tactical Tools**
>
> To ensure that the person you hire can do a job, the job specs should emphasize what you expect the applicant to have accomplished in previous jobs—not just the length of his or her experience.

♦ **Special factors.** Among the many other factors that may be included in the job specification are such requirements as fluency in a foreign language, willingness to travel, willingness to work on weekends, willingness to work overtime at short notice, and anything else an applicant must comply with to perform the job satisfactorily.

Eliminating Good Prospects for the Wrong Reasons

One of the most common problems in determining the specifications for a job is having the requirement of a higher level of qualifications than is really necessary, thus knocking out potentially good candidates for the wrong reason. This problem frequently occurs in these areas:

♦ **Education.** Suppose certain job specs call for a college degree. Is that degree necessary? It often is, but just as often having the degree has no bearing on a person's ability to succeed in a job. Requiring a higher level of education has more disadvantages than advantages. You may attract smart and creative people, but often a job doesn't challenge them, which results in low productivity and high turnover. More important, you may turn away the best possible candidates for a position by putting the emphasis on a less important aspect of the job.

♦ **Duration of experience.** Your job specs may call for 10 years' experience in accounting, but why specify 10 years? No direct correlation exists between the number of years a person has worked in a field and that person's competence. Lots of people have 10 years on a job but only 1 year's experience (after they've mastered the basics of the job, they plod along, never growing or learning from their experience). Other people acquire a great deal of skill in a much shorter period.

It's not that years of experience don't count for anything. Often, the only way a person can gain the skills necessary to do a good job, make sound decisions, and make mature judgments is by having extensive experience. Just counting the years, however, isn't the way to determine that ability.

Rather than specify a number of years, set up a list of factors a new employee should bring to a job and how qualified the person should be in each area. By asking an applicant specific questions about each of these factors, you can determine what he or she knows and has accomplished in each area.

♦ **Type of experience.** Another requirement job specs often mandate is that an applicant should have experience in "our industry." Skills and job knowledge often can be acquired only in companies that do similar work. In many jobs, however, a background in other industries is just as valuable and may be even better because the new associate isn't tradition bound and will bring to the job original and innovative concepts.

♦ **Preferential factors.** Some job specs are essential to perform a job, but other less critical factors could add to a candidate's value to your company. In listing preferential factors, use them as extra assets and don't eliminate good people simply because they don't have those qualifications.

It may be an extra benefit if a candidate already knows how to use a certain type of computer software, for example, but because that knowledge can be picked up on the job, eliminating a person who is otherwise well qualified might be a mistake.

♦ **Intangible factors.** Intangible factors can be as important (or even more important!) than some tangible requirements.

Of course, you want to hire people with high intelligence, creativity, integrity, loyalty, and enthusiasm, and who have a positive attitude. When you list the intangible requirements for a job, however, put them in proper perspective as they relate to a job.

Tactical Tools
To ensure that the person you hire can do a job, the job specs should emphasize what you expect the applicant to have accomplished in previous jobs—not just the length of his or her experience.

What Do I Have to Pay to Get the Person I Need?

Another part of job analysis involves determining the pay scale for a job. Most organizations have a formal job classification system in which various factors are weighed to determine the value of a job. These factors include level of responsibility, contribution of a job to a company's bottom line, type of education, and training and experience necessary to perform the job. Notice that the classification applies to a job, not to the person performing a job.

> **Words to Work By**
>
> To attract and keep good employees, your pay scale must be at least as high as the **going rate,** which is the salary paid for similar work in your industry or community.

Negotiating the Pay Package

The pricing of a job in smaller organizations is often done haphazardly: You pay what you have to pay in order to hire the person you want. You must have some guidelines about what a job is worth so that you don't pay more than necessary or offer too little and not attract good applicants. You have to determine the *going rate* for a job you want to fill.

This list shows some of the sources for obtaining information about the salary scales in your community or industry:

- **Trade and professional associations.** These groups conduct and publish periodic salary surveys. Members of these associations can discern how their pay scales compare with other companies in their field and in their geographic area. These surveys are best used when you seek salary information for specialists in your industry or profession.

> **Tactical Tools**
>
> Information on going rates by type of job, industry, and location can be obtained from the U.S. Bureau of Labor Statistics National Compensation Survey at www.bls.gov/comhom.htm. Other sources: Salary.com at www.salary.com, Wage Web at www.wageweb.com, and American Career Information Network at www.acinet.org.

- **Chambers of commerce.** Some chambers of commerce publish salary surveys for their locations. Because these surveys include a variety of industries, you can obtain salary information about jobs that exist in a variety of companies, such as computer operators and clerical personnel.

- **Employment agencies.** These agencies can inform you about the going rate for any type of position in which they place employees.

- **Networking.** Ask people you know who are managers in other companies in your community or industry. They often are willing to share information about going rates.

Once you have a clear understanding of what the job is worth, you are in a position to negotiate the specific starting salary with the candidate. In some cases, there is no negotiation. You make an offer and the candidate takes it or leaves it. However, when the salary is flexible, there may be some give and take.

Most people are offered a moderate increase over their current salary when hired for a new job. Occasionally, a higher increment is warranted for improved credentials, an advanced degree, or a professional license that the candidate has received since starting the previous job.

Sometimes applicants are unrealistic about what they can obtain. It is advisable to let the applicant know the salary range early in the interviewing process. If the candidate is totally out of line, he or she will withdraw or be eliminated before additional interviewing time is wasted. If the candidate is within range and is being seriously considered, the negotiation should take place before a final offer is made.

Throughout the interview, identify what is important to the applicant—for example, opportunity to accomplish his or her goals, advancement, or creative freedom. Show how those things can be attained on the job. In your negotiation, this often will persuade a candidate to accept a lower starting salary. Emphasize not just the salary but also the benefits package, the frequency of salary reviews, and opportunities for advancement. Most candidates don't make the decision to accept or decline an offer based on salary alone.

The Least You Need to Know

- Base your job requirements on job factors, not on the background of people currently doing the job.

- When you analyze a job, observe the people performing the job, and discuss with them and their managers what they do.

- Job descriptions are more than just guidelines. You should take them very seriously. To avoid stagnation, provisions for flexibility should be built in to the description.

- Base job specifications on the job description. This technique enables you to choose people for a position who are capable of doing the job.

- By overqualifying a job, you eliminate otherwise qualified people for the wrong reasons.

- Know the going rates for your jobs so that you don't overpay or underpay your associates.

12

Finding Top-Quality People

In This Chapter

- ◆ Your best bet may be in your own backyard
- ◆ Where are those great candidates?
- ◆ Using employment agencies and headhunters
- ◆ Sources you might not have thought of
- ◆ Temps—short term solutions
- ◆ Using the Internet—a bonanza or a disaster?

You have a job opening in your department, and you've prepared the job description and job specs. Now you're ready to screen applicants.

The first thing you should do is to contact your human resources department. The HR team is composed of experts in recruiting and choosing personnel and usually takes care of most of the initial steps in the hiring procedure. The HR department can provide you with advice that can save you the time and effort. They're aware of all the legal implications involved in this delicate area and can help you avoid problems.

Applicants can come from many sources. People working in other positions in your company may fit your needs—look there first. In addition, you can seek people from outside your organization through a variety of channels.

This chapter explains how to recruit personnel and provides some tips for evaluating application forms and resumés and conducting interviews that will give you meaningful information on which to base your hiring decisions.

Your Best Bet May Be Close By

People who work for your company may make valuable members of your team. They may work at jobs in which they don't use their full potential, or they may be ready for new challenges. Joining your team would be a move up for them. Even if an opening isn't an immediate promotion, a lateral transfer might enable that person to take a step forward in reaching her career goals.

Taking Advantage of Internal Transfers

Seeking to fill a team vacancy from within a company has many advantages:

◆ People who already work in your company know the "lay of the land." They're familiar with your company's rules and regulations, customs and culture, and practices and idiosyncrasies. Hiring these people rather than someone from outside your company saves time in orientation and minimizes the risks of dissatisfaction with your company.

◆ You know more about these people than you can possibly learn about outsiders. You may have worked directly with a certain person or observed him in action. You can get detailed and honest information about a candidate from previous supervisors and company records.

◆ Offering opportunities to current employees boosts morale and serves as an incentive for them to perform at their highest level.

◆ An important side effect is that it creates a positive image of your company in the industry and in your community. This image encourages good people to apply when jobs for outsiders do become available.

> **CAUTION**
>
> **Stop! Look! Listen!**
>
> The practice of restricting promotions to current employees tends to perpetuate the racial, ethnic, and gender makeup of your staff. Companies whose employees are predominantly white and male and who rarely seek outside personnel have been charged with discrimination against African Americans, other minorities, and women.

But It Has Its Share of Problems

Although the advantages of internal promotion usually outweigh the limitations, there are disadvantages to consider:

◆ The job may require skills not found in your company.

◆ If you promote only from within, you limit the sources from which to draw candidates and you may be restricted to promoting a person significantly less qualified than someone from outside your company.

◆ People who have worked in other companies bring with them new and different ideas and know-how that can benefit your team.

◆ Outsiders look at your activities with a fresh view, not tainted by over-familiarity.

Most companies use a judicious mixture combining internal promotion and transfers with outside recruitment to get and keep the best candidates for their openings.

One of the major problems in interdepartmental transfers is the reluctance of department heads to release efficient and productive workers to other departments. One of the first actions of a company planning a policy of internal recruitment should be to notify all department heads and team leaders that it will overrule any attempts to keep people who could be more valuable to the organization from transferring to another position. It should also be mentioned that people who are passed over for better positions in other departments are unlikely to remain with the company, and probably will seek another job elsewhere—so both the department and the company will lose a valuable employee.

Finding the Right Candidate from Within the Company

Many organizations have developed training programs that provide them with a steady stream of trained people for their expanding job needs. In some companies, there's a plethora of talent to choose from.

However, there are times when there are no obvious candidates for a vacant job. You may have people in the company who are qualified to do the job—and you don't know it. What can you do?

Search the Personnel Files

If properly maintained, personnel records can be a major resource. Examination of these records may uncover people working in jobs below their education or skill

---

Tactical Tools

Send periodic questionnaires to all employees to bring the personnel records up to date. Ask about new skills or knowledge acquired at the annual reviews. All this should be incorporated in the personnel records.

levels. It may also reveal people who have had additional training since they were employed.

Any training given by the company, whether internal or outside seminars or programs should be noted. If the company has a tuition reimbursement policy, any courses falling into this category should be noted. Employees should be encouraged to inform the human resources department of other courses, programs, or outside training they may have completed.

Personnel records can be an important means of locating people urgently needed by a company. A major aerospace firm spent several thousand dollars in advertising for specialized engineers needed for a new project in one division of the company. The recruiters were shocked to receive letters in reply to the ad from engineers in another division of the same company. The engineers claimed that their specialized knowledge wasn't being used in their current jobs and were seeking a position where it would be. Had the HR department known of them, it would have saved the company money and time.

Ask the Supervisors

Supervisors and team leaders know a good deal about their associates. Take advantage of this. Let them know what jobs are open in other departments. They may have associates who are qualified.

There are two dangers here. One is that supervisors or team leaders may be reluctant to lose a good worker, even if the transfer would be advantageous to both the worker and the company. It's not easy to overcome this. The company must have a strict policy on this, as noted earlier.

The other danger is that the supervisor may refer somebody he or she wants to get rid of. Give as careful screening to applicants referred by their team leaders as to every other candidate for the job.

Job Banks

To systematize internal searches, many firms have established databases listing all of the skills, talents, experience, education, and other background information of all of its employees. These are usually referred to as *job banks*, sometimes called *skill banks*.

For example, under "Excel," you would list the names of all employees who have worked with this program at any time in their careers, whether or not they are currently using it now. If a need arises for a team member with Excel experience, you can check the job bank to see if anyone in the company has that experience but is employed in another capacity. If so, you might see if they would be willing to transfer. Job banks are only useful if they are updated frequently. As employees gain new skills or complete internal or outside training programs, that information should be added to the database.

Words to Work By

A **job bank** or **skill bank** is a database listing all of the skills, education, experience factors, and other background information of all employees, which can be searched to match job openings against current work force.

Job Posting

Many companies make a practice of posting job openings on bulletin boards or listing them in company newsletters so that any employee who believes he or she is qualified can apply. Indeed, many union contracts require that job openings be posted.

Posting a job opening encourages current employees who may qualify for the job, but are not known to the manager or team leader seeking to fill the job, to apply. For example, Sandra L. worked in the order-processing department, but her career goal was in sales. Everybody tells her she has a "sales personality," and she had some part-time selling experience. When an opening for a sales trainee was posted, she applied.

The sales manager interviewed her and recognized her talent. She was transferred into the sales training program and in time became one of the company's star sales reps. Had the job not been posted, Sandra would not have known there was an opening, and the sales manager would not have known about Sandra, and the company would have missed a high potential employee.

Tactical Tools

Post jobs on the company intranet—the internal variation of the Internet that is accessed only by company employees.

There are still companies where minority and women employees are not usually considered for certain jobs. Job posting enables members of these groups to apply and be given serious consideration for them. For this reason, many compliance agreements with the EEOC include a requirement that all jobs be posted.

However, there's a down side to posting jobs. When a current employee applies for a posted job and is rejected, you may have a disgruntled employee. Some may quit, causing the loss of a good employee. Some of those who stay lose self-confidence and make little effort to build up their competence. Some go back to work and bad-mouth the company to their co-workers leading to low morale.

When rejecting an employee for an internal transfer or promotion, take the time to explain in detail why he or she did not qualify. Point out what might be done so that next time this type of job is posted, they will be better equipped to handle it and have a good chance of getting it. Suggest what additional training they need, and if pertinent, what the company will do to help them attain that training.

> **Stop! Look! Listen!**
>
> When several employees apply for a posted job—and there is only one opening—assure the unsuccessful candidates that they were seriously considered and, if true, that there will be future opportunities for which they will be considered. Guide them as to what they can do to improve their chances in the future.

Using Current Employees as a Recruiting Source

The men and women who work for you are an excellent source for getting people like themselves. Many of them have friends from school or from previous jobs who have similar backgrounds to theirs and who may be prospects for your open positions. Programs to encourage referrals by employees have been instituted in many companies.

This has not always been the case. In fact, many companies had policies to refuse employment to friends and relatives of current employees. Before the EEO laws banned such questions, application forms often inquired whether the applicant had relatives or friends within the company.

One reason this policy was instituted was the fear that if friends or relatives worked together, they might form cliques, which would disrupt the smooth flow of operations. A better understanding of group dynamics and greater decentralization of business functions—and labor shortages—has made this fear less valid.

> **Now Hear This**
>
> *Fortune* magazine (Jan. 22, 2001) reported that a least 20 percent of new hires in their list of the 100 Best Companies to Work For came from recommendations from employees. Eighty-three companies paid bonuses for successful new hires. Although most bonuses were modest, some companies paid up to $15,000 for hard-to-find specialists.

Encouraging Employee Referrals

The most important factor in developing a program of employee referrals is company morale. The morale and attitudes of the people in a company can make or break a referral campaign. If employees are discontent, it's unlikely they will refer friends.

Managers often kid themselves into thinking their organization is "one big, happy family," when under the surface it is seething with discontent. Periodic employee attitude surveys or evaluations by outside consultants can educe the true status of morale. If it is not satisfactory, the referral program will not work until steps are taken to correct the problems that cause the poor morale.

Some programs may be limited to occasional suggestions by the team leader and others in management that friends are welcome to apply for jobs. Others may involve formal campaigns with prizes, rewards, and publicity.

Stop! Look! Listen!

The morale and attitudes of the people in a company can make or break a referral campaign. If employees aren't happy, it's unlikely they will refer friends even if the rewards offered are substantial.

Tactical Tools

To keep employees alert to the referral program, give every employee who makes a referral a token gift such as a coffee mug, T-shirt, or key chain when the referral is made, and of course, a significant reward if the person is hired.

Reward Programs for Successful Referrals

Prizes or bonuses are offered for each person employed through the program— usually contingent on the new employee remaining with the firm for a specified period of time. How much the award should be varies from company to company and usually depends on the difficulty of locating qualified candidates. Most companies pay a set fee such as $100 for referring a semi-skilled factory worker or office clerk to several thousand dollars for technicians, engineers, and professional staff members.

Using Outside Sources

In addition to looking at internal candidates, it pays to look outside the company to ensure that you are selecting from the very best pool of available people.

Using Help Wanted Ads

Probably the most frequently used source for finding applicants is the classified ad section of a newspaper or trade magazine.

The selection of the most effective medium depends on the type of position that is advertised. If the job is one that is most likely to be filled by a local resident, the logical source is a local newspaper; if you are willing to relocate a candidate, your best bet would be in a publication that the type person you are seeking will most likely read.

Most industries have trade journals that cover its field. In addition, professional organizations have magazines devoted to their special needs.

Most classified ads are answered with resumés. However, if quick action is desired, you may request that applicants respond by e-mail. It's a good idea to establish a unique e-mail address for responses. This prevents accidental mixing up of company material with the hiring process. Also, at the end of the search, you can close down the address.

Tactical Tools

A great source of advertising for local people is "drive-time" radio. You have a captive audience. While riding in their cars, you hit them with your ad. If your ad sounds exciting enough, they'll contact you when they get home—or even immediately from their cell phones.

Employment Agencies

Your objective is to fill the open job as rapidly as possible with the best-qualified applicant at the lowest cost. Unless you are exclusively engaged in hiring, you have many other duties that may have to be neglected when searching for personnel. Employment agencies can cut down on the time needed to fill the job. However, they can be a waste of your time if you don't know how to use them effectively.

Employment agencies won't necessarily solve all your hiring problems, but they often can make the process less time consuming, costly, and frustrating. Employment agencies can benefit you in the following ways:

◆ They can save you money. Hiring is costly. Ads cost money. The time used in interviewing applicants costs money. Going out of town to interview applicants or bringing them to your facility costs money. The fee you pay the agency is usually considerably lower than the amount saved by the work they do.

◆ Employment agencies can save you time. Often agencies have files of qualified applicants who can be referred to you immediately.

♦ If your job opening is in a specialized field, agencies that frequently deal with people in that field have resources to reach top-level candidates who may be interested.

♦ They prescreen candidates and refer only those who are close to your specs. This saves you the time and energy of reading countless resumés and interviewing unqualified applicants.

♦ They can keep your company name confidential until you are ready to interview the applicant.

♦ If you develop an ongoing relationship with an agency, they will inform you about highly qualified people who become available even when you don't have an immediate opening. Often, it may be worthwhile creating an opening for a high potential individual.

> **Stop! Look! Listen!**
> Even greater than the direct costs of hiring (advertising, agency fees, and travel) are the indirect costs: the salaries for the time spent by the people engaged in the hiring process (reading resumés, interviewing applicants, checking references, and related work).

Employment agencies don't charge you a fee unless you hire a person referred by them and that person starts work. Most agencies charge fees based on the salary paid to the employee—usually a percentage (10 to 20 percent of annual salary).

Sometimes, however, it may cost you nothing. Although the employer pays most private agencies for their services, there are some agencies that charge the fee to the applicant. Whether the agency charges the company or the applicant depends on the job market. When jobs are hard to find, the applicant is more likely to pay the fee; when jobs are plentiful and applicants are hard to find, the burden of payment shifts to the employer.

Headhunters

Headhunters? Sounds barbarous. No, these are not savage tribes who cut off the heads of their enemies, but a nickname for a special type of recruiter who aggressively goes after candidates for their clients rather than waiting for applicants to come to them. The people in that field don't like being called *headhunters;* they prefer the more professional title: *executive recruiters.*

> **Words to Work By**
> Consultants who specialize in recruiting and screening executives and other top-level personnel are called variously **executive recruiters, executive search organizations,** or informally, **headhunters.**

Executive or technical recruiters differ from employment agencies in that they put their efforts into identifying and going after specific candidates, who are usually currently employed and not actively seeking jobs. These firms usually work on higher paying positions. Some recruiters charge a flat fee, paid whether or not they fill the job; most take a nonrefundable retainer and, if they succeed in filling the job, a percentage of the salary.

Job Fairs

Trade associations, private recruiting firms, colleges, and other organizations organize job fairs. They tend to specialize in specific types of jobs, such as those needed in a particular industry or jobs in a professional or technical area.

Companies rent booths at the fair to attract applicants, provide prospects with job information, and even conduct preliminary interviews.

Some firms conduct their own job fairs. They promote the fair in radio or newspaper ads for several weeks in advance, then set up a section of their facility for the fair.

Government Job Services

Every state has its own job service. They are aided and coordinated by the United States Employment Service (U.S.E.S.), a division of the U.S. Department of Labor. Unemployed people are required to register with the state job service in order to qualify for unemployment benefits. As a result, the public usually refers to these offices as "unemployment offices."

The state job services have always been a major source for hiring blue collar help. They usually know the needs of the companies in their areas and can serve them rapidly and effectively. In case of shortages of certain types of labor in one part of the state, they can recruit from another part of the state and occasionally from other states through the U.S.E.S.

However, many employers have found fault with the quality of referrals from the state job services. Persons not really interested in working accept referrals in order to maintain their unemployment benefits—a waste of time for the company interviewing them.

Professional and Technical Associations

Most professional associations have informal placement services for their members. Members seeking jobs send their resumés to the placement committee. When companies list jobs with the association, the placement service refers the appropriate resumés to them. The problem here is that the services or committees are often run by volunteers, and in some organizations the committee meets once a month or even less frequently. Furthermore, the members might not be trained in employment screening and so they may refer unqualified candidates to the company, wasting the employer's time.

Now Hear This

A good source to locate professional or technical associations in any field is Gale's Encyclopedia of Associations, which can be found in most libraries. Internet source: Gateway to Associations Online (info.asaenet.org/gateway/OnlineAssocSlist.html).

Some organizations do have full time professionals doing the placement. When contacting professional associations for referrals, learn how they are organized and operate.

Sources for Trainees

Most colleges, community colleges, and trade schools are anxious to place their graduates and offer placement services to them. It pays to contact the schools in your area and list jobs with them that you need to fill.

Most large companies make regular visits to college campuses throughout the country to recruit graduating students. If you seek trainees with specialized education, it pays to keep in regular touch with schools and colleges that teach those specialties.

Using Temps

You don't have to hire people to have them work for you. Almost all companies at some time or another use *temps*—people who work on their premises, but are on the payroll of a temporary staffing or employee leasing service. According to a survey made by the American Staffing Association, 90 percent of all companies in America use temporary help services.

Words to Work By

Temps (temporary personnel) are people who work for companies but are employed by—on the payroll of— temporary staffing or employee leasing services Usually they are used for short-term assignments such as filling in for absent employees or augmenting permanent staff when needed.

Temporary services differ from employment agencies in that they don't place people on jobs, but hire them themselves and "lease" them to employers who require either full-time or part-time workers for short periods of time. These jobs range from simple clerical or low-skill laborers all the way to professional and executive positions.

The temp services charge a fee to the company based on the skill level and the number of hours worked by the people they supply you. As the workers are not on your payroll, you pay no benefits or payroll taxes. You are free from the burden of withholding income taxes. They accrue no sick leave or vacation time. If they are absent, the temp service will send another person to do the work. If you are not satisfied, they will replace them. You don't have the hassle of hiring, disciplining, and perhaps firing people.

Most temp services have a reservoir of trained people for the jobs they fill. To ensure the quality of their people, they provide training programs in clerical and computer skills as well as other areas commonly needed by their clients.

Rent-a-Worker

Some business executives have a dream—to run a company without the problems of hiring, administering, and dealing with employees. Believe it or not, it can be done. Instead of hiring people, you can lease them just as you would a car or a piece of equipment.

Over the past few years this concept has spread. Some companies now only maintain a core group of key personnel and have most of their work done by leased employees. Many of the leading temp services have expanded into this field.

In many cases, leased employees work on company premises. They may even be employees, who had been downsized by the company and then were hired by the staffing service, and then leased to their former employer.

The advantages of leasing employees are that the company is relieved of having to recruit staff and deal with all of the administrative headaches.

Tactical Tools
One way of improving your odds on getting recommendations for open jobs is to network—to make connections with people who are likely to know people with the skills and experience your company usually hires.

However, there are many drawbacks to leasing people. When you lease a car, you're still responsible for maintaining it. When you lease personnel, you still have to train them and direct their work. They may not be your employees, but they are your associates. It's up to you to keep them motivated. This is not easy when you have no control over their compensation. It's tough to build up a sense of loyalty and ownership when the team member doesn't identify with the company.

Inasmuch as leased employees don't get most of the benefits given regular employees, a climate of resentment may develop that impairs morale and productivity. To overcome this, more and more leasing companies are providing equivalent benefits to their people—and of course, this is reflected in higher charges to the employer.

The Internet as a Source for Personnel

You can purchase all kinds of goods and services by clicking your mouse. So why not seek to fill your jobs via computer? The applicants you want are probably sitting at their terminals right now surfing the net looking at what career opportunities are around.

Using Your Web Pages

Many firms list their job openings on their company website. The trouble with many web pages is that it's not easy to access employment information. To attract applicants, design a special recruiting page and put a connecting link on the home page so applicants can easily access it.

> **Tactical Tools**
>
> Make your recruiting web page exciting and enticing. Give prospects an intimate look at the company through video clips, vignettes about successful employees, and meaningful job descriptions. Make it easy to contact the company. Provide an e-mail address where applicants can send their resumés.

Using Internet Referral Services

You may be thinking: "Web pages are okay for big companies. My company isn't that well known. Job seekers aren't likely to even know about it, let alone hit our web page."

The solution: Use one of the many Internet job referral services. These are the cyber-equivalent of the help wanted pages in newspapers or technical publications.

 **Now Hear This**

It is estimated that the Internet recruiting business will go from $250 million in 1999 to $5.1 billion by 2003—half the size of the traditional search industry.

Recruiting During Periods of Layoffs

Even when companies are downsizing, they still need to recruit. Why would you hire people on one hand while laying off on the other? Usually the needs are for specialists in skills that are needed to keep the company operating.

It would be great if you can train workers who might be laid off in these skills, but most times this isn't possible because of the nature of the job and the amount of schooling, experience, and skill needed.

Jobs in many technical, professional, and specialized areas are always hard to fill. Good managers are always on the lookout for candidates to fill these positions and grab them when they become available.

The Least You Need to Know

- The first place to look when a job opening occurs is within your own company.

- In seeking candidates for routine jobs, run ads in the help wanted section of a local newspaper. For specialized jobs, trade or professional journals are your best bet.

- Employment agencies can provide rapid service in filling jobs, and you only pay a fee if you hire the person referred by them.

- Headhunters (executive recruiters) are best used when a job is hard to fill and proactive steps are needed to find candidates.

- Don't overlook the Internet as a viable source for candidates.

- Even in times of downsizing, be alert to availability of hard-to-find personnel.

Chapter 13

Screening Candidates

In This Chapter

- ◆ How to evaluate resumés
- ◆ Getting significant information from application forms
- ◆ Making the application a legal protector
- ◆ Using the telephone as a prescreener
- ◆ Preparing for the interview
- ◆ Getting the most from the interview
- ◆ Giving information to the applicant

As a result of your recruiting efforts, you've received a number of resumés. Your next job is to determine which applicants are worth interviewing. In this chapter, you will learn how to pick the candidates whose backgrounds appear to be closest to those required for the open job, to prepare carefully for the interview, and to conduct it effectively.

The First Step: Screening the Resumés

Always remember that the resumé is a promotional piece written by the applicant to persuade you why he or she should be hired. It is not necessarily an objective recap of qualifications. Your job is to find among those glowing words, what the applicant has really done in his or her past jobs and schooling.

Tips on Rapid Screening

You may receive hundreds of resumés in response to an ad. It can take hours and hours of your time to read them and make your preliminary judgments. You can save time and uncover hidden problems in the resumés by following these guidelines:

> **Tactical Tools**
>
> Show some flexibility in using "knockout factors." For example, unless a specific degree is needed for legal or professional reasons, a person who lacks the degree but has extensive experience in a field may be better qualified than a person with a degree and less experience.

- Establish some "knockout factors." These are job requirements that are absolutely essential to performing the job. They include necessary educational qualifications and/or licenses, for example, a degree in electronics, certification as a plumber, or a pilot's license.

- Select key components of the job and screen for them. When you have many applicants for a position, you can narrow the field by looking for experience in those key aspects. For example, if one of the major requirements for success on a job is experience in marketing to major food chains, by scanning resumés for this experience, you will focus on qualified applicants.

- Look for gaps in dates. Some people who have had short duration jobs omit them from their resumés.

- Watch for candidates who give more space on the resumé to past positions than current ones. This may be due to the applicant just updating an old resumé instead of creating a new one. This could be a sign of laziness, or it may just mean that the more recent jobs were less pertinent than previous ones.

- Keep an eye out for overemphasis on education for experienced applicants. If a person is out of school five or more years, the resumé should primarily cover work experience. What was done in high school or college is secondary to what has been accomplished on the job. For such applicants, information about education should be limited to degrees and specialized programs completed.

- As you read the resumés, check to see if a significant amount of education and experience the applicant specifies includes the key factors the applicant must have to qualify.

◆ If these factors are mentioned, determine if this experience or training has been acquired in a setting comparable to that of your organization. (For example, cost accounting experience in a chemical company may not be of much value to an automobile parts company as the cost systems are entirely different.)

◆ Determine if the applicant has enough depth of experience to meet your requirements.

None of these are necessarily knockout factors. They simply suggest further exploration in the interview.

> **Stop! Look! Listen!**
>
> Resumés are only pieces of paper, which cannot possibly describe the whole person. If you choose not to see an applicant based on the resumé, you will lose this prospect— perhaps the best candidate— forever. If you have any doubts, before placing it in the reject file, telephone the candidate to obtain more information.

The Application Form

In addition to requesting resumés, some companies also require all candidates to fill out an application form. This form serves several purposes. It's a rapid means of providing the interviewer with the basic information about the applicant. It alleviates the need for the interviewer to take time asking for this routine information. It provides legal protection. It makes it easy to compare candidates. The following is a prototype application form, which you can adapt to your own particular needs.

Application for Employment

Date: _____

Name: _____   Social Security number: _____

Address: _____

City, State, ZIP: _____   Phone: _____

Position sought: _____   Salary desired: _____

EDUCATION

Level: _____ School/Location: _____ Course: _____

Number of years: _____ Degree or diploma: _____

continues

---

continued

College: _____

Other: _____

_____

EMPLOYMENT RECORD

1. Company/Address: _____

    Dates: _____ Salary: _____ Supervisor: _____

    Duties: _____

    _____

    _____

2. Company/Address: _____

    Dates: _____ Salary: _____ Supervisor: _____

    Duties: _____

    _____

    _____

3. Company/Address: _____

    Dates: _____ Salary: _____ Supervisor: _____

    Duties: _____

    _____

    _____

How were you referred to this company? _____

Are you 18 years of age or older? _____

If you're hired, can you provide written evidence that you are authorized to work in the United States? _____

Is there any other name under which you have worked that we would need in order to check your work record (if so, please provide): _____

APPLICANT'S STATEMENT

I understand that the employer follows an "employment at will" policy, in that I or the employer may terminate my employment at any time or for any reason consistent with applicable federal and state laws. This employment-at-will policy cannot be changed verbally or in writing unless authorized specifically by the president or executive vice president of this company. I understand that this application is not a contract of employment. I understand that the federal government prohibits the employment of unauthorized aliens; all persons hired must provide satisfactory proof of employment authorization and identity. Failure to submit such proof will result in denial of employment.

I understand that the employer may investigate my work and personal history and verify all information given on this application, on related papers, and in interviews. I hereby authorize all individuals, schools, and firms named therein, except my current employer (if so noted), to provide any information requested about me and hereby release them from all liability for damage in providing this information.

I certify that all the statements in this form and other information provided by me in applying for this position are true and understand that any falsification or willful omission shall be sufficient cause for dismissal or refusal of employment.

Signed: _____

All Applicants *Must* Fill Out the Form

Some candidates may be reluctant to complete an application. They might tell you that all of that information is in the resumé. And sometimes it is. But, as was pointed out earlier in this chapter, a resumé is designed to play up the strengths of the applicant—sometimes to cover up negative factors. If your company requires that candidates complete the form to be considered for the job, then stick to this policy.

CAUTION

Stop! Look! Listen!

"I don't have to fill out the application. I have a resumé." This is *not* a good argument. If an applicant doesn't want to take the time to complete your application form, he or she may be hiding something—or it may be an indicator of laziness or unwillingness to follow instructions.

It Provides Information You Need

It's convenient to have essential information in one easy to find place. The form provides name, address, phone number, Social Security number, and educational background. Most useful is the work history with dates of employment, positions, companies, and a brief description of duties and responsibilities. Usually it includes salary, reason for leaving, and the name of a person in the company who can provide information about the applicant.

It gives you enough basic information to determine whether or not the prospect is worthy of further consideration. Although most forms don't have enough space to give details about a person's activities, actions, and accomplishments, it provides, along with the applicant's resumé, adequate data to make preliminary judgments.

> **Now Hear This**
>
> Target Stores and Home Depot have substituted computer-based tools for paper job applications. Kiosks have been placed in the stores so shoppers can apply for jobs by answering the questions online. Then a formatted copy is sent electronically to the manager on duty who can set up an immediate interview.

> **Tactical Tools**
>
> Impressive resumés may make a candidate stand out, but when the resumé and application together are considered, you may find that the applicant with a less impressive looking resumé actually has a better background.

It Makes It Easy to Compare Candidates

While resumés are written in a variety of styles, applications for jobs in a company are all formatted in the same way. This makes it easy to compare applicants. Placing application forms side by side, you can immediately measure the education and experience of each candidate against the others. You can compare duration and types of experience and note salary variations.

Application Clauses to Protect You

In addition to being a selection tool, the application form is a contract. Of course, it's a one-sided contract in that it's written to protect the employer. Courtrooms have been filled with lawsuits against companies by job applicants who have claimed that companies discriminated against them in the hiring process. Others have claimed that companies jeopardized their current job by calling their employer for a reference, or that their privacy was invaded by having their backgrounds investigated.

Properly designed application forms can protect companies. For example, if no questions on your application request age or related information, applicants will have a tough time proving that a company discriminated against them because of age. If the application form requests permission to contact current employers or to perform background checks, then companies are protected on that front.

> **Tactical Tools**
>
> Before reprinting your application form each time more copies are needed, have your legal counsel review it to ensure it's in compliance with the latest laws and regulations.

Let's look at some of the important clauses attorneys strongly recommend be included in this document. You will find suggested wording in the sample application form in this chapter, but it is always advisable to consult your attorney, as wording may have to be adapted to union contracts, local laws, and court rulings.

Permission to Investigate Background

This covers two different types of investigation: checking references and using an investigative service to look into the applicant's background.

♦ **Reference checks:** Because of their concerns about litigation, many companies refuse to give information about former or current employees. By getting a release from the applicant authorizing the employer to provide information, you obviate this concern. Many companies have a clause to cover this on their application form; some have this on a separate document.

> **Stop! Look! Listen!**
>
> Some lawyers suggest that even if a release clause is incorporated in the application form, a separate form should be signed for each school and employer to be contacted.

See the sample application form in this chapter for an example of such a clause.

♦ **Investigative reports:** Under the Fair Credit Reporting Act, a federal law, if you consider using the services of an outside credit or investigative reporting agency, you must provide the applicant with a written notification stating that such a report may be ordered. The applicant must be advised that he or she has the right to request a copy of such a report from the agency that conducts the investigation and that the name of such agency will be provided on request. If you plan to use this type service on a regular basis, this clause should be printed on the application form in print that is no smaller than the rest of the application and should have a space for signature of the applicant and of a witness. If you use investigative reports for only a few positions, rather than print it on the application, develop a separate form to use when appropriate.

Employment at Will

Unless an employee is protected by an individual contract with the employer, a negotiated contract between the employer and a labor union, or is civil service employee, that person falls under the employment-at-will status. This means that the employer has the right to terminate the services of that employee at any time, for any reason, or for no reason at all so long as it complies with applicable laws such as the civil rights laws. Most employees in American companies fall in this category. However, to ensure that new employees are aware of this, it should be indicated on the application form. By having the applicant sign the application form, he or she acknowledges understanding and acceptance of "employment at will" (for more on this topic, see Chapter 24).

Certification of Truth

If after you hire a person, you find out that he or she had lied in his or her application or resumé about an important factor, you should have the option to take immediate action to terminate that person.

Have your company's legal advisors word the certification of truth clause to meet all appropriate laws.

The Telephone Screening Interview

Once you've sifted through all the applications and/or resumés and put together a stack of likely candidates, it's time to pick up the telephone. Probably the most frequently used screening tool is the telephone. In a relatively brief telephone interview, you can acquire a lot more information about a candidate than can be obtained from the application and/or resumé.

It's not a good idea to call the applicant at his or her place of work to discuss your job opening. This is not only unethical, but it puts the applicant in an awkward position as other people may be nearby who can hear the conversation. Instead, call the applicant at home in the evening. This may mean you have to make these calls from your home or work late at the office. It's just one of the sacrifices that recruiters and managers have to make to get the people they want.

Plan the phone call as carefully as an in-person interview. Read the application and/or resumé carefully and note the areas that require elaboration. Don't be afraid to ask hard questions, such as why the applicant wants to leave his or her current position, why the candidate was unemployed for lengthy periods of time, what his or her relations with superiors were like, and specific details about work or educational background. Suggestions on how to conduct an interview will be covered later in this chapter—adapt these techniques to the telephone interview.

Take Notes

In a telephone interview, it's even more important than in a personal interview to note the answers to your questions. It's not a distraction to the interviewee as it might be in a face-to-face interview, so you have more freedom to be thorough in your note taking. We tend to remember people and what they tell us more easily when we see them in person than when we just hear them over the phone.

Closing the Telephone Interview

In closing the interview, review your notes to ensure that you have all the information you need. If you're sure you want to extend the invitation, do so. If you have some reservations or wish to discuss your reaction with others in your organization, tell the applicant you'll be in touch with him or her. Give a specific time when your next contact should be expected, and be sure to keep your promise. If you have decided to reject the applicant, either say so immediately, or notify the applicant in a reasonably short time after the phone call.

It's Show Time

You've done the preparatory work. You've studied application forms and resumés and completed a preliminary phone interview. Now you're ready to see the applicant. Interviewing is both an art and a science. It's a science because it can be structured to bring out the information desired. It's an art because the interviewer must be able to tailor the questions and interpret the responses.

Interviews are more than just pleasant conversations between you and the applicant. How the interviewing process is planned and followed can make the difference between hiring the best candidate and just selecting one by instinct.

Preparing for the Interview

Before an applicant enters the interviewing room, you should study the application and resumé. Note any areas that require more information or are indicators of strengths or weaknesses so that you will remember to ask questions about them.

Keep in mind the objectives of the interview: first, to determine whether the candidate has the technical qualifications needed for the position; second, to find out if the applicant has the personality traits needed to be successful in the job.

Plan Your Questions

Well-designed questions based on the job specs can help determine skill qualifications. Personality qualifications are much more difficult to measure. Some of these intangibles may be listed in the job specs. For example, "must be able to work under pressure," or "should be able to present public speeches." It's not easy to reduce personality factors to a simple statement. The interviewer's knowledge of the job, the people with whom the applicant will have to work, and the company culture must be taken into consideration.

Some interviewers sit down with the applicant with only a general idea of what questions they plan to ask. They may start with a general question such as "Tell me about yourself." From the response, they then pick aspects of the background to explore. This may be OK for an experienced interviewer who just uses that question as an opening device and has thought out what added questions to ask. However, the danger here is that the applicant may tell you only what he or she wants you to hear and you may never get around to asking about areas not mentioned.

Make a List of Key Questions

In planning for the interview, develop a list of questions you plan to ask. An effective interview is well planned. The interviewer doesn't ad lib questions.

Some interviewers write down the questions they plan to ask and refer to it during the interview.

Others make notes on the applicant's application form to remind them about areas they wish to explore. Still other interviewers depend on their knowledge of the field to develop questions as they move along in the process. Later in this chapter, you'll find a structured interview form listing questions that are effective in obtaining good information.

The Structured Interview

Most good interviews have some kind of structure. If not, they result in a chaotic exchange of questions and answers with little possibility of making reasonable decisions. However, some companies use specially prepared *structured interview* forms, which interviewers must follow virtually line by line.

Advantages of Using a Structured Interview

Some labor lawyers argue that asking each applicant exactly the same questions in exactly the same order will be a defense against charges of discrimination. Some psychologists have designed structured interviews with the objective of uncovering patterns of behavior. Others use structured interviews simply to make the interview process as easy as possible. Whether the reason is legal, psychological, or just pragmatic, there are some advantages to using some form of structured interview.

By asking questions from a printed list, you won't miss asking an important question. In addition, structured interview forms provide space next to the questions to record answers. This helps the interviewer remember the responses. In addition, as all applicants are asked the same questions, it makes it easy to compare applicants when making the final decision.

Consider the Downside

The negative side of a formal structured interview is that it stifles creativity and flexibility. In the formal structured interview, you are not allowed to deviate from the

Stop! Look! Listen!

It's important to prepare questions to ask an applicant at the interview. However, don't limit yourself to asking just those questions. Be alert to responses and ask additional questions based on answers received. Review the list of legal and illegal questions in Chapter 7 to ensure you keep within the law.

Words to Work By

Structured interviews are conducted using a list of questions that must be asked in exactly the same way in exactly the same order. They are also called **patterned interviews, diagnostic interviews,** and **guided interviews.**

form. Both those forms developed for legal reasons and those with psychological implication require strict adherence to the structure.

Sometimes an applicant's answer to one question may make it advisable for you to depart from the structure and follow-up to obtain more or better information.

Using a Less Formal Structure

I suggest that you use the structured interview only as a guide. This cannot be done if the format you use is one in which the psychologist requires the interviewer to phrase questions exactly as printed or if you're company requires strict adherence. However, most structured interviews are not of this nature, and variations and flexibility can be built into them.

The following is an example of a modified structured interview form. It is designed to serve as a guide and gives the interviewer freedom to be flexible. Feel free to adapt this for your own use. Follow the instructions at the beginning of the form.

> **CAUTION**
>
> **Stop! Look! Listen!**
>
> When using a structured interview form, don't fall into the trap of reading the question as if it were a questionnaire. Present the questions in a conversational tone and rephrase where necessary to put the question into the context of the conversation.

To use this system effectively, it must be personalized for each specific job and for each applicant. The suggested questions are to be used only as guidelines. They might or might not be asked of each applicant depending upon pertinence.

Most important: Specific questions relating to job requirements should be developed for each job based on *your* job description, company needs, and interviewer's follow-up to responses given by the applicant.

Structured Interview Questions

(Complete this section before the interview begins.)

Name of applicant: _____

Address: _____

_____

Telephone/fax/e-mail: _____

_____

Position: _____

Department: _____

Interviewed by: _____

Date: _____

Note: In designing the form to use in your company, leave spaces between questions to note answers.

Education

Ask questions in Part A of applicants who did not attend college. Use questions in Part B for college graduates or those who have had same college. For applicants who have been out of college five years or more omit A or B and ask only questions in Part C.

A. For Applicants Who Did Not Attend College:

1. What was your highest level of schooling completed?

2. Why did you decide not to continue your formal education?

3. How were your overall grades?

4. What extracurricular activities did you participate in?

5. If you worked during school, how many hours per week? Summers? What kind of jobs?

6. What steps have you taken to acquire additional education since leaving school?

7. What training have you had in high or other schools that helped in your career?

8. What was the first significant job you held after leaving high school?

9. How did this lead to your present career?

B. For College Graduates or Those with Some College:

1. I see that you attended (name of college). Why did you select that school?

continues

continued

2. What was your major? Why did you choose it?

3. What were your overall college grades? How did they compare with your high school grades?

4. What courses did you start in college and later drop? Why?

5. In what types of extracurricular activities did you participate in college? What offices did you hold?

6. How did you finance your college education?

7. If you worked in high school or college, how many hours per week? Summers? Kind of jobs?

8. What were your vocational plans when you were in college?

9. If your vocational plans are different now, when did you change your thinking? Why?

10. What additional education have you had since college?

11. How do you think college contributed to your career?

12. (If college was not completed.) When did you leave college? Why? Do you plan to complete your degree? (If so, ask about plans.)

13. What was the first significant job you held after leaving (graduating from) college?

14. How did this lead to your current career?

C. For Persons out of School Five Years or Longer:

1. What educational background have you had that has contributed to success in your career?

2. What courses or seminars have you taken recently? (If job-related, how did you apply them to your job?)

3. What are you doing now to keep up with the state of the art in your field?

4. What magazines and types of books do you read regularly?

Work Experience

Ask these questions for *each* job held:

1. On your application you indicated you worked for (name of company) Are you still there? (Or: When were you there?)

2. Describe your duties and responsibilities in each of your assignments with this company?

3. What were some of the things you particularly enjoyed about that job?

4. What were some of the things you least enjoyed in that position?

5. What do you consider your major accomplishment in that assignment?

6. Tell me about some of your disappointments or setbacks in that job.

7. Tell me about the progress you made in that company.

8. If progress was significant, ask: To what do you attribute this fine progress? If not, ask: Were you satisfied with this progress? If not satisfied, ask: How did you attempt to overcome this?

9. Why did you leave (or: why do you want to leave) that company?

Specific Questions

On a separate sheet of paper, list specific questions to be asked-based on the job description. (See section immediately following this form.)

Intangible Factors

In addition to the questions on job qualifications, ask some questions to elicit information about the applicant as a person:

1. What are you seeking in this job that you are not getting in your present job?

2. Tell me about your short- and long-term career goals.

3. In what way could a job with our company meet your career objectives?

4. If you had to do it over again, what changes would you make in your life and your career?

continues

continued

5. Think of a supervisor you particularly respected. Describe his/her management style? Describe your least effective supervisor?

6. What have supervisors complimented you for? What have they criticized you for?

7. Tell me about some of the significant problems encountered? How did you solve them?

8. If hired for this position, what can you bring to it that will make you productive right away?

9. In what areas could we help you become even more productive?

Preparing Specific Job-Related Questions

The responses to the general questions in your interview will give you enough information to determine if the candidate is basically qualified for your job. However, there are in every job certain very specific areas of knowledge, experience, and expertise that the applicant must demonstrate to be capable of becoming productive rapidly. To determine this, you should also prepare a list of questions that will probe for these details.

> **Tactical Tools**
>
> Read your job specs carefully. Discuss the job with the department head or team leader. Frame questions that will enable you to get the information needed to determine whether this applicant is best for the open position.

As the questions differ from job to job—even jobs with the same or similar titles may require different specific factors—you must develop appropriate questions for each job.

To do this, study not just the job specification, which lists the qualifications required, but also the job description, which gives details of job functions.

> **Now Hear This**
>
> Lists of specific questions to ask applicants for more than 70 different jobs can be found in *Be a Better Employment Interviewer* by Dr. Arthur R. Pell. It sells for $14.95 and can be ordered from Personnel Publications, PO Box 301, Huntington, NY 11745.

For example, if your opening is for a medical technician, prepare questions about the types of medical equipment the applicant has learned to operate in school, his or her experience in operating the equipment, and the venues in which the person worked (Hospital? Clinic? Physician's office?). If you are not fully knowledgeable about the job, have the person to whom the person would report design these questions for you—and, of course, the appropriate answers.

Getting Started

In order to obtain the best results from an interview, the interviewer must put the applicant at ease. To do this takes a little time, but even in a brief interview is well worth it.

Establish Rapport

To make the applicant feel at ease, the interviewer must be at ease and feel comfortable about the interviewing process. An ideal setting for an interview is a private room, comfortably furnished with a minimum of distracting papers on the desk. To avoid telephone interruptions, turn on your voicemail or have somebody else answer your phone.

It's much better to personally go to the reception area than to send a secretary to fetch him or her. So get up from your chair and get out there. Introduce yourself and escort the applicant to the interviewing room.

When greeting the applicant, use his or her full name. "David Livingston. Hi, I'm Henry Stanley." This makes the applicant feel that you identify him or her as an individual, not just another candidate. Dale Carnegie put it best when he said, "Remember, a person's name is to that person the sweetest and most important sound in any language."

By using both the first and the last name in addressing the applicant and in introducing yourself, you are putting both of you on equal footing. If you call yourself Mr. or Ms., and call the applicant "Dave" it sounds condescending.

The opening should be related to the interview, but should not make the applicant defensive or upset. Don't start with such questions as "What makes you think that you could handle this job?" or "Why were you fired from your last job?"

A better approach would be to select an innocuous area from the application and comment on it. It may be based on something in the background that you relate to. For example, "I see you went to Lincoln High School. Did you know Mr. Salkin, the drama teacher?" or "I see you live in Chelsea. That neighborhood is growing rapidly."

Guidelines for Better Interviewing

To get the most out of the interview, here are some guidelines to follow when asking questions:

◆ Don't ask questions that can be answered with a simple "Yes" or "No." This stifles information. Instead of asking, "Have you any experience in budgeting?" ask, "Tell me about your experience in budgeting?"

◆ Don't put words in the applicant's mouth. Instead of asking: "You've called on discount stores, haven't you?" ask, "What discount stores have you called on?"

◆ Don't ask questions that are unrelated to your objectives. It might be interesting to follow up on certain tidbits of gossip the applicant volunteers, but it rarely leads to pertinent information.

◆ Do ask questions that develop information as to the applicant's *experience* ("What were your responsibilities regarding the purchasing of equipment?"), *knowledge* ("How did you, or would you cope with this problem?"), and *attitudes* ("How do you feel about heavy travel?" Or "Why do you wish to change jobs now?").

Now Hear This

An important objective of the interview is to create a favorable image of the company in the eyes of the applicant. The reputation of the firm may be improved or harmed by the manner in which applicants are treated. You want your top candidate to accept a job offer and who knows, even rejected applicants may be potential customers.

An effective way of probing for full information is to use the "W" questions: "What," "When," "Where," "Who," and "Why." With the addition of "How," you can draw out most of the information needed. For example:

"What computer software was used?"

"When did you design that program?"

"Where was the program installed?"

"Who was responsible for supervising that project?"

"Why did you make that decision?"

"How did you implement the new system?"

Stop! Look! Listen!

Glib applicants may come up with high-sounding solutions to situations, but they may not be really practical. Follow through by asking what problems might be encountered if the idea were implemented.

Ask Situational Questions

Give the applicant a hypothetical situation and ask how he or she would handle it. The situations should be reasonably close to actual problems found on the job. Judge the response by knowledge of the subject, approach to the solution, value of the suggestions, and clarity in communicating the answer.

Summary Questions

After you have asked the applicant about a phase of his or her background, ask another question that will summarize what has been presented. For example "You certainly have extensive background in quality control, briefly summarize what you can contribute to make our company more effective in that area."

Using Non-Directive Techniques

It's not always possible to obtain necessary information by direct questioning. Nondirective approaches may help in these cases. Nondirective questioning uses open-end questions such as "Tell me about ..." The applicant then tells whatever he or she feels is important. Instead of commenting about the response, you nod your head and say "uh-huh," "yes," "I see." This encourages the applicant to keep talking without your giving any hint as to what you are seeking.

In this way, the applicant may talk about problems, personality factors, attitudes, or weaknesses that might not have been uncovered directly. On the other hand, it may bring out some positive factors and strengths that were missed by direct questioning.

Another way of using the nondirective approach is to be silent. Most people can't tolerate silence. If you don't respond instantly, the applicant is likely to keep talking.

> **Tactical Tools**
>
> Try this: After the applicant responds to your question, count to five slowly (to yourself, of course) before asking the next question. By waiting five seconds, you'll be surprised how often an applicant adds something—positive or negative—to the response to the previous question.

Giving Information to the Applicant

An important part of the interview is giving the applicant information about the company and the job. All the work and expense undertaken to get good employees is lost if the applicants you want don't accept your offer. By giving them a positive picture of the job at the interview, you're more likely to have a higher rate of acceptances.

When and What to Tell About the Job

Some interviewers start the interview by describing the job duties. Some give the applicant a copy of the job description in advance of the interview. *This is a serious error.* If an applicant knows too much about a job too soon, he or she is likely to tailor the answers to all of your questions to fit the job.

For example, suppose you tell a prospect that the job calls for selling to department store chains. Even if the applicant has only limited experience in this area, when you ask, "What types of markets did you call on?" guess which one will be emphasized?

The best way to give information about duties and responsibilities is to feed it to the applicant throughout the interview—*after* you have ascertained the background of the applicant in that phase of the work. For the sales job that involves calling on department store chains, you might first ask the candidate to state the types of markets he or she called on.

You should then ask specific questions about the applicant's experience in each of these markets. If the department store background is satisfactory, you might then say: "I'm glad you have such a fine background in dealing with department store chains as they represent about 40 percent of our customer list. If you're hired, you'd be working closely with those chains."

If the background in this area was weak, you might say: "As a great deal of our business is with department store chains, if we hire you, we would have to give you added training in this area."

Stop! Look! Listen!

Don't give the applicants copies of the job description before an interview. Their responses to your questions will be influenced by what they read.

At the end of the first interview, the interviewer should have a fairly complete knowledge of the applicant's background and the applicant should have a good idea of the nature of the job. At subsequent interviews, the emphasis will be on obtaining more specific details about the applicant and giving the applicant more specific data about the job.

Answering Applicants' Questions

Most interviewers give the applicant an opportunity to ask questions about the job and the company at some point (usually at the end) of the interview. The questions asked can give some insight into the applicant's personality and help you in your evaluation.

Are the questions primarily of a personal nature? (Such as vacations, time off, raises, and similar queries), or are they about the job? People who are only concerned about personal aspects are less likely to be as highly motivated as job-oriented applicants. Their questions can also be clues to their real interest in the job. If you feel, from these questions that a prospective candidate might not be too enthusiastic about the job, it gives you another chance to sell the prospect on the advantages of joining your company.

You are always "selling" when you interview. It's important that you present your company and the job in a positive and enthusiastic manner. This doesn't mean that you should exaggerate or mislead the applicant. Tell the applicant the negatives at the interview, but show how the positive aspects outweigh them. Remember that you, the interviewer, will be working with this candidate. An honest interview discussing positive and negative aspects helps to build trust.

> **Tactical Tools**
>
> Every job has its negative aspects, and if you hide them, the applicant will find out sooner or later. This could lead to rejection of the job offer, or worse, acceptance and early resignation.

Closing the Interview

Once you have all the information you need, and you've told the applicant about the job and given him or her an opportunity to ask questions, it's time to bring the interview to a close.

End on a Positive Note

All interviews should end on a positive note. The applicant should be told what the next step would be: Another interview? Testing? A final decision?

Informing the Applicant of Your Decision

If, on the basis of the interview, you have decided not to hire the candidate, it's only fair to tell him or her. In most cases, the reason may be obvious. During the interview, it became clear to both of you that the applicant was not qualified. Just say: "As you don't have experience in area X and Y, which are essential to being able to do this job, we cannot consider you for it."

If the reason is not directly job related, such as lacking personal characteristics or your reaction to the applicant, rather than reject him or her outright, say, "We have several more applicants to interview. Once we've seen them all, we'll make a decision." Then, after a reasonable period, let them know they were rejected.

> **Tactical Tools**
>
> Don't keep applicants on a string waiting to hear from you. If you are not interested in a candidate, write or phone him or her no later than a week after the interview. If the applicant is still being considered, but the decision is delayed, keep the applicant advised of the status.

Remembering the Applicant

You've seen a dozen applicants for the open position. Unless you take notes, it's unlikely to remember what each one has told you and your reaction to them.

Good Notes Keep You Out of Trouble

If you've kept good records of the interviews, it's easier to compare candidates. By rereading your notes rather than depending on your memory, you are more likely to make sounder judgments. When several people interview the same candidate, a consistent system of recording information will facilitate an in-depth analysis of the applicant's qualifications.

Good records also come in handy if you face legal problems. In case of an investigation by government agencies such as the EEOC or state civil rights divisions, good records of the interview can be your most important defense. Where no records or inadequate records have been kept, the opinion of the hearing officer is dependent on the company's word against the applicant's. Good, consistent records provide solid evidence.

Taking Notes

Taking notes often has a negative effect on applicants. Some get very nervous when they see you write down everything they say. They may be inhibited from talking freely and hold back on important matters.

Taking notes also may have a negative effect on you, the interviewer. You're so busy writing what the applicant just said, that you don't listen to what is now being said.

Write brief notes during the interview. Immediately after the interview review them and write a summary, while the interview is still fresh in your mind.

List the reasons for accepting or rejecting each candidate. Succinctly stating a reason helps overcome intuitive decisions based on some vague like or dislike. Don't forget that the EEOC or other agencies may challenge the reasons.

Some companies have special forms designed for interview record keeping. Others suggest you make notes on the application form or on a paper to attach to the form after the interview. In any case a summary form should be completed *immediately* after the close of the interview.

The Least You Need to Know

◆ Before evaluating resumés, set up a series of knockout factors. Unless the applicant meets these specs, there's no point arranging for an interview.

◆ Don't take a resumé at face value. Read between the lines. Look for hidden negative factors.

◆ Before conducting an interview, review the job specs and description application as well as the applicant's resumé and application form.

◆ Prepare a list of key questions.

◆ A good interview should be structured, but flexible enough so that follow-up questions can be asked.

◆ Telephone interviews can provide enough information to determine whether it's worthwhile to invite the applicant for a face-to-face meeting.

◆ Put the applicant at ease by asking nonthreatening questions at the start of the interview.

◆ To get full information, use the "W" questions: "What," "When," "Where," "Who," and "Why." With the addition of "How," you can draw out most of the information needed.

◆ Use nondirective approaches to elicit additional information about candidates.

Chapter 14

Who Should I Hire?

In This Chapter

- ◆ Multiple interviews
- ◆ Tests? Yes or No?
- ◆ References checks that provide real information
- ◆ Overcoming roadblocks to making good hiring decisions
- ◆ Comparing applicants
- ◆ Making a job offer

An interview is one of the primary tools for choosing new employees, but it's not the only one. After all, an interview is, by its very nature, subjective.

To supplement your reaction to applicants, it's a good idea to have other managers or staff members interview them. Because each person tends to look for different facets of an applicant's background, if several people do the interviewing, you will uncover much more about a candidate than any one interviewer can find. In a team set-up, it's particularly helpful for team members to interview people who may join their team. Other techniques for obtaining information about prospective employees are to check their references and, in some cases, have them undergo testing.

This chapter discusses these and other approaches to learning as much as possible about applicants before making your hiring decision.

Multiple Interviews

Hiring an employee can be the most important decision you make as a manager. The people who comprise your staff can make or break your endeavors. No matter how good you may be as an interviewer, it's a good idea to seek the reaction of others before making a final decision.

> **Tactical Tools**
>
> Before making a hiring decision, have an applicant interviewed by other people who will work closely with that person.

In larger companies, a member of the human resources department usually conducts preliminary interviews with applicants. Only people who meet basic job requirements are referred to the manager.

If HR isn't involved in the interview process, it's still a good idea to have the applicant interviewed by at least one other person. You may have missed important facts or been overly influenced by one factor or another.

The person (or persons) you ask to be the other interviewer should have the appropriate type of job and level of responsibility. To interview for jobs of a technical or specialized nature, a person with expertise in that area is the best choice. If a new employee will work closely with another department, the opinion of the manager of that department will be meaningful. Many companies require finalists to be interviewed by the manager at the next higher level (your boss).

When You Work in Teams

Because the team concept involves every member of a team, the process of choosing members for the team should be a team activity. The danger is that interviewing takes time: If every team member interviews every applicant, other work will suffer.

It's not necessary for every team member to conduct a full interview. Each team member should concentrate on the part of an applicant's background in which she or he has the greatest knowledge. All team members will have the opportunity to size up an applicant, and to share their evaluations with the rest of the team. It also gives a candidate a chance to meet the people with whom he or she will be working, and can help the candidate make the best decision as to whether to join your team.

Have each interviewer fill out an interview summary sheet so that evaluations can be compared more easily.

Employment Tests: A Panacea or a Waste of Time?

Do tests help in choosing employees? Some companies swear by testing; others swear at them. In companies in which tests are used extensively as part of the screening process, the HR department or an independent testing organization does the testing. Except for performance tests (discussed later in this chapter), it's unlikely that you will have to administer tests.

Let's look at the most frequently used preemployment tests.

Intelligence Tests

Like the IQ tests used in schools, these tests measure the ability to learn. They vary from simple exercises (such as the Wunderlic tests) that can be administered by people with a minimum of training, to highly sophisticated tests that must be administered by specialists with a Ph.D. in psychology.

The major flaw in using general intelligence tests is that two individuals who receive the same score can earn it in very different ways. One may be high in reasoning, low in numerical skills, and average in verbal skills. The other may be high in numerical skills, low in reasoning, and high in verbal skills. They display entirely different intelligence profiles. Judging them by the total score can be misleading. To get the true picture, the test has to be evaluated by the scores of its components.

Tests often create other problems, too. For instance, some people believe that highly creative people score lower on standardized exams.

Another problem is that some tests violate the equal opportunity laws. To ensure that a test is in compliance, it must be validated to be free from *cultural bias*, and the score on the test must be directly related to the ability to do the job. Most test publishers have taken steps to eliminate cultural bias, but it is up to the company itself to prove that the test does have relevance to job success. For example, a test may contain questions about Greek mythology—a subject biased against minorities who come from cultures where this subject is less likely to be studied—and such questions are not relevant to ability to learn the job. The Equal Employment Opportunity Commission has issued guidelines on validation of tests, which can be obtained directly from its office in your area.

Aptitude Tests

These tests are designed to determine the potential of candidates in specific areas such as mechanical ability, clerical skills, and sales potential. Such tests are helpful in screening inexperienced people to determine whether they have the aptitude in the type of work you plan to train them for.

Performance Tests

These tests measure how well applicants can do the job. Examples include operating a piece of machinery, entering data into a computer, writing advertising copy, or proofreading manuscripts. Such tests are usually not controversial, and in most instances give the employer a realistic way of determining the ability of the applicant to do the job.

Designing performance tests for more complex jobs isn't easy. There are no performance tests for managerial ability or for most advanced jobs. Some companies, as part of the screening process, have asked applicants for such jobs to develop programs or projects for them. This makes sense. Asking an applicant for a marketing position to develop a marketing program for a new product can provide insight into his or her methods of operation, creativity, and practicality. However, such tests can be carried too far. One company asked an applicant for a training director's position to create a leadership-training program for team leaders. He worked on it for several days and submitted it, but didn't get the job. Some months later, he learned that the company was using his plan to train team leaders. He billed the company for providing consulting services. When the company ignored his bill, he sued and won the case.

Stop! Look! Listen!

If performance tests are used, the exact same test, under the same circumstances, must be used for all applicants. For example, in a recent case a company testing applicants for a clerical job gave each candidate a spelling test. However, black applicants were given words that were much more difficult than those in the test given white applicants.

Personality Tests

Personality tests are designed to identify personality characteristics. They vary from quickie questionnaires to highly sophisticated psychological evaluations. A great deal of controversy exists over the value of these types of tests. Supervisors and team leaders are cautioned not to make decisions based on the results of personality tests unless experts make the full implications clear to them.

Selecting tests or similar assessment tools must be done very carefully. In buying a published test, ascertain the legitimacy of the publisher and the test by checking with the American Psychological Association and by contacting current and, if possible, past users of the test for their opinions.

Managers should always remember that the administration of one or more personality tests is not the same thing as a comprehensive pre-employment assessment by an industrial psychologist. Such assessments include ability and personality measures, plus an extensive interview. These assessments typically cost in the neighborhood of $500–$1,000 per candidate, and are usually based on an hourly rate charged by the psychologist.

Are these tests worth the cost? It depends on whom you speak to. Most of the companies that use some form of testing report mixed results. However, as many factors—not just the test results—are considered before making the hiring decision, it's difficult to determine just how valuable the tests are.

Now Hear This

A large number of personality tests are available. You can obtain information about approved tests from the American Psychological Association, 1010 Vermont Ave, Washington, D.C., 20005-4907. Phone: (202) 783-2077. Website: www.

Stop! Look! Listen!

Sometimes you can't win. If you hire someone whose test score is low and that person fails, management may blame you for not considering the test results. If you have someone whose score is high and he or she succeeds, management often credits the test instead of complimenting you for using good judgment.

Who Uses Employment Tests?

The American Management Association (AMA) administered a survey about workplace testing to nearly 1,100 human resources managers. Because AMA corporate members are mostly mid-sized and large companies, the data does not reflect the policies and practices of the U.S. economy as a whole, where small firms predominate. Nevertheless, 48 percent of respondents say they use some form of psychological testing to assess abilities and behaviors for applicants as well as employees. Tests measured cognitive ability, interests/career paths, managerial abilities, personality, and simulated job tasks/physical ability.

Despite the advances in computerized psychological testing, face-to-face interviews or interpersonal exchanges designed to create a psychological profile remain the most frequent types of such tests used (43 percent of respondents test applicants this way).

Nearly 65 percent of surveyed employers test applicants' job skills. This includes skill tests such as typing, computing, or specific professional proficiencies (for example, accounting, engineering, or marketing).

Making Meaningful Reference Checks

Applicants can tell you anything they want about their experiences. How do you know whether they're telling the truth? A reference check is one of the oldest approaches to verifying a background, but is it reliable? Former employers unfortunately don't always tell the whole truth about candidates. They may be reluctant to make negative statements, either because they don't want to prevent the person from working—as long it's not for them—or they fear that they might be sued. Still, a reference check is virtually your only source of verification.

<table>
<tr><td>

Tactical Tools

To make reference checks more successful, talk to an applicant's supervisor, not to a member of the HR staff. Prepare good questions. Begin with verification questions. Advance to detailed questions about job duties, and comment on responses. Then ask for opinions about performance, attitudes, and so on.

</td><td>

Unless your company policy is that the human resources department checks references, it's better for you, the person making the hiring decision, to do it. You have more insight into your staffing needs and can ask follow-up questions that will help you determine whether the applicant's background fits your needs. Be careful to follow the same guidelines in asking questions of the reference as you do in interviewing applicants. Just as you can't ask an applicant whether she has young children, for example, you can't attempt to get this type of information from the reference.

</td></tr>
</table>

Getting Useful Information from a Reference

Most reference checks are made by telephone. To make the best of a difficult situation, you must carefully plan the reference check and use diplomacy in conducting it.

The following list provides some tips for making a reference check:

◆ **Call an applicant's immediate supervisor.** Try to avoid speaking to the company's HR staff members. The only information they usually have is what's on file. An immediate supervisor can give you details about exactly how that person worked, in addition to his or her personality factors and other significant traits.

◆ **Begin your conversation with a friendly greeting.** Then ask whether the employer can verify some information about the applicant. Most people don't mind verifying data. Ask a few verification questions about date of employment, job title, and other items from the application.

♦ **Diplomatically shift to a question that requires a substantive answer,** but not one that calls for opinion. Respond with a comment about the answer, as in this example:

You: Tell me about her duties in dealing with customers.

Supervisor: [Gives details of the applicant's work.]

You: That's very important in the job she is seeking because she'll be on the phone with customers much of the time.

By commenting about what you have learned, you make the interchange a conversation—not an interrogation. You're making telephone friends with the former supervisor. You're building up a relationship that will make him or her more likely to give opinions about an applicant's work performance, attitudes, and other valuable information.

> **CAUTION**
>
> **Stop! Look! Listen!**
>
> Never tell an applicant that he or she is hired "subject to a reference check." If the references are good but you choose another candidate, an applicant will assume that you received a poor reference. Also, never tell a person that the reason for rejection is a poor reference. Reference information should be treated as confidential.

"All I Can Tell You Is That She Worked Here"

If a former employer refuses outright to answer a question, don't push. Point out that you understand any reluctance. Make the comment, "I'm sure that you would want to have as much information as possible about a candidate if you were considering someone." Then ask another question (but don't repeat the same one). If the responses begin coming more freely, return to the original question, preferably using different words.

What happens if you believe that the person you're speaking to is holding something back? What if you sense from the person's voice that he or she is hesitating in providing answers or you detect a vagueness that says you're not getting the full story? Here's one way to handle this situation:

> **Now Hear This**
>
> One of the great paradoxes in reference checking is that companies want full information about prospective employees from former employers, but because of their fear of being sued for defamation, when asked for information about their former employees, they give little more than basic information—dates of employment and job title.

> Mr. Controller, I appreciate your taking the time to talk to me about Alice Accountant. The job we have is very important to our firm, and we cannot afford to make a mistake. Are there any special problems we might face if we hire Alice?

Here's another approach:

> Ivan will need some special training for this job. Can you point out any areas to which we should give particular attention?

From the answer you receive, you may pick up some information about Ivan's weaknesses.

Dealing with Poor References

Suppose everything about Carlos seems fine, and in your judgment he's just right for the job. When you call his previous employer, however, you get a bad reference. What do you do?

If you have received good reports from Carlos's other references, it's likely that the poor reference was based on a personality conflict or some other factor unrelated to his work. Contact other people in the company who are familiar with his work and get their input.

Maybe Carlos's previous boss tells you that he was a sloppy worker. Check it out some more. The ex-boss may have been a perfectionist who isn't satisfied with anyone.

Perhaps you hear a diatribe about how awful Carlos was. However, you notice that he had held that job for eight years. If he had been that bad, how come he worked there for such a long time? Maybe his ex-boss resents his leaving and is taking revenge.

Knowing When to Check References

Check references after you believe that an applicant has a reasonable chance of being hired. If you have more than one finalist, check references for each one before making a final decision. A reference check may turn up information that suggests a need for additional inquiry. Arrange another interview to explore it.

Determining Whether an Applicant Can Do the Job

By the time to make a decision comes, all of those under consideration are basically qualified to do the job. Your responsibility is to select the best one.

Who's Best for Your Job?

Although all the surviving applicants meet the basic specs, they all offer different degrees of expertise in the key areas as well as additional qualifications. For example, Betty and Sue both have been operating room nurses. Betty's experience has been in a hospital in a small community. She hasn't worked with the sophisticated equipment that Sue, who worked in a large hospital, has. Your hospital doesn't have this equipment at this time, but is planning to install it. Your decision between Betty and Sue would depend on their total backgrounds. Sue's experience is an asset, but perhaps Betty is a better overall candidate with the potential to learn to use the new equipment when it is installed.

Do They Have Those Critical Intangibles?

Meeting the job specs is just part of the decision-making process. Equally important is having those intangible factors that make the difference between just doing a job and doing it well. Let's look at a few of these factors and how to evaluate it when interviewing the candidates:

◆ **Self-confidence.** When Jeremy was interviewed he exuded self-confidence. He wasn't afraid to talk about his failures and didn't brag about his accomplishments. Jeremy was matter-of-fact about his successes. He projected an image of being totally secure in his feelings about his capabilities. It is likely that Jeremy will manifest this self-confidence on the job, enabling him to adapt readily to the new situation.

◆ **Fluency of expression.** Laura was able to discuss her background easily and fluently. She didn't hesitate or grasp for words. When the interviewer probed for details, she was ready with statistics, examples, and specific applications. Not only does this indicate her expertise, but her ability to communicate.

◆ **Maturity.** Maturity cannot be measured by the chronological age of a person. Young people can be very mature and older people may still manifest child-like emotions. Mature applicants are not hostile or defensive. They do not interpret questions as barbs by a "prosecutor out to catch them." They don't show self-pity or have excuses for all of their past failures or inadequacies. They can discuss their weaknesses as readily as their strengths.

CAUTION

Stop! Look! Listen!

Some applicants can talk a good game, but can they perform? To determine if an applicant is a talker but not a doer, ask depth questions and probe for specific examples of his or her work. Glib phonies cannot come up with meaningful answers.

◆ **Intelligence.** Although some aspects of intelligence may be measured by tests, you can pick up a great deal about the type of intelligence a person has at an interview. If the job calls for rapid reaction to situations as they develop (such as a sales rep), a person who responds to questions rapidly and sensibly has the kind of intelligence needed for the job. However, if the person is applying for a job where it is important to ponder over a question before coming up with an answer (such as a research engineer), a slow, but well thought out response may be indicative of the type of intelligence required.

Choosing Among Several Top-Level Applicants

In a tight job market, you may have only one viable candidate. Your choice now is easy. Hire or don't hire. However, in most cases, you have several good people from which to make your final selection.

The Final Selection

To systematize making the decision, compare applicants by placing their backgrounds side by side. One way of doing this is to create a worksheet such as the following:

Final Selection Worksheet			
Job Specs			
	Education	Experience	Intangibles	Other (specify)
Applicant 1 Name:				
Applicant 2 Name:				
Applicant 3 Name:				
Applicant 4 Name:				

Intuition or Gut Feelings

Often candidates are very close in their qualifications for the job. You have to make a choice among relatively equally competent people. Now it is a matter of your judgment. Choosing a candidate purely on gut feeling without systematically analyzing each prospect's background in relation to the job specs is a mistake. When the decision is choosing the best among equals, you have to trust your gut feelings on which one to pick. As we said, hiring is both a science and an art. When you've exhausted the "science"—the systematic comparison of candidates, then the "art"—your gut feelings—takes over.

Avoiding Decision-Making Blunders

In making a hiring decision, avoid letting irrelevant or insignificant factors influence you. These factors include:

- **Overemphasizing appearance.** Although neatness and grooming are good indicators of personal work habits, good looks are too often overemphasized in employment. This bias has resulted in companies rejecting well-qualified men and women in favor or their more physically attractive competitors.

- **Giving preference to people like you.** You may subconsciously favor people who attended the same school you did, who come from similar ethnic backgrounds, or who travel in the same circles as you.

- **Succumbing to the "halo effect."** Because one quality of an applicant is outstanding, you overlook that person's faults or attribute unwarranted assets to him or her. Because Sheila's test score in computer know-how is the highest you've ever seen, for example, you're so impressed that you offer her a job. Only later do you learn that she doesn't qualify in several other key aspects of the job.

In making a final decision, carefully compare each candidate's background against the job specs and against each other. Look at the whole person (you might have to live with your choice for a long time).

Making the Offer

Once you've decided which candidate you want to hire, you are ready to make a job offer.

Review the Job Specs

Don't take anything for granted. During the entire process, the candidate has been enthusiastic about the job, has expressed sincere interest, and seems anxious to start work. Before making the offer, it's important to review the job and make sure that both you and the applicant are on the same track.

Stop! Look! Listen!

Don't make a job offer unless you are sure that you and the candidate know exactly what the job entails and that the applicant not only is qualified for it, but the job fits his or her career goals.

Go over the job description point by point. Although the candidate may have read it already, most job descriptions are not comprehensive and there are many facets not specified. Discuss each aspect of the job to ensure that it is what the applicant has understood.

What the Company Expects

In addition to the job duties expected of a staff member, most companies have policies and practices that should be made clear to an applicant before making a job offer. As noted previously, if the job requires travel, overtime work, work on weekends, or unusual working conditions, this should be made clear to the applicant. Indeed, this should have been brought up early in the process, so if there is a problem in complying, the applicant could withdraw before reaching this point.

"Sell" the Job

In today's competitive market, applicants often have to be sold on accepting job offers. Salary and the entire compensation package are important, and these will be discussed in the next section. Often, it isn't money that will make the difference between acceptance and rejection of a job offer by the person you really want. Learn about the applicant's goals, aspirations, special needs, and anything else that may affect his or her job satisfaction.

The Compensation Package

Most companies have a clearly defined compensation program. Before making an offer, check all the arrangements with your boss to avoid misunderstandings.

In negotiating salary, keep in mind what you pay currently employed people for doing similar work. Offering a new person considerably more than that amount can cause serious morale problems. There are exceptions to this rule, of course. Some applicants have capabilities that you believe would be of great value to your company, and to attract these people, you may have to pay considerably more than your current top rate. Some companies create special job categories to accommodate this situation. Others pay only what they must and hope that it won't lead to lower morale.

Salary alone isn't a total compensation package. It includes vacations, benefits, frequency of salary reviews, and incentive programs. All these items should be clearly explained.

> **Tactical Tools**
>
> Even when the salary you offer is less than an applicant wants, you may persuade that person to take your offer by pointing out how the job will enable him or her to use creativity, engage in work of special interest, and help reach career goals.

CAUTION

Stop! Look! Listen! _____

Don't let your anxiety over losing a desirable candidate tempt you to make an informal offer—promising a higher salary or other condition of employment that hasn't been approved—with the hope that you can persuade management to agree to it. Failure to get this agreement will not only cause the applicant to reject the offer but can also lead to legal action against your company.

Overcoming Obstacles

What do you do if at the time you make the offer, the applicant brings up new objections? Just as a salesperson must be prepared to overcome last minute reservations to buy a product, you must be ready to face and overcome these objections. Let's look at some common problems.

The Salary Is Too Low

Your first choice is Hillary. Early in the interview process, you explored her salary requirements, and your offer is in line. At least that's what you thought. Now Hillary demurs. "If I stay where I am, I'll get a raise in a few months that will bring me above that salary. You'll have to do better."

Having received approval of the hire at the salary offered, you have to either reject her, persuade her to take the job by selling her on other advantages, or go back to your boss for approval of the higher rate. What you do depends on many factors. Do you have other viable candidates for the job? If not, how urgent is it to fill the job?

Determine whether you can legitimately offer other benefits, such as a salary review in six months, opportunity for special training in an area in which she is particularly interested, or other perks. Think over the situation carefully, and discuss it with your manager. Caution: Don't make commitments you don't have the authority to honor.

If you and your boss agree that Hillary should still be considered for the position, determine how much above your original offer you're willing to pay and what else you can offer. With this in mind, you can negotiate with her and try to reach an acceptable arrangement. If this new negotiation doesn't lead to agreement, discontinue the discussion and seek another candidate. Continuing to haggle over terms of employment is not advisable.

I Need Flexible Hours

Some companies have an established policy on flextime. If the job for which the candidate is being considered falls into this policy, there's no problem. All that has to be worked out are the hours. However, if there is no policy, whether to grant this request depends on a variety of circumstances. If you give a new employee flexible hours, will the current staff also want their hours changed? There are some jobs in which flexible hours are more appropriate than in others. Is filling this job so difficult that it pays to bend the rules?

What Are My Opportunities for Advancement?

Of course, you can't promise automatic advancement in most jobs. Employees have to earn promotions. You should point out that the company conducts periodic performance reviews and that advancement is based on these reviews. If the company has a career-pathing program, take this opportunity to describe how it works.

I'm Considering Other Offers

It's not unusual for a good applicant to be looking at several possibilities. All through the interviewing process, you should be feeling the applicant out to determine what he or she is really seeking in the new job. Keep a record of this. Does he seek rapid advancement? Does she want special training? Has he commented on a particular type of job interest? Has she expressed concern about health benefits? Here is where you can use that information to persuade the candidate you want to accept your offer.

One way to counteract other offers is to ask the prospect to list all the advantages of joining the other company or staying on the present job. Then, you list all the advantages of joining your team. Be prepared to show how your job—which may even pay less or have fewer benefits than other offers—is still the best bet. Use all the information gleaned at the interviews about what the candidate desires, and show how your job will help the prospect meet the goals he or she has set for the future. If this prospect is the one you really feel will be the best for your team, it's well worthwhile to make this effort.

Countering the Counteroffer

You've knocked yourself out reading resumés, interviewing applicants, and comparing candidates. You make the decision that you'll hire Barbara, and she accepts your offer. A week later she calls to tell you that she has changed her mind: When she told her boss that she was leaving, her boss made a counteroffer.

Frustrating? You bet. To minimize the possibility of a counteroffer, assume that any currently employed candidate will get one. At the time you make your offer, bring it up and make these points:

 ◆ You know that she has done a great job in her present company. You also realize that when she notifies her company that she's planning to leave, it will undoubtedly make a counteroffer. Why? Because they need her now.

 ◆ If the company truly appreciated her work, it wouldn't have waited until she got another job offer to give her a raise. It would have given it to her long ago.

 ◆ Many people who have accepted counteroffers from a current employer find out that, after the pressure is off the company, it will train or hire someone else and let her go.

 ◆ From now on, she will always be looked on as a disloyal person who threatened to leave just to get more money.

 ◆ When the time for a raise comes around again, guess whose salary has already been "adjusted"?

When these arguments are used, the number of people who accept counteroffers decreases significantly.

In many companies, the final offer, including salary, is handled by the HR department. Usually the HR representative discusses directly with the applicant the starting salary, benefits, and other facets of employment. If you're responsible for making the offer in your company, however, it's a good idea to check all the arrangements with your boss and the HR department to avoid misunderstandings.

Arranging for Medical Exams

Many companies require applicants to take a medical exam before they can be put on the payroll. You cannot reject an applicant on the basis of a medical exam, however, unless you can show that the reason for the rejection is job-related. If a job calls for heavy lifting, for example, and the candidate has a heart condition that could be aggravated by that task, it's a legitimate reason for rejection. On the other hand, rejecting an applicant, not because of the work, but because it will increase your insurance premiums, isn't acceptable.

> **Now Hear This**
>
> The Americans with Disabilities Act (ADA) requires that a medical exam be given only after the decision to hire is made. The exam cannot be used as a reason for rejection unless a person's physical condition is a job-related issue and your company cannot make accommodations for it.

Most companies arrange for a medical exam close to a person's starting date. They tell applicants that they are hired subject to passing a physical exam. If this is your policy, caution applicants not to give notice to a current employer until after examination results have been received.

Congratulations—You Made an Offer!

Although most companies make job offers orally (no letter and no written agreement), an oral offer is just as binding as a written one. Some companies supplement an oral offer with a letter of confirmation so that there are no misunderstandings about the terms.

> **Stop! Look! Listen!**
>
> When you make a job offer, the salary should be stated by pay period—not on an annual basis. Rather than specify $30,000 per year, specify $1,250 per half-month. Why? Because some courts have ruled that if you quote a salary on an annual basis, you're guaranteeing the job for one year.

A job offer letter should contain these elements:

♦ Title of job (a copy of the job description should be attached)

♦ Starting date

♦ Salary, including an explanation of incentive programs

♦ Benefits (may be in the form of a brochure given to all new employees)

♦ Working hours, location of job, and other working conditions

♦ If pertinent, deadline for acceptance of offer

Employment Contracts—Yes or No?

In some situations, the employer and employee sign a formal contract. These contracts are often used with senior management people and key professional, sales, or technical personnel. Although it's rare, some organizations require all salaried employees to sign a contract—often little more than a formalized letter of agreement concerning conditions of employment. In many cases, they're designed for the benefit of the company, and the employee has little room for negotiation.

One of the most controversial areas covered in contracts is the so-called "restrictive covenant," which prohibits employees who leave the company from working for a competitor for a specified period of time. Although these types of contracts have been challenged, they're usually enforceable if they're limited in scope. Prohibiting a person from working for a competitor for a limited period of time, for example, is more likely to be upheld than prohibiting that type of employment forever.

Senior managers and other employees who hold critical positions in a company and applicants who have skills that are in great demand have the clout to negotiate personal contracts with the company. Any contract, whether it's generic or a negotiated special agreement, should be drawn up by a qualified attorney, not by HR or other managers.

Rejecting the Also-Rans

Some companies just assume that if applicants don't get an offer, they will realize that they were rejected. It's not only courteous but also good business practice to notify the men and women you have interviewed that the job has been filled.

You don't have to tell applicants why they didn't get the job. Explanations can lead to misunderstandings and even litigation. The most diplomatic approach is just to state that the background of another candidate was closer to your needs.

> **Tactical Tools**
>
> Don't notify unsuccessful applicants until shortly after your new employee starts work. If, for some reason, the chosen candidate changes his or her mind and doesn't start, you can go back to some of the others without having them feel that they were a second choice.

The Least You Need to Know

♦ All candidates should be interviewed by more than one manager and/or staff member.

♦ Tests can be a helpful screening tool, but use them as an aid, not as the chief source, for making your decision.

♦ Whenever possible, check the references of a prospective employee by speaking to the person to whom he or she reported, not to the HR department.

♦ When you compare candidates, consider the whole person, not just one aspect of his or her background.

♦ In making a job offer, make sure that the candidate fully understands the nature of the job, the salary and benefits, and other conditions of employment.

Part  Laying the Groundwork for Superior Performance

Hiring the right people is a good beginning, but now you have to get them started on the right foot—trained to do their work superbly and motivated to become enthusiastic performers. And once they're up to speed, you need to make sure that they stay with the company. This isn't an easy task! But we'll show you how to do it.

In the following chapters, you will learn how to make newcomers feel comfortable in the their new environment and acclimate them to the customs and culture of the company, department, and team.

You'll also get hands-on approaches to training and retraining staff members, selecting and utilizing mentors, and establishing a collaborative and cooperative workforce.

Chapter 15

Getting Started on the Right Foot

In This Chapter

- ◆ Acclimating the new employee to the organization
- ◆ Training for skill development
- ◆ Selecting the right person to do the training
- ◆ Techniques and tools you can use

You've done everything right in attracting, screening, and finally hiring someone for the open job. A starting date has been set, and at last, the new employee reports to work. What you do those first few days may determine whether that person becomes a loyal, dedicated, enthusiastic staff member or a half-hearted worker already on the way to disillusionment and potential problems.

Let's look at this from the viewpoint of the new employee. Starting a new job is both exciting and scary. The new person doesn't know just what to expect. During the period of interviews and preemployment discussions, impressions and expectations were developed, and now comes the reality check: Does the job live up to what was expected?

When the company hired Ken, he was told the job would involve creative approaches to the work, but from day one, he was told not to deviate from what the manual specified. When Dorothy was interviewed, she was given the impression that the company believed strongly in employee participation. When she was hired, she found that her boss usually ignored suggestions from employees.

Sometimes the reason for this may be poor leadership by the immediate supervisors. However, often the problems could have been alleviated if the new workers were properly oriented so that they fully understood the company's policies, the true nature of their jobs, and what they might expect over time.

The First Critical Days

Most companies have some type of orientation program for new employees. The human resources department usually conducts the program on the first day the new employees report to work, before they are sent to the department they will work in. They may be shown videos, be given a tour of the facilities, receive literature, or attend a lecture. They learn the history of the organization, further details about their benefits, and the company's rules and regulations. This is a good start, but it's not enough.

Now Hear This

Recent studies have shown that one of the key reasons a whopping 55 percent of newly hired employees fail or voluntarily leave their new organizations within the first two years is due to a failure to properly introduce and assimilate them into the new culture.

The team leader or supervisor must augment this with an orientation to the team or department. This should include a detailed discussion of the nature of the specific job the new worker will be performing and an understanding of what the supervisor plans to do to train the employee and help him or her to become productive.

On-Boarding

Words to Work By

On-boarding is a systematized approach to orienting a new employee to the company, the department or team, and the job.

A relatively new approach companies are using is known as *on-boarding*. This process supplements and makes more effective the traditional orientation program. Originally designed to bring newly hired executives into the mainstream rapidly and thoroughly, it is now being extended to technical, professional, and administrative personnel, and in some companies, to all new hires.

Let's look at how a successful on-boarding process works.

The Development of a Plan

The single most important aspect of successful on-boarding is the development of a comprehensive plan to shepherd the new employee through the first several months. Unfortunately, most organizations are not very good in doing this, and few that have a plan rarely take the time to describe it in writing.

The best plans contain the following elements:

1. A Very Clear Sense of What They're Trying to Accomplish

All of the best plans and on-boarding strategies contain a *statement of purpose*. Obviously, this is very important in helping bring focus to the on-boarding effort, and as insurance against some future misunderstanding. In many cases, the purpose statement is no more than a sentence or two, but the effect is always the same: *To make clear the reason a successful on-boarding effort is important to both the company and to the new employee.* Rather than using a boilerplate plan for all new employees, the most effective on-boarding plans are tailored to the special needs of the new employee and the organization.

2. An Honest, Objective Assessment of the Current Environment

A careful assessment of the current environment is a particularly important element of a good on-boarding plan. Every company culture has positive and negative qualities, and every new employee is likely to experience both. The best, most successful on-boarding plans carefully evaluate both the forces that tend to work in favor of a new employee to increase the likelihood of a successful introduction, and those that work against it. Being sure which is which, and to what extent, can have as much to do with success and failure as anything else.

During the on-boarding process, the new employee should be given a full and honest assessment of the situation that he or she will face. For example, Jason expected to take over an ongoing collections program that "needed a little sharpening up." When he started the job, he found that the system was in shambles and collections were well behind schedule. Had he been given the true picture, he would have been far better prepared for the work he had to do.

3. Key Critical Objectives

One of the biggest contributors to failed on-boarding attempts is taking on too much too soon. It's not at all unusual for new employees to feel as though they're "in the spotlight" for some period of time. People are watching. They're forming impressions—and making judgments. It's important that the first few months of a new employee's tenure be orchestrated, at least to some appropriate extent. One of the best strategies in this regard is identifying and clarifying the three or four (seldom more) key objectives that are critical to the success of the new employee in those first months of the job.

4. Short-Term, Intermediate, and Long-Term Goals with Timetables

In addition to identifying key critical objectives, good on-boarding plans also specify a series of key goals, and the dates by which they should be achieved.

5. Mentor

One very important step in successfully on-boarding a new employee is the selecting of a mentor. Obviously, it's important that this person be intimately familiar with the internal workings on the firm, including the key political players and the leaders of the informal organization.

> **Tactical Tools**
>
> The most successful on-boardings have always included a mentor with some level of prestige within the organization, and this is particularly important when assimilating someone in the more senior ranks of the organization.

Mentors provide important advice for new employees on a range of topics. Their overall mission is to "pave the way" for the new person, make sure they're introduced to the right people, and run interference should the going get tough. Later in this chapter, we will discuss the use of mentors in more detail.

Some Additional Successful On-Boarding Practices

When a person starts a new job, he or she is naturally ill at ease. They don't know their new colleagues, they are unfamiliar with the company culture, and they are anxious to make a good start. As a manager, you want that person to begin producing rapidly and become successful. Here are some suggestions for easing this transition:

- **Arrange for some early successes.** One of the biggest problems new employees face in assimilating to the culture of a new company is a lack of initial focus. One way organizations have found that helps a new hire get off on the right foot is to enable them to achieve some significant successes during the first couple of weeks on the job.

  Let's see how this worked with one company. As part of the on-boarding process for Ben, an assistant marketing manager, he was given an assignment to study

the possibility of using e-marketing outlets for the company's products. As Ben
had worked with e-markets in his previous
job, he had a good deal of knowledge in
this area. By enabling him to use his
expertise immediately, the company gave
him the opportunity to demonstrate his

> **Tactical Tools**
>
> Give the new employee a
> chance to show early successes
> by assigning projects in which
> they can utilize their expertise.

value to the organization early on. This not only was a benefit to the company,
but also made Ben feel like part of a winning team from the beginning. It also
enabled his colleagues and teammates to observe their new team member at his
very best—ensuring his acceptance by the group.

◆ **Develop a job description, with clear performance standards.** Few things
are more helpful to a new employee—and contribute more to a successful
assimilation—than the development of a well-conceived job description, which
focuses on the results expected and how they will be measured.

◆ **Give new employees at all levels ample time to learn, study, and plan
before assuming any major responsibilities.** Successful companies often give
new employees, particularly in the management and technical areas, up to three
months (and even more in some instances) to settle into their jobs and "learn the
ropes" before they assume major responsibilities.

◆ **Overcome resentment of "bypassed" employees.** When outsiders are hired
for higher-level jobs, it's not uncommon for it to lead to jealousy or resentment
of the new hire by a current employee or group of employees. They may feel
they were unfairly "overlooked" for the job. In some cases, it may lead to flagrant attempts to undermine the new person through whispering campaigns,
unjustified criticisms, rumor-mongering, and subtle refusals to cooperate, and a
general lowering of morale in the
department and perhaps the company
itself.

Companies must prepare to cope with
these and other major internal obstacles to
success, and to swiftly minimize their
impact.

◆ **Provide unwavering support.** There
seems to be little question that the single
most valuable contribution company executives can make to the assimilation of a
new hire is the offering of unwavering

> **CAUTION**
>
> **Stop! Look! Listen!**
>
> Don't expect immediate
> results from new people. No mat-
> ter how experienced they may
> be, they need time to adapt your
> company's culture and style of
> work. Providing the new em-
> ployee with full support, training,
> and encouragement over the first
> few months will maximize the
> chances of developing a produc-
> tive and loyal staff member.

support. Too many organizations badly underestimate the importance of this, and as a result, begin encouraging, however unintentionally, subtle challenges to their decisions.

The Training Process

In most organizations, training is done on the job by supervisors and team leaders—not professional trainers. Training is not an innate talent, but it can be learned. In the following section, I'll tell you about several successful techniques that you can use.

The Four Cs of Skill Training

Training cannot be a haphazard process. It must be planned and systemized. Over the years I have worked with and refined an effective and simple program to train people to perform tasks. It consists of four steps: conditioning, communication, conduct, and conclusion.

Conditioning

To condition the trainee to learn and to accept what is being taught, you should tell a trainee, before the training begins, what will be taught, why it's performed, and how it fits into the overall picture. When people can see the entire picture, not just their small part in it, they learn faster and understand more clearly, and they're more likely to remember what they've been taught.

Communication

You can't say to a trainee, "Just watch me, and do what I do." It's not that simple. Work is much too complex to learn just by observation. The following four steps can guide you in showing someone how to perform a task:

1. Describe what you're going to do.

2. Demonstrate step-by-step. As you demonstrate, explain each step and explain why it's done (for example, "Notice that I entered the order number on the top right side of the form to make it easy to locate.").

3. Have the trainee perform the task and explain to you the method and reason for each step.

4. If the trainee doesn't perform to your satisfaction, have him or her repeat the task. If he or she performs well, reinforce the behavior with praise or positive comments. All employees are "on probation" officially or unofficially for the first few months on any job. Make every effort to help that person succeed, but if he or she just can't do the job, it's best to transfer them to a job for which they are better qualified or just let them go.

Conduct the Work

After you're satisfied that a trainee can do a job, leave him or her alone, and let them do it. The trainee needs an opportunity to try out what he or she has learned. They will probably make some mistakes, but that's to be expected. From time to time, check out how things are going and make necessary corrections.

Conclusion

The final step is important because people tend to change what they have been taught. Careless people may skip some steps in a procedure, causing errors or complications. Smart people may make changes that they believe are better than what they were taught. Although you should encourage your associates to try to find more effective approaches to their job, caution them not to make any changes until they have discussed them with you. They often may not be aware of the ramifications of their suggested changes.

Schedule concluding discussions of new assignments three to four weeks after the conduct step. At that time, review what the associate has been doing, and, if changes have been made intentionally or inadvertently, bring the person back on track.

Who Should Do the Training?

Usually the supervisor does the training, but this isn't always the case. Some organizations encourage an entire team to participate in the task of training new members; others assign one person to act as a mentor.

Whether you are team based or not, it may be advisable to assign somebody other than the supervisor to do or assist in the training. Determining who will train new members or be assigned to retrain others depends on what people are being trained to do. *Caution:* A person who knows the job best isn't always the most qualified person to train others. It takes more than job knowledge to be an effective trainer.

Job know-how *is* essential for the person who will do the training, but it's only part of the picture. Look for these additional factors:

- **Personal characteristics:** Patience, empathy, and flexibility are good qualities to look for.

- **Knowledge of training techniques:** If a team member has the right personal characteristics, he can learn the training techniques. Some companies provide "Train the Trainer" programs to build up the communications skills of people who will do training.

- **A strong, positive attitude toward the job and the company:** If you assign a disgruntled person to do your training, that person might infect the trainee with the virus of discontent.

Training Tools and Techniques

Today's leaders have available to them a variety of aids and techniques to facilitate their training efforts. Some have been around for years; others were developed more recently.

Training Manuals That Really Train

Training manuals, or "do it by the numbers" handbooks, are helpful for teaching routine tasks. They make the training process easy for both the trainer and the trainees; you can always refer to them when you're in doubt about what to do.

Unfortunately, training manuals can be poorly written and confusing; some are laced with technical terminology intelligible only to the engineers who wrote them.

Because jobs today are becoming less and less routine, training manuals are often inadequate—to the point that they even stifle creativity. Don't rely on a book because it's easy; rather, think out new and possibly better approaches to training.

Interactive Computer Training

Many companies have developed a variety of interactive computer programs to train employees. Such programs were initially designed for use in schools to enable students to learn at their own pace. Slower learners could take their time and repeat sections until they understood them. Fast learners or students who had more background could move ahead quickly, and students could test themselves as they progressed.

Because most companies have their own ways of doing things, generic programs, such as the ones used by schools, haven't been of much value. However, there are generic programs, such as those that teach basic accounting skills and various computer operations, which can be an asset to any organization. Check software catalogs to determine which programs might be valuable to you.

Some larger organizations have customized programs to suit their own needs. These programs are usually not available outside the companies that developed them. Perhaps you can customize programs to meet your own requirements.

Walk into any computer store and you'll find a variety of standard courses on CD-ROM. You'll find courses in all types of computer functions, typing, general office skills, accounting, marketing, business planning, and general management. These can be used at the workplace or given to employees to use at home.

The Internet—the School of the Future

Computers have moved training from the classroom to the desk, the kitchen table, and even the lap of each individual.

Universities and private organizations offer courses and individual study programs on hundreds of subjects. You can study a foreign language, learn basic or advanced math, acquire technical know-how, and even obtain a college degree. The Internet makes it possible for students to engage in classroom interaction, even when they're participating from home.

Teleconferencing

Sometimes the most effective way to train or retrain staff members is to hold classes that bring together employees from several locations. This is a common practice among national and global organizations. It's also one of the most expensive ways to train. Not only do the participants take time off from their regular work, but they also spend additional time getting to and from the training site. Travel, hotel, meals, and often the cost of renting the training facility (for example, a conference center) add to the expense.

One way to reduce the cost and time involved is teleconferencing. Using specially designed computer and TV equipment, participants can see, hear, and interact with the instructor and each other without going far from their base. Larger organizations may have teleconferencing technology available on-site. Smaller companies can use the services of teleconferencing firms that can set up such conferences wherever needed.

At the University of Notre Dame, for example, executive MBA courses are held simultaneously via satellite at three corporate facilities: Ameritech, Carrier Corporation, and Owens-Illinois.

Case Studies

A *case study* is a description of a real or simulated business situation presented to trainees for analysis, discussion, and solution.

Case studies are used in graduate schools, seminars, and corporate training programs to enable trainees to work on the types of problems they're most likely to encounter on the job. The studies are often drawn from the experiences of real companies. The experience of working out these types of problems in a classroom instead of learning by trial and error on the job pays off in fewer trials and less costly errors.

> **Tactical Tools**
>
> To make case solving most effective, design cases that are related to the job. Make them complex and challenging, and make their solutions necessitate collaboration and teamwork.

A significant advantage of using case studies in management development is that trainees work on the case collaboratively. They learn how to organize and use teams to solve cases.

Role-Playing

In today's companies, most jobs require interaction with other people. Perhaps the best way to train people for this type of interaction is through role-playing.

As in case studies, role-playing should be based on realistic situations a trainee may face on the job: dealing with a customer, resolving a dispute among team members, or conducting a performance review. Role-playing should be fun, but if it's only fun and not a learning experience, you're wasting your time.

Effective role-playing must be carefully structured. Participants should be briefed on the goals of the exercise, and each participant should be given a specific part to play. Don't give people scripts—improvisation makes the exercise more spontaneous and allows for flexibility. Just make sure you establish limits, so participants don't stray from the goal of the exercise.

To get everyone—not just the players—involved, give each role to a group of people. Have the group study and discuss how the role should be played. Appoint one member of the group to play the role and have the other group members step in to supplement the primary player. For example, if the person playing the role of a personnel interviewer fails to ask a key question, one of the members of that group can intervene and ask the question.

After the role-playing is completed, have all the group critique what has transpired and discuss what they've learned from the experience.

Using Video

Videotapes, like training manuals, are most appropriate for training people to do routine jobs. For example, you can purchase videos for training people in basic computer skills, accounting, and other general subjects. For situations in which flexibility and initiative are necessary, tapes can impede creativity. In such cases, customizing videotapes to meet your own needs is a more effective option. This list describes some ways to use customized video to enhance the effectiveness of your training programs:

- ◆ **Tape demonstrations:** For work of a physical nature (most factory or maintenance jobs and some clerical jobs), a good demonstration is an important part of the training. You can tape yourself or one of the best workers performing the job. Show the tape in real time to demonstrate the pace at which a job should be carried out. Use slow motion to better explain each step of the task. Once you have a good demonstration on tape, you can show it to any of your trainees at any time.

- ◆ **Tape job performance:** One of the best ways to help people recognize exactly what they're doing on the job is to videotape them at work. Rather than trying to verbally describe a person's strengths and weaknesses, let her review the tape and see for herself.

- ◆ **Tape team meetings:** Here's an example of how taping a team or group meeting can lead to improvement. When Diane studied the tapes of meetings she had participated in, she noticed that she tended to dominate group discussions. She pushed her ideas across, shut off opposing arguments, and was sometimes rude to other participants. She told her team leader that although she knew she was an assertive person, until she saw the tape she didn't realize the way she came across to others and agreed to attend a human relations training course.

- **Tape role-playing:** Role-playing is an excellent way to develop interpersonal relations. By videotaping role-playing and reviewing the tapes, role-playing becomes an even more effective training tool.

- **Tape presentations:** If you're required to make presentations at internal meetings or outside functions, there's no better way to improve your oratory skills than to study videos of your practice deliveries.

Using Audio

One of the best ways to train people whose jobs require lots of telephone use—telemarketers, customer service representatives, order clerks, credit checkers—is to record telephone conversations.

You can purchase a component that connects the telephone to a voice-activated tape recorder. Some voice mail and answering machines have this capability built in.

Tape several conversations, and then review them with the trainee. Listen to what is said and how it's said. Pay close attention to the way the trainee reacts to what the other party says—and how that person reacts to him or her.

Stop! Look! Listen!

In some states, taping telephone conversations is illegal without the consent of the party being recorded. Check your state laws.

Cross-Training

When teams are the operating units in an organization, it's helpful for everyone on a team to be able to perform the work of any other member. The whining comment "It's not my job" is no longer valid.

If your team consists of people from various disciplines, you cannot always expect them to be able to do work in other areas: A multidepartmental team consisting of people from marketing, engineering, and finance doesn't easily lend itself to cross-training.

Most teams, however, are made up of people who do similar work. One sales support team consists of order clerks, customer service representatives, and computer operators. All are trained in every aspect of the team's work and can move from job to job as necessary.

Although that team's order clerks spend most of their time processing orders and the customer service reps are almost always on the phone, if the pressure is on processing orders, customer service reps can work on order processing between calls. If a customer service rep is out of the office, any team member can fill in at a moment's notice.

Preparing for Advancement

Training isn't limited to teaching job skills. Training team members to become team leaders or rank-and-file employees to become supervisors is an important aspect of organizational development.

The Cadet Corps

For many years, training for management positions was limited to people who were on a special management track. They usually were hired as management trainees after graduating from college and went through a series of management training programs within an organization, often supplemented by seminars, courses, and residencies at universities or special training schools.

One of the most commonly used cadet programs was job rotation. After basic orientation, trainees were assigned to work for a short period in each of several departments. The objective was to give them an overview of the company so that when they moved into regular positions, they would have a good concept of the entire operation.

Makes sense? Sometimes. In many companies, the time spent in each training assignment was not long enough to give the trainees any more than a superficial knowledge. They never really got their feet wet. They wasted the time of the department heads, which had to divert their energies from working with their own teams. The regular team members, knowing that the trainees would be gone shortly, often resented their intrusion. Resentment was compounded by people's feelings that these cadets were of a privileged class and would someday be their bosses without having worked their way up.

Everybody Is a Potential Manager

In recent years, the special management track has been supplanted by employee development, in which training for management is open to any employee. And why not? Even the military has learned that graduation from

Words to Work By

A **mentor** is a team member assigned to act as counselor, trainer, and "big brother" or "big sister" to a new member.

military academies isn't essential to be a top leader. Companies have recognized that latent leadership talent exists in most people and can be developed in them.

Mentor, Mentor—Where Is My Mentor?

Earlier in this chapter, mentors were mentioned as a key factor in on-boarding. However, the role of the mentor is much broader. It's a well-known fact that when a high-ranking manager takes a younger employee under his or her wing—becomes that person's mentor—the protégé not only has a head start for advancement, but will acquire more know-how about the work, the workings of the company, and the "tricks of the trade" than others.

Why shouldn't everybody have a mentor? Why leave it to chance that some senior managers choose a protégé while others don't? Why not make mentoring a job requirement—not only for senior executives, but for all experienced staff members? By structuring a mentoring program and assigning the best people on your team the responsibility of mentoring a new member, you take a giant step forward in encouraging productivity and growth in the newcomer.

A structured mentoring program requires that chosen mentors be willing to take on the job. Compelling someone to be a mentor is self-defeating. Not everybody is interested in or qualified for this assignment. New mentors should be trained in the art of mentoring by experienced people.

Now Hear This

Both the mentor and the mentored benefit from the process of mentoring. Those who are mentored learn the new skills while mentors sharpen their skills in order to pass them on. It heightens the mentor's sense of responsibility as he or she guides his or her protégé through the maze of company policies and politics. It also makes the

Ten Tips for New Mentors

If you're a first-time mentor, you're probably unsure of how to deal with this new responsibility. If you have had your own successful experience with a mentor, use that as a guide. If not, seek out a member of your organization who has a reputation as a great mentor and ask for advice, counsel, and guidance. Ask him or her to be your mentor in mentoring.

In any case, here are 10 tips to start you on the right track:

1. Know your work. Review the basics. Think back on the problems you've faced and how you dealt with them. Be prepared to answer questions about every aspect of the job.

2. Know your company. One of the main functions of a mentor is to help the trainee overcome the hurdles of unfamiliar company policies and practices. More important, as a person who's been around the organization for some time, you know the inner workings of the organization—the true power structure—the company politics.

3. Get to know your protégé. To be an effective mentor, take the time to learn as much as you can about the person you are mentoring. Learn about his or her education, previous work experience, current job, and more. Learn his or her goals, ambitions, and outside interests. Observe personality traits. Get accustomed to his or her ways of communicating in writing, verbally, and, most important, nonverbally.

4. Learn to teach. If you have minimal experience in teaching, pick up pointers on teaching methods from the best trainers you know. Read articles and books on training techniques.

5. Learn to learn. It is essential that you keep learning—not only the latest techniques in your own field, but developments in your industry, in the business community, and in the overall field of management.

6. Be patient. The person you are mentoring may not pick up what you teach as rapidly as you would like. Patience is key for successful mentoring.

7. Be tactful. You are not a drill sergeant training a rookie in how to survive in combat. Be kind. Be courteous. Be gentle—but be firm and let the trainee know you expect the best.

8. Don't be afraid to take risks. Give your protégé assignments that will challenge his or her capabilities. Let the person know that he or she won't succeed in all the assignments, but that the best way to grow is to take on tough jobs. We learn through failure, after all.

9. Celebrate successes. Let the trainee know you are proud of the accomplishments and progress he or she makes.

10. Encourage the person you are mentoring to become a mentor.

Laying the Foundation for Self-Training

It wasn't long ago that when you were trained for a job, you were considered fully trained after you mastered the skills and functions of the job. This training was augmented by occasional technology updates. Now, just a few years later, many formerly routine and highly structured jobs are dynamic and flexible.

Look at the position of "secretary." It used to connote a woman taking dictation, making appointments for her boss, answering the phone, filing papers, and acting as a gofer. Today that secretary is more of an executive assistant. She or he may prepare the agenda for a meeting, supervise clerks, compile information and write reports, and make important business decisions. It's a considerably different job. Traditional secretarial training isn't adequate preparation for this type of work.

> **Words to Work By**
>
> **Training** people is often a one-way process. The teacher presents information; the student absorbs it (you hope). When training is replaced by **learning,** the emphasis shifts to developing the trainee's ability to identify and solve problems, seek knowledge, and take the initiative to continue self-development.

Training must be replaced by *learning.* The difference between training and learning is that training is a one-way transfer of information from trainer to trainee. Learning involves not only absorbing information but also knowing how to identify potential problems, seeking the knowledge and information that are necessary to solve problems, and creating new concepts. This process is the focus of modern training and development.

The Least You Need to Know

- Start the new employee using a well-designed on-boarding program.

- Use the Four Cs (Condition, Communicate, Conduct, Conclude) to train skills.

- Incorporate into your training program techniques such as case studies, role-playing, interactive computer programs, and audio- or videotaping to make the training experience more exciting, more meaningful, and more productive.

- Encourage experienced team members to become mentors for new employees, and experienced managers to mentor potential team leaders.

- Redesign your training programs to meet today's challenges. Emphasize problem solving and creative thinking and help participants become self-learners.

Chapter 16

Developing an Excited and Enthusiastic Staff

In This Chapter

- ◆ Getting to know your associates
- ◆ Recognizing your staff as a motivational force
- ◆ Making the transition from boss to leader
- ◆ Learning how to lead when you don't work in teams
- ◆ Building motivation into the job

Once your new employee is oriented and trained, your next job is to meld the new person and the incumbents into a cooperative, cohesive group or team. Your goal is to develop that inner motivation that will propel them toward accomplishing the department's goals. Whether your company works on a team basis or uses the traditional supervisor/subordinate format, managers should consider their employees as a team.

Successful managers start the process of developing team spirit by taking the time to get to know each of their employees as individuals. Team members are humans, not robots, each with his or her strengths and weaknesses, personal agenda, and style of working. Learning and understanding each person's individualities are the first steps in building a motivated group of people.

Different Strokes for Different Folks

Maybe you think that all you really have to know about your associates is the quality of their work. Wrong! Knowing the people with whom you work requires more than just knowing their job skills. Sure, that's an important part, but it's *only* a part of their total make-up. Learn what's important to each person—his or her ambitions and goals, families, special concerns—in other words, what makes each of them tick.

Learn Each Person's M.O.

If you've ever watched crime shows or read detective stories, you know the term *M.O.* (*modus operandi,* or method of operation). Detectives can often tell who has committed a crime by his or her M.O., or the manner in which it was committed, because criminals tend to use the same M.O.s in all of their crimes.

M.O.s aren't limited to criminals. We all have M.O.s in the way we do our work and the way we live our lives. Study the way each of your people operates, and you'll discover his or her M.O. For example, you might notice that one person always ponders a subject before commenting on it; another rereads everything she's worked on several times before turning it in.

> **Words to Work By**
>
> A person's **M.O.** is his or her method, or mode, of operation (the patterns of behavior that a person habitually follows in performing work).

Psychologists don't call them M.O.s; they call them "patterns of behavior." No matter what you call M.O.s, being aware of them helps you understand people and enables you to work with them more effectively.

Getting to Know Your Associates

The best way to get to know people is to speak to them, ask questions, and get their opinions on various matters. Maybe you think that this is too intrusive. You don't want to be nosy. Okay, you don't have to *ask* personal questions directly. By observing and listening, you can learn a great deal about your colleagues.

Listen when they speak to you: Listen to what they say, and listen to what they *don't* say. Listen when they speak to others. Eavesdropping may not be polite, but you can learn a great deal. Observe how your team members do their work and how they act and react. It doesn't take long to identify their likes and dislikes, their quirks and eccentricities. By listening, you can learn about the things that are important to each of them and the "hot buttons" that turn them on or off.

By observing and listening, you might realize that Claudia is a creative person. If you want to excite her about her role in an assignment, you can do so by appealing to her creativity. You notice that Mike is slow when he's learning new things but that, after he learns them, he works quickly and accurately. To allow Mike to do his best, you know that you'll need patience.

It's easy to remember these individual characteristics when you supervise a small number of people, but if you're involved with larger groups or have high turnover in your department, set up a notebook with a page for each staff member. For each person, list spouse's name, children's names and ages, hobbies and interests, and any behavioral traits or facets of their personality to help you "reach" them.

> **Tactical Tools**
>
> Encourage your associates to express their ideas, especially when they differ from yours. Their disagreements not only provide you with new ideas but also give you insight into the ways in which they approach problems that will help you to work more effectively with them.

Making Your Team Self-Motivating

If your organization is changing from the traditional supervisor/subordinate mode to the team mode, it's essential that your employees understand their new roles and that they begin to apply the team system on the job.

Let's look at how Denise did this. As sales manager, her primary role had been to train, motivate, and lead her sales force. Denise discovered that, as in most companies, without the support of the office staff to obtain and maintain sales production, sales were lost and customers became dissatisfied.

The salespeople in Denise's company were paid on a commission basis. They worked long and hard to acquire and keep accounts. They were often frustrated, however, when the order department stalled deliveries or when indifferent customer service representatives antagonized customers.

She organized regional teams made up of salespeople, order clerks, and customer service

> **Tactical Tools**
>
> One thing in a person's make-up that really gets him or her excited—positively or negatively—is a hot button. Find a person's hot button, and you can really get through to him or her.

personnel and trained them to work together and understand each person's role. The compensation system was changed so that rather than a salesperson alone being rewarded for making a sale, bonuses and raises for all team members were based on the team's productivity. Denise developed self-confident, enthusiastic teams that worked together to assure customer satisfaction. This resulted in increased sales and high morale in the department.

Making the Transition from Boss to Team Leader

Many traditional supervisors find it difficult to make the transition to team leader. "If I'm going to be held accountable when anything goes wrong, how can I give up control?"

Yes, it's still the team leader's job to ensure that the goals of the team are met, but you can still accomplish this task in a team environment. The key to team control is self-control.

You, the team leader, must keep every member of your team aware of what is expected from him individually and from the team as a whole. Team members should be kept alert at all times on how the team is doing. In this way, they monitor their own activities.

Overcoming Hurdles

So all you have to do is convert from traditional methods to team concepts and all your troubles are over, right? Of course not. Teams aren't a cure-all for management problems. They have their share of troubles.

One common problem occurs when team members don't carry their weight and other members have to work harder to maintain their team's productivity. Team members can often overcome this situation themselves, by working with the weaker person to help him develop the necessary skills. If the reason for poor performance isn't a lack of skill but is instead a lack of motivation, the others may encourage—or in some cases, shame—the slacker into better production. Peer pressure is a powerful tool. If all else fails, the person will have to be removed from the team.

Teams in the workplace have many advantages, but they're not a panacea. People who learn to work together in teams produce more, enjoy their work more, and are less likely to quit for superficial

> **Tactical Tools**
>
> To turn a team into a self-motivated unit, create "team spirit" among members by getting everyone on your team involved in every aspect of a job. Team members will then work together to meet goals.

reasons. Teams create a motivational environment and help build the *esprit de corps* that is important to success.

When Your Company Doesn't Use Teams

Your company may not be organized in teams. No matter what the organizational structure, you can use any and all of the techniques in this chapter and in this book to improve your effectiveness as a manager. Just learn the suggested techniques and begin applying them today!

After José returned from an intensive management development weekend at the university, he bubbled with enthusiasm about all the ideas he had learned. He wanted to take immediate action in restructuring his department into teams.

"Whoa," José's boss said. "Take it easy. We're not making any radical changes now." Rather than give up in frustration, José asked himself, "What can I do within the current structure to adapt what I've learned?"

Within the first few weeks, José made the following changes in his management style:

♦ He became more available to the people who reported to him. Rather than brush off their questions and suggestions, he took time to listen, evaluate, and respond to them.

♦ He overcame the temptation to make every decision. When asked for a decision, he threw the decision back to the person requesting it. "What do *you* think should be done?"

♦ Rather than plan the work himself when new assignments were received, he enlisted the participation of his entire team.

♦ He encouraged associates to acquire skills outside their usual work duties. He used cross training and assigned them work that required interaction with others in the group with different types of work.

♦ He conferred with all staff members to ensure that they understood what was expected of them on the job and how their performance would be evaluated. Most important, he learned more about their individual goals and aspirations.

♦ He periodically held exciting and productive department meetings.

♦ He visited suppliers and subcontractors and invited them to visit the company and attend meetings.

Now Hear This

Good management consists of inspiring average people to do the work of superior people.
—John D. Rockefeller

The payoff didn't take long. Within a few months, productivity increased, quality improved, and cooperation and collaboration among the group members became a way of life. All this—without changing the structure.

Building Motivation into the Job

Extensive studies over the years by behavioral scientists have shown that motivational programs that really work include recognition, control over one's own work, and obtaining satisfaction from the job. Let's explore how this can be accomplished.

Make the Job "Worker Friendly"

If you enjoy your work, if the job gives you job satisfaction, if you can't wait to go to work every morning and hate to leave each evening, there's no need for any other type of motivation. Are there such jobs? Although many new jobs being created in growth industries have the ingredients that lead to enjoyment and satisfaction, a large number of people have jobs that are routine, dull, and sometimes tedious. It's difficult, if not impossible, to generate excitement about these jobs.

One way to make dull jobs more "worker friendly" is to redesign them. Rather than look at a job as a series of tasks that must be performed, study it as a total process. Make the job less routine by enlarging the scope of the job. Focus on what has to be accomplished rather than on the steps leading to its accomplishment by redesigning the manner in which the job is performed.

Enriching the Job

Here's an example of how *job enrichment* works. When Jennifer was hired to head the claims-processing department at Liability Insurance Company, she inherited a department with low morale, high turnover, and disgruntled employees. The claims-processing operation was an assembly line. Each clerk checked a section of the form and sent it to other clerks, each of whom checked another section. If errors were found, the form was sent to a specialist for handling. Efficient? Maybe, but it made the work dull and not very challenging.

Jennifer reorganized the process. She eliminated the assembly line and retrained each clerk to check the entire form, correct any errors, and personally deal with problems. Although operations slowed down during the break-in period, it paid off in a highly

Words to Work By

Job enrichment means redesigning a job to provide diversity, challenge, and commitment and in some cases, to alleviate boredom.

motivated team of workers who found gratification in working through the entire process and seeing it completed satisfactorily.

When associates are trained to perform all aspects of the jobs their group handles, it gives managers the flexibility to assign any part of the work to any staff member and, because associates do different work at different times, breaks the boredom of routine.

Stop! Look! Listen!

Don't assume that just because an employee is an "expert" in one phase of the work that he or she is not trainable in other aspects. Make an effort to expand the capabilities of each member of your group.

Involving Everyone in Planning

There are many types of work for which production quotas are established. Word-processing operators are given the number of letters they must complete each day; production workers are given hourly quotas; salespeople must meet monthly standards. Management usually sets these quotas. Most workers don't like having quotas imposed on them. Worse, if management wants to raise quotas, employees are resentful and resistant.

A solution is to have your staff participate in setting quotas for their own jobs. You might think that they'll set low quotas that are easy to meet, and this may happen. That's why the process is *participatory*. As a manager, you don't step out of the picture completely, but are one of the participants. Your role is to ensure that realistic goals are set. In most cases, however, people do set reasonable quotas, and because it's their goal, they accept it and work to achieve it.

Another example of participation in planning is the experience of Ford Motor Company, in its development of the Taurus. Ford didn't follow the usual industry practice of having a group of specialists design the car. Workers representing every type of job that would be involved in building the car were brought in to work with designers during the planning stage. The suggestions culled from workers' experience on the production line brought forth ideas that might never have occurred to the specialists. When the Taurus was brought to the factory floor, workers looked on it as their car. The result: The Taurus became the most trouble-free and profitable car Ford has introduced in recent years.

Now Hear This

No one likes to feel that he or she is being sold something or told to do something. We much prefer to feel we are buying of our own accord or acting on our own ideas. We like to be consulted about our wishes, our wants, our thoughts.

—Dale Carnegie

Twenty-One Motivators That Really Work Well

Here are some of the best techniques for motivating people to commit themselves to superior performance:

Encourage participation in setting goals and determining how to reach them.

Keep all employees aware of how their job relates to others.

Provide all employees with the tools and training necessary to succeed.

Pay at least the going rate for jobs that are performed.

Provide good, safe working conditions.

Give clear directions that are easily understood and accepted.

Know each person's abilities and give assignments based on the ability to handle those assignments.

Allow people to make decisions related to their jobs.

Be accessible. Listen actively and empathically.

Give credit and praise for a job well done.

Give prompt and direct answers to questions.

Treat employees fairly and with respect and consideration.

Help out with work problems.

Encourage employees to acquire additional knowledge and skills.

Show interest and concern for people as individuals.

Learn employees' M.O.s and deal with them accordingly.

Make each person an integral part of the team.

Keep people challenged and excited by their work.

Consider your associates' ideas and suggestions.

Keep people informed about how they're doing on the job.

Encourage your people to do their best and then support their efforts.

> **Tactical Tools**
>
> The best way to determine what works best in motivating the people you supervise is to get feedback from them on the various approaches you use and revise them based on your findings.

Avoid Negative Motivation

Threatening to fire people if they don't work is sometimes effective—at least temporarily. When jobs are scarce and people know that they won't have a job if they get fired, they'll work in some pretty unsatisfying conditions. However, how much work do they do? Some folks work just enough to keep from getting fired and not one bit more. Fear isn't real motivation; *real* motivation spurs people to produce more than just what's necessary to keep their jobs. In addition, fear of being fired becomes less of a motivator as the job market expands. If comparable jobs are available in more amenable environments, employees working for managers who use fear as a tool won't stick around long.

However, some people do respond best to negative motivation. Maybe they've been raised by intimidating parents or have worked under tyrannical bosses for so long that it's the only way of life they understand. Good leaders must recognize each person's individualities and adapt what they use to motivate that person to what works best for him or her.

Career-Pathing: A Motivator for the Ambitious

Everybody isn't interested in promotion. Lots of workers are happy to just do their jobs, get their annual raises, and not worry about taking on added responsibilities. For these people, offering opportunity for advancement is not a motivator. However, if a person is ambitious and looks forward to moving ahead in the company, opportunity for advancement can be a major motivator.

As mentioned in Chapter 15, some companies have formalized the offering of opportunity by identifying promotable people early in their careers and worked with them to enhance their opportunities.

A good example is that of Kevin, an employee of Southeast Utilities. When he was hired, Kevin went through a series of evaluations and was assigned to a training program. When the program was completed, he was assigned to a team in the technical support department. Over the first few years he was progressively given more responsibilities and performed them very well.

Words to Work By

In order to promote the careers of their employees, companies have instituted **career-pathing** programs. Employees are assessed to determine their potential and what steps they must take to move up in positions that will be of greatest value to both the company and to themselves.

At his third annual performance review, he was informed that because of his excellent record, he was chosen to participate in the company's *career-pathing* program. This program served the dual purpose of giving top-level employees the opportunity to advance and to ensure that the expanding needs of the company would be met. Each year several men and women were selected to be assessed and trained to move up the corporate ladder.

The first step in this process was to report to an assessment center where Kevin was given a series of tests, interviews, and participated in interactive exercises with other participants.

After the results were analyzed, he met with the career-pathing team of the human resources department to discuss their findings, his own ambitions, and the opportunities available in the company.

> **Tactical Tools**
>
> To make the career-pathing program even more effective, assign a mentor to each "career-pather"—a senior manager to guide him or her over the bumps and hurdles that may be encountered.

> **Stop! Look! Listen!**
>
> Competence on a job by itself is not a good reason for promoting somebody to a supervisory position. More important are leadership ability, communication skills, and superior interpersonal relations.

Kevin was told that there were many opportunities in the organization for a person with his talents and suggested several areas he should consider for his career path. They pointed out that to become better equipped for growth within the company, he should acquire more knowledge in the information technology areas and develop managerial skills.

To start the ball rolling, he was advised to sign up for an advanced computer training program. Once he completed it successfully, he would be transferred to a position in the IT department where he could hone those skills. In addition, to prepare him for eventual promotion to management, he was counseled to enroll in an MBA program at the local university under the company's tuition reimbursement plan.

Career-pathing programs take much time and effort on both the part of the management and the selected employees. They pay off in building a highly motivated group of potential managers.

The Least You Need to Know

- Learn and remember what's important in the lives of each member of your group.

- By identifying your associates' M.O.s, you'll understand them and work more effectively with each one.

◆ Develop team spirit to make your team self-motivated.

◆ The key to group control is self-control. If all associates are aware of what's expected and are informed of what has been accomplished, they'll monitor their own activities.

◆ If your organization isn't team structured, you can still create an atmosphere of collaboration and participation to motivate the people you supervise.

◆ One way to make dull jobs more worker friendly is to redesign the jobs and change their focus.

◆ To promote the careers of employees, institute career-pathing programs.

Chapter 17

Does Money Motivate?

In This Chapter

- ◆ Understanding when money does and doesn't motivate
- ◆ Knowing when money is the scorecard
- ◆ Determining whether benefits are motivators or satisfiers
- ◆ Tying money to performance as keys to employee satisfaction
- ◆ Telecommuting and work-life programs

Here's a mini-lesson in logic:

A: The more money you earn, the happier you are.

B: The more work you produce, the more money you earn.

Therefore:

C: People will produce more to earn more money and become happier.

Sounds logical, but is it true? Sometimes, but not always. Assume A and B are both true. It should logically follow that C is true, right? Sometimes it is, but often it's not.

Motivators vs. Satisfiers

Remember that the word *motivate* begins with the same three letters as *motion*. Motivation is the incentive to get into motion, or making things move.

A team of behavioral scientists led by Frederick Herzberg studied what people want from their jobs and classified the results in two categories:

♦ **Satisfiers (also called maintenance factors):** Factors people require from a job to justify minimum effort. These factors include working conditions, money, and benefits. After employees are satisfied, however, just giving them more of the same factors doesn't motivate them to work harder. What most people consider motivators are really just satisfiers.

♦ **Motivators:** Factors that stimulate people to put out more energy, effort, and enthusiasm in their jobs.

To see how this concept works on the job, suppose you work in a less than adequate facility, in which lighting is poor, ventilation is inadequate, and space is tight. Productivity, of course, is low.

> **Words to Work By**
>
> When managers **motivate,** they stimulate people to exert more effort, energy, and enthusiasm in whatever they're doing. The best motivation is self-motivation. Your job as a team leader is to provide a climate in which self-motivation flourishes.

In a few months, your company moves to new quarters, with excellent lighting and air conditioning and lots of space, and productivity shoots up.

The company CEO is elated. He says to the board of directors, "I've found the solution to high productivity: If you give people better working conditions, they'll produce more, so I'm going to make the working conditions even better." He hires an interior designer, has new carpet installed, hangs paintings on the walls, and places plants around the office. The employees are delighted. It's a pleasure to work in these surroundings—but productivity doesn't increase at all.

Why not? People seek a level of satisfaction in their jobs—in this case, reasonably good working conditions. When the working environment was made acceptable, employees were satisfied, and it showed up in their productivity. After the conditions met their level of satisfaction, however, adding enhancements didn't motivate them.

So What Does This Have to Do with Money?

Money, like working conditions, is a satisfier. You might assume that offering more money generates higher productivity. And you're probably right—for most people, but not for everyone. Incentive programs, in which people are given an opportunity to earn more money by producing more, are part of many company compensation plans. They work for some people, but not for others.

The sales department is a good example. Because salespeople usually work on a commission, or incentive, basis, they're in the enviable position of rarely having to ask for a raise. If salespeople want to earn more money, all they have to do is work harder or smarter and make as much money as they want. Therefore, all salespeople are very rich. Right? Wrong!

Why doesn't this logic work? Sales managers have complained about this problem from the beginning of time. They say, "We have an excellent incentive program, and the money is there for our sales staff. All they have to do is reach out—and they don't. Why not?"

You have to delve deep into the human psyche for an answer. We all set personal salary levels, consciously or subconsciously, at which we are satisfied. Until we reach that point, money does motivate us, but after that—no more. *This level varies significantly from person to person.*

Some people set this point very high—money is a major motivator to them; others are content at lower levels. It doesn't mean that they don't want their annual raise or bonus, but if obtaining the extra money requires special effort or inconvenience, you can forget it.

Suppose Derek is in your production group and that his salary is 60 percent of yours. His wife works, but you know by the nature of her job that it doesn't pay much. Derek drives a 12-year-old car and buys his clothes from thrift shops. The only vacations his family has ever taken are occasional camping trips. You feel sorry for him. Now you can help Derek: You need several workers for a special project to be done over the next six Saturdays at double-time pay. When you ask Derek whether he wants the assignment, he says "No," and you can't understand why. It seems to you that he should be eager to make more money, but he has already reached his level of satisfaction. Spending Saturdays with his family is more important to him than the opportunity to earn more money.

> ### Tactical Tools
>
> Supervisors and team leaders rarely have control over the basic satisfiers: working conditions, salary scale, employee benefits, and the like. These factors are set by company policy, but they do have the opportunity to use the real motivators: job satisfaction, recognition, and the opportunity for their associates to achieve successes.

This example doesn't mean that money doesn't motivate at all. The opportunity to earn money motivates everyone to the point that they are satisfied. Some people, like Derek, are content at lower levels. As long as they can meet their basic needs, other things are more important to them than money. To other people, this point is very high, and they "knock themselves out" to keep making more money.

By learning as much as you can about your associates, you learn about their interests, goals, and lifestyles and the level of income at which they're satisfied. To offer the opportunity to make more money as an incentive to people who don't care about it is futile. You have to find other ways to motivate them.

Money as a Scorecard

Barney was unhappy. As vice president of marketing in his company, he earned $250,000 per year in combined salary and bonus but he believed that he was underpaid. "Our company had its best year in a decade," he said, "and it was chiefly due to my marketing efforts. I should be paid more."

When Barney was asked about his current quarter-of-a-million-dollar salary, he said, "I don't need the money. But my salary is the score that measures my success."

You don't have to be in the six-figure income bracket to consider your pay a scorecard. A merit raise given to a trainee or a production bonus paid to a factory worker is as much of a boost to that person's ego as is the money.

As discussed in the next chapters, intangible motivators are extremely effective, and supplementing them with a reward in the form of a raise or bonus adds to their value. It's not only the money itself but also the tangible acknowledgment of success.

When a person is promoted to a higher level position, the increase in pay that goes with the promotion is a recognition of the person's new status. Being in a higher salary classification adds prestige both within and outside a company.

Benefits: Motivators or Satisfiers?

Benefits are important in today's companies. Most companies provide some form of health insurance, life insurance, pension, and other benefits to their employees. In fact, the benefits package is one of the factors that potential employees consider when they evaluate a job offer—but it isn't a motivator. (Have you ever known anyone who worked harder because the company introduced a dental insurance program?)

Benefits are satisfiers. Good benefits attract people to work for a company, and they also keep people from quitting. (Sometimes, the people you wish would quit don't.)

Now Hear This

A happy team is not necessarily a productive team. Permissiveness and indulgence lead to carelessness and poor work. A manager's challenge is to develop, with associates, high performance standards that challenge and motivate them.

Raises, Cost-of-Living Increases, and Other Adjustments

In most companies pay raises are given as part of the performance review system. They're rarely given out otherwise. Unless specified in a union or personal contract, companies have no legal obligation to give employees raises at all. The amount of an increase, and how and when it's given, depend on each company's policy.

It is a common practice to give employees who meet minimum performance standards an annual raise based on increases in the cost of living. However, as often occurred in the past few years, when business becomes more competitive and inflation stays relatively low, even this expected annual raise is often discontinued, at least temporarily.

When people don't get as high a raise as they expect—or no raise at all—it leads to low morale. It's not easy for team leaders to keep members motivated in the face of disappointing compensation. You can't ignore the situation and hope that it will go away. Encourage any dissatisfied team members to express their concerns. If the reason a member didn't get the raise is poor performance, discuss it and pledge to help him or her improve enough for a raise the next time around. If the reason is a company freeze on pay increases, explain it and point out that it's a temporary situation that should be alleviated soon.

Old and New Incentive Pay Programs

In an economy that is moving rapidly away from mass production and manufacturing-based businesses to custom-engineered production and service-type industries, new types of incentive programs have had to be developed, but old programs still have value in some industries.

Piecework

Wages based solely on the number of units produced was the primary pay plan in some industries in the past. The harder you worked, the more money you received. Speed of production was the primary factor in determining wages, and this method worked well. Abuse in the piecework system, however, was rampant. Often, when workers mastered their work and produced more than quotas required, companies reduced the price paid per piece or raised the quota to keep overall costs down. This practice led to reduced motivation; workers would only do a fixed amount of work, which defeated the purpose of the incentive program.

As work became more complex, paying by the piece was no longer practical. Because of pressure from unions and, later, minimum wage laws, hourly rates replaced piecework rates in most industries.

Quota Pay Plans

Industrial engineers in the age of scientific management (the 1920s and 1930s) introduced a variation of piecework. Quotas were established based on time and motion studies, and people who exceeded quotas received extra pay. These types of programs still exist and, properly designed and administered, succeed in motivating some people. Even the best of these programs, however, may not alleviate company practices of raising quotas when workers master the job and frequently exceed them.

Sometimes it's the workers who manipulate the quota system. I saw how this system worked during the summers of my college years, when I worked in a factory that used it. Because I was young and energetic and wanted to make money to pay my college expenses, I quickly mastered the work and soon exceeded my quota. One of my co-workers pulled me aside and said, "Hey, you're working too fast. You're making it bad for the rest of us." His implication was that if I didn't slow down, he would break my arm.

Incentive Programs for Salespeople

Most sales jobs are paid on an incentive basis. Salespeople earn a commission or bonus based on their personal sales. This system should motivate people to knock themselves out to make more sales, but, as mentioned, it doesn't always happen. Many salespeople set limits for themselves, and, when they reach that limit, they "take it easy."

Another adverse result of sales incentives is that it encourages salespeople to concentrate on getting new business, often at the expense of neglecting established customers.

Effective sales incentive programs present challenges to the sales reps. They may vary from one period to another, depending on what the company wants to emphasize at any one time. The incentives may be based on one or more of the following:

- ◆ Number of new accounts opened

- ◆ Increase in volume of sales of current accounts

- ◆ Sales of specific items the company is pushing

- ◆ Introduction of new markets (for instance, the company has sold primarily to drug stores and now is promoting sales to food outlets)

Stock Options

Stock option programs provide opportunity for employees to benefit from an increase in the company's stock value. They are given "rights" to purchase the stock at a price that is lower than the market price. They do not pay for the "rights." Let's say the stock is currently selling for $25 per share. They are given options to buy the stock at $22 per share. If they exercise the options immediately, they make a $3 per share profit. However, the incentive is to keep the options until the stock rises higher in value. A year later, the stock is selling at $40 per share. They can still purchase it at $22 and sell it immediately for a profit of $18.

Stock options usually are not offered to lower-level employees, but often are a major part of executives' compensation packages.

The incentive is to help the company grow through their efforts, which will result in higher stock prices.

The downside is that stock price doesn't necessarily reflect the company's profitability. Other market factors may influence it. If the stock falls below the option price, the rights are worthless. In the bear market starting in 2000 and continuing as this book is being written, stock options have become worthless in many companies. In addition, as we saw in the scandals exemplified by Enron and other companies, management sometimes has engaged in illegal accounting practices, which eventually results in the significant losses to employees.

> **Stop! Look! Listen!** _____
>
> The benefits and incentive-pay area is complex and regulated by federal and state laws. Few companies have the expertise to institute effective programs without professional help. Some of the top consultants in this field are Towers Perrin (335 Madison Avenue, New York, NY 10017-3388); Hay Group (100 Penn Square East, Philadelphia, PA 19107-3388); and Hewitt Associates (100 Half Day Road, Lincolnshire, IL 60069).

Hiring Bonuses

If you follow sports, you know all about signing bonuses. The sports pages are always reporting fabulous amounts of money paid not only to top players, but also to promising rookies just out of high school or college.

To attract hard-to-find specialists, such as computer whizzes or financial geniuses, and sometimes just to get people who qualify for high-demand positions, companies have paid hundreds, and sometime thousands, of dollars in signing bonuses.

Incentive Plans That Work

In our tough, competitive economy, businesses need incentive plans. Even if money isn't the only, or even the best, way to motivate people, it can play an important role. Money combined with other types of motivation enhances the value of that approach. These programs may be based on exceeding predetermined expectations, rewarding special achievements, or sharing in the company's profits.

Special Awards for Special Achievements

The Footloose Shoe Store chain has instituted periodic campaigns to emphasize various aspects of its work. One campaign, for example, centered on increasing sales of "add-ons" (accessories for customers who have already bought shoes from the company). The campaign, which lasted four weeks, began with rallies at a banquet hall in each region in which the chain operated. Staff members from all the stores in the region assembled in a party atmosphere, where food, balloons, door prizes, and music set the mood as the program was kicked off.

Footloose announced that prizes would be awarded, including $2,000 to be divided among all the staff members (both sales and support) of the contest-winning store. The sales clerk who made the most personal add-on sales in the region would receive

$500, and the sales clerk who made the most add-on sales in each store would receive $100. The campaign was reinforced by weekly reports on the standings of each store and each sales clerk.

The result was not only a significant increase in accessory sales for that period but also an increase in regular sales, attributed to the excitement and enthusiasm generated by the campaign. Another party was held to present awards and recognize winners. Footloose runs three or four campaigns every year (too many parties would lessen the novelty).

Xerox is another company that adds financial reward to recognition. To encourage team participation, special bonuses are given to teams that contribute ideas leading to gains in production, quality, cost savings, or profits.

Tactical Tools
Tailor your incentive plan to what the company wants to accomplish. Create innovative programs that will motivate workers to help the company meet its goals.

A company that has instituted a total quality management (TQM) program, in which it puts special emphasis on providing high-quality products or services to customers, often augments the program by offering financial rewards based on reduction of product rejects, measurable improvements in quality, and increased customer satisfaction.

Profit Sharing

Companies use many variations of profit-sharing plans—that is, plans that distribute a portion of the company's profits to the employees. Many of these plans are informal. The executive committee or board of directors sets aside at the end of the fiscal year a certain portion of profits to be distributed among employees. Other, more formal, plans follow an established formula.

In many organizations, only managerial employees are included in a profit-sharing plan; in others, all employees who have been with the company for a certain number of years are also included; in still others, the entire workforce gets a piece of the profits. Some profit-sharing plans are mandated by union contracts.

A number of profit-sharing programs are based on employee stock ownership. Various types of stock ownership plans are used, including giving stock as a bonus, giving employees the option to buy company stock at below market rates, and employee stock ownership programs (ESOPs), in which employees own their company.

Perks: The Extras That Add Up

In many companies, employees have been given perks—those little extras that may not seem like much, but they often are significant additions to the traditional compensation package—and have been a great help in keeping people from leaving.

Why do perks motivate people to stay on a job? Why not give the employees cash bonuses and let them purchase or lease their own car, pay their own dues to the country club, or buy what they wish? Companies have found that most employees like receiving perks. If they did get cash equivalent, they would probably use it to pay bills or fritter it away. Perks keep reminding them that the company is giving them something. Every time they step into the company car, it reinforces their loyalty to the company. Every time they pass the day care bill to the accounting department, they thank the company for taking that burden off them.

Perks shouldn't be confused with benefits. Benefits such as pensions, health care, and life insurance are part of the compensation package. Today almost all large companies provide these standard benefits. Perks usually are add-ons to make life more pleasant for employees.

The Perk Buffet

Company perks vary. Here are some of the more commonly provided perks:

- **Company cars.** Cars are leased for executives, sales people, and sometimes other staff members.

- **Memberships in professional associations.** To encourage technical and specialized personnel to keep up with the state of the art in their fields, the company will pay their dues in appropriate associations.

- **Subscriptions to professional and technical journals.** Offered for the same reason as memberships in associations.

- **Membership in social clubs.** Because much business is conducted on the golf course or over a meal, for years many companies have paid the enrollment fees and annual dues for country clubs and dining clubs for executives and sales representatives. In recent years, such memberships have been extended to other employees as an added incentive.

- **Subsidized lunchrooms.** I recently had lunch in the cafeteria of a large insurance company. The bill for a salad, entree, coffee, and dessert was less than half of what is normally charged at a restaurant. This is a great savings for employees.

- **Coffee and snacks.** Many companies provide a never-empty coffee pot for employees. Often the company offers free doughnuts, bagels, or sweet rolls at break time.

- **Child care.** With the great number of families in which both parents are working, child care is a major problem. Some companies have child care facilities right on premises or arrange for child care at nearby facilities and subsidize the cost.

> **Now Hear This**
>
> According to the U.S. Chamber of Commerce, the fastest growing areas of benefits over the past five years have been day care for working parents and flexible hours.

- **Transportation.** Vans or buses are made available to employees to bring them to and from work. It's cheaper for the employees to use the company's transportation than to take public transportation or drive one's own car. Some companies will take employees to and from the nearest railroad station or bus depot at no cost to them.

> **Tactical Tools**
>
> Reward longevity. Give loyalty bonuses to employees who have completed long-term projects or years of service. Let employees know you appreciate their tenure.

- **Tuition.** Companies often pick up the entire bill for courses taken by employees—even if not specific to their job training. If the company doesn't pay in full, it may pay a portion of the cost of education.

- **Scholarships.** Some companies provide funds for college scholarships for children of employees.

- **Flextime.** A very effective perk is giving team members control over their own time. Some companies have company-wide flexible hours, but others allow supervisors or team leaders to set the hours for their staffs. For example, if there is a lot of pressure to complete a project, don't insist that everybody be on the job from 9 to 5. Some people may be more productive if they can work at home for a few hours before reporting to the office. Others may want to complete work away from the office during the day. Others may do their best work in the evening. Letting each person set time schedules for the project gives that person control over his or her hours and usually pays off in higher productivity.

> **Tactical Tools**
>
> Rather than just copying what other companies do to add perks to your buffet, talk with your employees to determine their real interests. What may work for one group may not be effective for another.

Less Common Perks That Some Companies Give

In order to attract and retain good people, some organizations have become creative and offer unusual and sometimes unique perks. Among these are ...

◆ **Birthday celebrations.** There are a few companies that give employees a day off on their birthday. That's a nice gesture, but it can disrupt team production. Many more companies celebrate the birthday on the job—at a break, lunch, or after work—with a mini-party: cake (no candles, age is confidential), soft drinks, and a little fun. When the group is relatively small, they may go out together after work for a little party.

◆ **Pets at work.** Bringing pets to the office can be very distracting, especially if they get restless. However, some companies permit employees to bring the dog or cat to work if they are kept under control. One company sets aside one day each week as "pet day" for employees who wish to take advantage of it.

◆ **Casual dress days.** Offices have always been formal places. Men wore suits and ties; women wore conservative outfits. Today many companies—particularly in the high-tech fields—have no dress code. Employees can wear whatever they feel comfortable in—except perhaps beachwear or "indelicate" attire. However, most offices still have traditional dress codes, modified somewhat. Sports jackets and slacks are okay for men and blouse-skirt outfits or slacks for women. To appease and attract the younger generation, companies have instituted casual dress days, usually Fridays, in which men can replace business suits with open-necked sports shirts and slacks and women can wear sporty outfits.

◆ **Exercise rooms.** With so many people engaging in regular exercise routines, many large firms have built complete gymnasiums for use of employees. Smaller organizations, of course, have neither the space nor funds for a gym, but an exercise room with a stationary bike, a treadmill, or other equipment for use by employees is feasible.

◆ **Recreation rooms.** To give employees a chance to relax after work, during breaks, or at lunch, some organizations have recreation rooms. In an article in *The Wall Street Journal*, one firm reported that it provided a billiard table and a Ping-Pong table; another, beanbag chairs; another a Velcro wall at which employees can throw sticky toys.

◆ **Financial counseling.** Companies provide seminars on managing money, investment basics, credit management, and means to achieve financial security. Some companies arrange for private counseling of employees by experts in the field.

◆ **Banking.** Many companies now have automatic teller machines on premises, while some large companies have arranged with a local bank to set up a branch at the company's facilities.

◆ **Charter schools.** To help retain parents who are concerned about the quality of education in the community, Ryder Systems, Inc. in Florida established a charter school at its Miami facility. Ryder made the initial investment to build the school, which will be recovered over time as the schools are funded by state education taxes. The school now enrolls 300 students from kindergarten to third grade. It has resulted in retaining many employees who might have left but for this perk.

◆ **Laundry facilities.** The Wilton Connor Packaging Company of Charlotte, North Carolina, offers an unusual perk. They learned that a large number of employees didn't own washers and dryers and spent an inordinate amount of time going to and from public laundromats. The company arranged with a local laundry to let employees drop off their wash in the morning and pick it up at the end of the workday at a minimum charge, subsidized by the company. The company reported that the laundry perk is one of the most popular among their employees.

◆ **Concierge services.** A growing trend, particularly in companies in larger cities, is the concierge service. Just as most top grade hotels have staff members who can care for the needs of their patrons, these firms provide equivalent facilities for their employees. What exactly do some of these services provide? Concierge staff can be called on to purchase tickets to theater or sports events, arrange for personal travel, make reservations at restaurants, provide messenger service, and do many of the time-consuming chores that complicate the lives of employees. In *Fortune*'s magazine's list of 100 best companies to work for, 26 offered concierge services, up from 15 just a year earlier.

Some of the more unusual chores reported by some companies include bringing employees' cars to be serviced, arranging pet care, waiting at an employee's home for a repairman to come, making arrangements for weddings and parties, and locating hard-to-find collectibles.

Rather than have company staff act as concierges, most concierge services are outsourced. Concierge services are available in most cities. Costs vary. Some services charge a per-employee rate, some charge hourly fees for actual time spent, others charge the company nothing, but take a percentage of the receipts on anything employees order from approved vendors. Some companies pay the entire cost, but may require the employee to pay a "co-payment" similar to that charged on health insurance.

Just as benefits add to the compensation package, perks provide both financial advantages and convenience factors that display the company's concern for its employees.

Unfortunately, in periods of decline in business, many companies will drop some or all of these perks to save money. This lowers morale of the employees who have become accustomed to them.

Telecommuting

Many people prefer working at home over having to fight traffic to and from their office. Some parents have turned to *telecommuting* to enable them to spend more time with their children and reduce day care expenses.

> **Words to Work By**
>
> The process of **telecommuting** uses technology to enable people to perform their work at home or at a remote location from the central office by receiving assignments and submitting completed work through a computer equipped with a modem.

Companies have discovered that it's often advantageous to let employees telecommute: It allows them to retain experienced workers who might not be able to come to the office regularly. These workers include parents with young children, people who can't leave their homes because they care for elderly or ill relatives, and people with a temporary or permanent disability.

Not every type of job is suitable for telecommuting. Many jobs require constant interaction with others on the job or the use of expensive or complex equipment that cannot be provided for home use.

Here are some types of jobs that *can* be done at home:

- ◆ Various types of clerical work
- ◆ Data entry
- ◆ Telemarketing
- ◆ Customer service
- ◆ Certain accounting functions
- ◆ Design and drafting
- ◆ Creative work such as writing advertising copy, writing technical manuals, artwork, and editing

With a little imagination, jobs that seem to be limited to the office often can be redesigned so that they can be done at home, or the person can telecommute certain days of the week and come into the office other days of the week.

Making Telecommuters Part of Your Team

Dr. Frank Ashby, a consultant who has worked with many companies that use telecommuters, suggests that the key to success is a well-designed plan for orienting and training all telecommuters. This plan should be followed by ongoing interaction between the leader and the telecommuter.

Provide guidelines for dealing with the special problems of working at home. Many people who are accustomed to the routine of an office find that they flounder when they have to work without direct supervision.

Ashby recommends training in at least the areas of time management and priority setting. He recommends these guidelines for telecommuters:

> **Tactical Tools**
>
> Make sure prospective telecommuters are fully aware of the negative as well as the positive aspects of working at home. Have the employee try it for a trial period before agreeing to a permanent arrangement.

- ◆ **Set specific hours that you plan to work—and stick to them.** Although some telecommuters are paid on an hourly basis and must keep time logs, most work in salaried jobs in which their work is measured not by hours worked but by their achievement of key results areas (see Chapter 20).

  Some jobs require telecommuters to be available at the telephone or at the computer during normal business hours; in others, the specific hours worked aren't important as long as the work is done and the manager knows when the employee can be contacted.

- ◆ **Set up working hours when children are in school or napping.** If you have children who aren't in school, arrange working hours for times when you're less likely to be disturbed or when another adult is available to take care of them.

- ◆ **Set priorities so that you're always aware of deadlines and progress on each assignment.**

Managers should make telecommuters as much a part of the team as people who work side by side in the office, and should treat them accordingly:

- ◆ Keep telecommuters informed of all team activities, even those in which they're not directly involved.

- Have them come to the office for business meetings, training programs, and company or department social events.

- Invite them to participate in such extracurricular activities as bowling leagues, softball teams, and family picnics.

- Put them on the distribution list for all the same materials they would receive if they were in-house employees.

- Require that they visit the office regularly—not just for discussion of their own work but also for in-person discussions about departmental activities and to give them an opportunity to interact with other staff members.

- Make yourself easily accessible by telephone, and return voice mail or other messages promptly. Many leaders call telecommuters periodically just to show a personal interest and to give them the opportunity to exchange ideas about overall activities—not just specific work assignments.

The Downside to Telecommuting

Prospective telecommuters should be made aware of the many potential problems of working at home. One home-based computer programmer complained that her friends and neighbors barged in for friendly chats or to ask her to accept deliveries, be available for service people, and even watch their children. She had to make clear to them that she was an at-home worker, not a lady of leisure. Being assertive cost her some "friends," but it was essential.

Another at-home worker, Dave, soon found that the freedom of working at home, setting his own time schedule, and avoiding rush hour didn't make up for the socialization of the workplace. He missed the interaction of daily contact with colleagues, the gossip around the water cooler, and even the daily parrying with his boss. He chose to return to the office.

Unlike Dave, Betty thrived on telecommuting. She was a well-disciplined, self-sufficient person, and even with two toddlers at home she accomplished a great deal.

However, two years later, when her supervisor moved up to a higher management position, Betty wasn't even considered for the promotion. When she complained, she was told that the job required being in the home office all of the time and as a telecommuter, she couldn't do it.

Betty agreed that being the supervisor would have meant giving up working at home, but her gripe was that she wasn't even given the opportunity to make the choice. She learned one of the hard lessons of being a telecommuter. Make sure that prospective telecommuters are fully aware of the negative as well as the positive aspects of working at home. Have them try it for a trial period before agreeing to a permanent arrangement.

Although some leadership jobs can be done via telecommuting, most cannot. Career-oriented people should keep this in mind when opting for working at home. People who work at home one or two days a week are more likely to be considered for promotion than those who work exclusively at home.

Now Hear This

The more enterprises come to rely on people working together without actually working together—that is, on people using the new technologies of information—the more important it will become to make sure that they are fully informed.

—Peter F. Drucker, management consultant and author

Work/Life Programs

To attract and retain top-level employees, more and more employers are turning to work/life programs that assist employees with balancing the demands of their personal and professional lives. Companies have come to recognize that increasingly employees are complaining about not having enough time for family, personal needs, community involvement, and household tasks—while work demands continue to increase.

Successful companies are reaping more than financial rewards from work/life programs. Work/life balance solutions can foster the three key characteristics common to *Fortune's* 100 Best Companies. Those characteristics are: engaging employees in business decisions that affect their hours, travel, time-off, and related issues; creating a supportive and inclusive company culture and environment; and giving greater consideration to their employees' quality of life. Work/life solutions have become a major new benefit, supplementing health care and 401(k)s.

Work/life programs represent a change in attitude of management toward their employee's life outside of the job. Traditionally, companies have expected their employees to make their job the top priority. Workers were expected to defer personal desires if overtime work was required. Professional, administrative, and management level people were often considered on duty 24/7, ready and willing to be available at the beck and call of their boss. Indeed, many companies still follow this concept.

When a company embraces a work/life philosophy it accepts that employees have other priorities, such as family and community commitments. Work/life programs are not limited to but may include many of the perks noted earlier in this chapter. The key factor is accepting and giving consideration to these needs of their people.

These employer-sponsored programs help employees balance their work and home responsibilities, and enhance employees' overall quality of life. They can boost employee loyalty, morale, and productivity, which in turn can improve the company's bottom line. During the last five years, the number of employers offering work/life programs has grown significantly.

A survey by *Working Mother* magazine and the Work & Family Connection Inc. reported that 70 percent of surveyed employees at a manufacturing company said they remained with their company because of its work/life benefits. In addition, 60 percent of workers surveyed at another large employer reported that the ability to balance work with personal and family responsibilities was "of great importance" in their decision to stay with the company.

Work/Life Programs = Employee Productivity

Several studies have noted the link between work/life programs and employee productivity. One study, for example, reported that work/life initiatives enable employees to better manage their life responsibilities, and as a result, they can be more focused and productive at work.

Now Hear This

According to a recent survey by Hewitt Associates, 74 percent of the respondents now offer flexible schedules. In addition, 90 percent of the respondents offer some type of child care benefits. Other work/life benefits noted in the survey were adoption assistance and various provisions for elder care.

Work/life programs build loyalty, and employees who are strongly committed to their company are more productive. For example, Scott Paper Co. stated that work/life programs and other efforts to support employees increased productivity by 35 percent.

Other studies have shown that often employees value work/life balance assistance more than salary. According to JobTrak.com's Career Values Poll, a great number of students and alumni consider balancing work and personal lives more important to them than money, location, and advancement potential.

It's Up to the Employer to Balance Work and Life

A survey by *Fast Company* magazine and Roper Starch Worldwide reported that 89 percent of college-educated, employed adults placed the responsibility of enabling people to balance their work and personal lives on their employer. With expectations like that, employees will reward the companies that reward them, through their loyalty and productivity.

The Least You Need to Know

- Motivation means getting into motion—getting moving in whatever endeavors you undertake.

- Money, benefits, and working conditions are satisfiers. Employees must be satisfied with these aspects of their jobs or else they don't work effectively. After people are satisfied, however, giving them more of the same factors doesn't necessarily motivate them.

- Everyone sets a level of income at which he or she is satisfied. Money motivates people up to that point, but after it's reached—no more.

- A program of bonuses for productivity combined with other motivational factors is more effective than the bonus by itself.

- Profit-sharing plans give team members a vested interest in keeping their company profitable.

- Perks can be an effective way of attracting and retaining top-level people.

- Consider instituting work/life programs as a motivator.

Chapter 18

Let Them Know You Love Them

In This Chapter

- ◆ Understanding that people are *people*, not cogs in a machine
- ◆ Recognizing achievement and making praise effective
- ◆ Creating recognition programs that work
- ◆ Motivating people under unfavorable circumstances
- ◆ Motivating people who work away from the base facilities

As pointed out in the last chapter, many things people once considered to be motivators are now seen as satisfiers. Money, benefits, and working conditions are important in keeping employees satisfied, but they don't motivate people beyond a certain point. To get your employees to work harder once they are satisfied, you need to concentrate on less tangible things, such as recognition of each person's individuality and giving people an opportunity for growth. Let's take a look at some of those intangibles.

People Crave Recognition

Human beings crave recognition. People like to know that others know who they are, what they want, and what they believe. Recognition begins when you learn and use people's names. Of course, you know the names of the men and women in your group, but you will be coordinating work with other groups, with internal and external suppliers, subcontractors, and customers. Everyone has a name. Learn them. Use them. It's your first step in recognizing each person's individuality.

> **Tactical Tools**
>
> By focusing on positive things—by giving attention and appreciation to the good things people do—you reinforce their desire to "do the right thing." You also help build their self-image and spur positive thoughts, which help develop a positive attitude.

However, just knowing and using an employee's name is only the beginning. Effective supervisors respect each of their staff members. They listen attentively to their comments, complaints, and suggestions about the work. They encourage them to be frank and honest without fear that disagreement will jeopardize their careers.

In Tony's exit interview after quitting his job with the Building Maintenance Company, he was asked what he liked most and least about the company. Tony responded that, although the salary and benefits were good, he never felt that he was part of the organization. "I always felt that I was looked at as nothing more than a cog in the machine," he said. "During the nine months I worked in the department, I made several suggestions, offered to take on extra projects, and tried to apply creative approaches to some of the work assigned to me. My boss didn't recognize all that I could have contributed."

Providing Positive Reinforcement

An autocratic boss continually criticizes, condemns, complains, and never forgets negative performance. However, he or she always takes good performance for granted. Managers today are more aware of the value of reinforcing the good things their associates do than of harping on their mistakes and inefficiencies.

When people hear continual criticism, they begin to feel stupid, inferior, and resentful. When someone does something that isn't satisfactory, your objective should be to correct the behavior, not to make the person feel bad.

The famous psychologist B. F. Skinner noted that criticism often reinforces poor behavior (when the only time an offender gets attention is when he or she is being criticized). He recommended that we minimize our reaction to poor behavior and maximize our appreciation of good behavior.

Rather than bawl out an associate for doing something wrong, quietly tell the person, "You're making some progress in the work, but we still have a long way to go. Let me show you some ways to do it more rapidly." When the work does improve, make a big fuss over it.

Now Hear This

Enthusiasm is one of the most powerful engines of success. When you do a thing, do it with all your might. Put your whole soul into it. Stamp it with your own personality. Be active, be energetic, be enthusiastic and faithful, and you will accomplish your objective. Nothing great was ever achieved without enthusiasm.

—Ralph Waldo Emerson

Showing That You Care

Just as you have a life outside the company, so does every member of your staff. A job is an important part of our lives, but there are many aspects of life that may be of greater importance: health, family, and outside interests, for example. Show sincere interest in an employee's total person.

Virginia, the head teller of a savings-and-loan association in Wichita, Kansas, makes a point of welcoming back associates who have been on vacation or out for several days because of illness. She asks them about their vacation or the state of their health and brings them up-to-date on company news. She makes them feel that she missed them—and it comes across sincerely because she really did miss them.

Now Hear This

Some supervisors fear that giving praise indicates softness on their part: "We don't want to coddle our subordinates."

Praise is *not* softness—it's a positive approach that reinforces good performance. When you stop thinking of your staff members as subordinates and instead think of them as partners all working to reach the same goals, appropriate praise will become a natural part of your behavior.

Jacob, a grandfather, realizes that children are the center of most families. He takes a genuine interest in the activities of his co-workers' children and has even accompanied associates to school events in which their children participate. Some people may consider this situation paternalistic or intrusive, but Jake's true concern comes across as positive interest and has helped meld his associates into a "working family."

Everyone Needs Praise, but What If It Hasn't Been Earned?

Human beings thrive on praise. Although all of us require praise to help make us feel good about ourselves, you can't praise people indiscriminately: Praise should be reserved for accomplishments that are worthy of special acknowledgment. So, how do you deal with people who never do anything particularly praiseworthy?

Maria faced this situation in her group of word processors. Several marginal operators had the attitude that, as long as they met their quotas, they were doing okay. Praising them for meeting quotas only reinforced their belief that nothing more was expected of them. Criticism of their failure to do more than the quota required was greeted with the response "I'm doing my job."

Maria decided to try positive reinforcement. She gave one of the operators a special assignment for which no production quota had been set. When the job was completed, Maria praised the employee's fine work. She followed this practice with all new assignments and eventually had the opportunity to sincerely praise each of the word processors.

Looking for Praiseworthy Situations

Some managers tend to look for things to criticize rather than things to compliment. Because they expect their staff to perform well, they concentrate on strengthening areas of weakness. Douglas, a regional supervisor for a California supermarket chain, made regular visits to the eight stores under his jurisdiction. He reported that when he went into a store he looked for *problems*. He criticized store managers for the way products were displayed, for slow-moving checkout lines, and anything else he noticed. "That's my job," he said, "to make sure that everything is being done correctly."

As you can guess, everyone working in the stores dreaded his visits. Douglas's boss acknowledged to him the importance of improving what was wrong but also pointed out that, because the stores exceeded sales volume forecasts and kept costs down, the managers needed to hear compliments on their success. His boss suggested that Douglas seek out good things and express his approbation. Douglas

> **Tactical Tools**
>
> People need praise. If employees do nothing that merits praise, assign them projects in which they can demonstrate success and then praise their accomplishments.

> **Stop! Look! Listen!**
>
> Beware of over-praising. When you praise every little thing, you dilute the power of praise. Save it for significant improvements, exceptional accomplishments, and special efforts.

was encouraged to make suggestions for improvements, but not to make them the focus of his visits.

Although it wasn't easy, Douglas followed his boss's advice. Within a few months, store managers looked forward to his visits. They began to share new ideas and seek his counsel about store issues. Clerks and other store staffers soon overcame their fear of the "big boss" and welcomed his comments and suggestions.

Five Tips for Effective Praise

As important as praise is in motivating people, it doesn't always work. Some supervisors praise every minor activity, diminishing the value of praise for real accomplishments. Others deliver praise in such a way that it seems phony. To make your praise more meaningful, follow these suggestions:

1. **Don't overdo it.** Praise is sweet. Candy is sweet, too, but the more you eat, the less sweet each piece becomes—and you may get a stomachache. Too much praise reduces the benefit that's derived from each bit of praise; if it's overdone, it loses its value altogether.

2. **Be sincere.** You can't fake sincerity. You must truly believe that what you're praising your associate for is actually commendable. If you don't believe it yourself, neither will your associate.

3. **Be specific about the reason for your praise.** Rather than say, "Great job!" it's much better to say, "The report you submitted on the XYZ matter enabled me to understand more clearly the complexities of the issue."

4. **Ask for your associate's advice.** Nothing is more flattering than to be asked for advice about how to handle a situation. This approach can backfire, though, if you don't *take* the advice. If you have to reject advice, ask people questions about their inadequate answers until *they* see the error of their ways and reissue good advice.

5. **Publicize praise.** Just as a reprimand should always be given in private, praising should be done (whenever possible) in public. Sometimes the matter for which praise is given is a private issue, but it's more often appropriate to let your entire group in on the praise. If other staff members are aware of the praise you give a colleague, it spurs them to work for similar recognition.

In some cases, praise for significant accomplishments is extremely public, such as when it's given at meetings or company events.

The Mary Kay cosmetics company is known for its policy of giving recognition to associates who have accomplished outstanding performance. In addition to receiving awards and plaques, award winners are feted at company conventions and publicized in the company magazine. Attending a Mary Kay convention is similar to attending a victory celebration: Winners are called to the stage and presented with their awards to the cheers and applause of an audience. Award winners report that recognition from senior executives and acclaim from peers is as rewarding as the award itself.

Give Them Something They Can Keep

Telling people that you appreciate what they've done is a great idea, but *writing* it is even more effective. The aura of oral praise fades away; a letter or even a brief note endures.

You don't have to spend much money. It doesn't take much time. This section looks at how writing the praise has worked for some team leaders.

Writing Thank-You Cards

At the A&G Merchandising Company in Wilmington, Delaware, team leaders are given packets of "thank-you" cards on which the words *Thank You* are printed in beautiful script on the front flap and the inside of the card is left blank. Whenever someone does something worthy of special recognition, that person's team leader writes a note on one of the cards detailing the special accomplishment and congratulating the employee for achieving it. The recipients cherish the cards and show them to friends and family.

Something to Hang on the Wall

No matter what type of award you give employees—large or small (cash, merchandise, tickets to a show or sports event, or a trip to a resort)—it's worth spending a few more dollars to include a certificate or plaque. Employees love to hang these mementos in their cubicles or offices, over their workbenches, or in their homes. The cash gets spent, the merchandise wears out, the trip becomes a long-past memory, but a certificate or plaque is a permanent reminder of the recognition.

Success Files—the Scorecard

Hillary, the sales manager of a large real estate office in Florida, makes a practice of sending letters of appreciation to sales staffers who do something special—selling a property that has been difficult to move, obtaining sales rights to a profitable building, or taking creative steps to make a sale.

With the first of these letters that Hillary sends to a salesperson, she encloses a file folder labeled "Success File" with this suggestion: "File the enclosed letter in this folder. Add to it any other commendatory letters you receive from me, from other managers, from clients, or from anyone else. As time goes on, you may experience failures or disappointments. There may be times when you don't feel good about yourself. When this happens, reread these letters. They're the proof that you're a success, that you have capability, that you are a special person. You did it before; you can do it again!"

The recipients of Hillary's letters repeatedly tell her how rereading the letters helps them overcome sales slumps, periods of depression, and general disenchantment when things aren't going well. It "reprograms" their psyche by reinforcing their self-esteem and enables them to face problems with new strength and confidence.

Creating Recognition Programs That Work

Any form of sincere recognition can be effective—some for short periods of time; others, much longer. Recognition programs that affect the entire organization are usually developed and administered by the human resources department. You participate in implementing the programs in your team. But even if there's no company-wide program, with a little imagination and initiative, you can create a variation just for your own staff. This section discusses a few of these techniques.

Employee of the Month

Choosing an associate every month for special recognition is probably the most popular form of formal recognition. The method of choosing employees and deciding which rewards and recognition to offer vary from company to company.

In most companies, each team leader or department head nominates candidates for an award. A committee weighs the contributions of each candidate and chooses the winner. In some organizations, peers make nominations in each department; increasingly, all employees are encouraged to make a nomination by writing a note or filling out a form. The committee makes its choice by comparing the nominees against a list of criteria and against each other.

Awards vary from company to company. The most frequently awarded prizes are cash, a day off with pay, or merchandise.

Almost all companies with employee-of-the-month programs have a permanent, prominently displayed plaque on which the winner's name is engraved. In some companies a photo of the winner is also displayed during the month. In addition, individual certificates or plaques are given to monthly winners.

Awards often are presented at luncheons to which all nominees for that month are invited. The winner is interviewed for an article in the company newsletter, and press releases are sent to local newspapers, radio, and TV stations.

As with anything else, there are drawbacks to the employee-of-the-month program. Here are a few:

♦ **Resentment.** Some people may believe that they were more suited for the award than the winner and resent not having been chosen. Resentment and envy are difficult to overcome, and there will always be unhappy losers.

♦ **Overexposure.** After a while any monthly program can become overdone—it's difficult to maintain excitement and enthusiasm month after month.

♦ **Lack of team recognition.** When people work in teams, individual efforts are subordinate to team efforts. When recognition belongs to a team, no single member of that team should be singled out for recognition.

Team Recognition

When individual commendation is undesirable, companies institute team recognition programs. In Xerox's successful program, individuals receive awards for special achievement, but, to encourage teamwork, recognition is also given to teams. These awards include honors to teams that perform outstanding work and special recognition to teams for "Excellence in Customer Satisfaction."

Another way Xerox recognizes teams is by holding an annual Teamwork Day. On the first Teamwork Day, held in 1983 in a company cafeteria in Webster, New York, the objective was to teach managers the results of planning team activities and fostering a truly competitive team spirit. Thirty teams showed off projects that year and received *no rewards or cash*, just thank-yous. A combination of word-of-mouth and a company newspaper article helped ensure the participation of 60 teams the following year and an audience of 500 visitors.

In the third year of Teamwork Day, hundreds of teams wanted to participate, but there was room for only 200 (1,000 people attended the exhibits). In the fourth year, the company rented the convention center in Rochester, New York, and 5,000 people attended. In its fifth year, the program expanded internationally; teamwork fairs were held in Rochester, Dallas, London, Amsterdam, and elsewhere. Teamwork Day is now a highly anticipated annual event.

Peer Recognition

Another successful motivational approach is peer recognition—when associates praise or give formal recognition to colleagues who have made their job easier or more satisfying. One way to encourage peer recognition in your company is to have employees consider co-workers as *internal customers* or *internal suppliers*.

Encourage your associates to recognize efforts of their internal suppliers and customers that enabled them to work more effectively.

Supervisors, managers, and team leaders aren't the only people who see the special efforts their associates make. All team members and co-workers are exposed daily to each other's efforts. Enabling them to recognize the work of peers not only brings to the forefront any accomplishments that may not have been recognized by managers but also makes both the nominator and the nominee feel that they are part of an integrated, interrelated, and caring organization.

Minicircuit Labs, which has plants in Brooklyn, New York, and Hialeah, Florida, encourages this concept by providing all its members with the following "You Made My Day" forms.

> **Words to Work By**
>
> An **internal customer** is another employee to whom you provide materials, information, or services. An **internal supplier** is another person in your organization who provides you with materials, information, or services. You may be a "customer" in some aspects of your work and a "supplier" in others.

> **Tactical Tools**
>
> When companies are organized on a team basis, a program of recognizing team accomplishments should be judiciously incorporated into any formal recognition programs.

You Made My Day!

Date: _____

To: _____   Dept: _____

From: _____   Dept: _____

What you did: _____

_____

What it meant to me: _____

_____

Signed: _____

Copy to human resources

Copy to team leader

Special Awards for Special Achievements

To win one of Mary Kay's highest and most coveted awards—those famous pink Cadillacs—at its award celebrations, its salespeople must meet a series of challenges and criteria (see the section "Five Tips for Effective Praise," earlier in this chapter). It's not easy to win the award, but every year more Mary Kay associates "make the grade."

Mary Kay doesn't *give* the cars away, however—it *lends* them for one year. Anyone who wants to keep a car or upgrade to the next year's model must continue to meet the standards. What an incentive to keep up the good work! As a result, relatively few winners have to give up their cars.

In some organizations, special awards are given not as part of a formal program, but on a manager's initiative. During the pre-Thanksgiving rush at Stew Leonard's food market in Norwalk, Connecticut, several office personnel noticed the long, creeping lines at checkout counters and—with no prompting from management—left their regular work duties to help cashiers bag the groceries, which helped speed up the lines.

Stew, the owner of the market, resolved to do something special for the employees who helped out. After the holiday rush was over, he bought for each of the employees a beautifully knitted shirt with the embroidered inscription "Stew Leonard ABCD

Award." The inscription stands for "*above* and *beyond* the *c*all of *d*uty." By giving special recognition to associates who do more than their jobs require, he not only gave credit where credit was due but also let everyone—the associates and their co-workers and supervisors, in addition to customers—know that he appreciated the extra effort.

Words to Work By

ABCD awards are given for performance that's truly Above and Beyond the Call of Duty. This type of special recognition pays off in continued efforts to achieve superior performance.

Motivating the Unmotivated

You have to accept that some people just can't be motivated (short of putting a stick of dynamite under their chairs). However, with the right approach, many men and women who seem to be complacent and unmovable might be spurred toward improved performance.

Some employees have been with their organization for many years. They've gone as far as they can go—and they know it. They also know that it's unlikely they'll ever be fired as long as they meet minimum performance standards, because most companies don't fire long-term employees except under dire circumstances. People with the attitude "I'll do as little as I can get away with" are called *coasters*.

Words to Work By

Long-term employees who have gone as far as they can and are not likely to be fired because of their tenure may become **coasters** until they retire.

Unfortunately, coasting isn't limited to "old-timers." People of all ages can fall into this category. They meet your minimum standards, but make no effort to do more.

It's difficult to motivate people who really don't want to be motivated, and many managers and team leaders don't even try. They just look at these people as crosses they have to bear.

Learning Not to Give Up

One often-successful approach to motivating coasters is giving them challenges—assignments or projects they can really "sink their teeth into."

Realistically, not everyone gets excited by challenges. Some people, faced with a challenge, turn away from it—it's too much trouble. However, for those who enjoy a challenging assignment, it can be a powerful motivator. Here are some guidelines:

◆ **Make the coaster a mentor to a new associate.** Many "old-timers" are flattered when asked to pass on their know-how and experience to the next generation. To ensure that they train newcomers properly, they hone their own skills and brush up on the latest developments in their field. Serious mentors do more than just train—they set good examples for their new associates.

◆ **Assign special projects.** Before the Associated Merchandise Company introduces a new product, it conducts a test market in key cities, a task it usually subcontracts to a market research firm. In testing its latest product, Associated tried a new approach: Rather than subcontract the job, it chose six men and women who had good marketing backgrounds but were now coasting. The six employees were relieved from their regular duties for four weeks. After a week of special training, each was sent to a test site to run the project. The challenge of a special assignment, enhanced by the success of the test, gave the coasters new enthusiasm that carried over into their regular work.

> **Tactical Tools**
>
> The downside of challenge as a motivator is that after a challenging assignment ends, the excitement it generates gradually fades. After a task is no longer a challenge, it's no longer a motivator either. You have to keep presenting new challenges.

◆ **Plan future projects.** Coasters often feel left out. "I'll be retiring in a few years, so why worry about what the company will do then?" Their attitude is exacerbated by the fact that their managers have already given up on them. By bringing coasters into the process of planning projects along with younger employees, you let them know that they are valued staff members and that they can bring to the group the value of their experience. An added benefit is that the coasters will learn from other members.

Motivating Off-Site Employees

Motivating telecommuters, independent subcontractors, and others who do most of their work away from the central facility, while keeping them from feeling like outsiders, is a challenge for managers. Here are a few suggestions:

◆ Schedule meetings either monthly or every other month with all employees working on a project. If the people are scattered all over the country, regional meetings at a convenient location would be more feasible. This enables them to get to know each other and to discuss ideas face-to-face. It also gives people a feeling of community and a closer relationship to the company. They don't feel left out.

◆ Encourage managers to telephone off-site people—frequent but brief calls to touch base and occasional conference calls to the entire project team.

◆ People working off-site should be invited periodically to come to the home office to meet with staff. The personal contacts between on-site and off-site employees create feelings of belonging.

◆ Managers should make periodic visits to the locations where off-site people work.

◆ Send a weekly newsletter to all off-site people, telling them about the latest developments in the company. Make it newsy and include human-interest stories about employees.

   In addition to, or instead of, a newsletter, provide a website, updated daily, to keep everybody current on company activities. Add some humor. Make it a site they'd want to read every day.

Motivating People Under Unfavorable Circumstances

Things don't always go well. Businesses go into slumps. Companies downsize and eliminate jobs. Large companies swallow smaller ones. How can morale be maintained and staff members motivated when they see their economic world toppling down around them? It's not easy, but, as you'll learn in this section, there are ways to do it.

When the Company Downsizes

When business is slow, companies reduce costs by laying off employees or downsizing. Layoffs have always been an element of the job world, particularly among blue collar industries. When business picks up, workers are likely to be rehired.

Downsizing differs from traditional layoffs in that total job categories are eliminated: There's little chance that people who have held these jobs will ever be rehired. Downsized positions are increasingly white collar and managerial jobs.

Elliot left his boss's office in shock. He had been told that the company was downsizing and that he would have to cut his team from 20 people to 15. He had worked hard to build a highly motivated team. Not only would he lose five good members, but also the remaining employees would feel insecure, stressed, and unmotivated.

After the trauma of the layoffs subsided, Elliot took these steps to begin the rebuilding process:

◆ Reassured team members that management had completed the downsizing process and that their jobs were secure.

◆ Set up a series of meetings to restructure the team so that all work would be covered.

◆ Assigned projects to subteams to implement the new structure with minimum loss of productivity in ongoing activities.

◆ Personally counseled team members who showed signs of unusual stress.

Within a short time, Elliot's team again functioned at optimum capacity.

When Your Company Is Merged or Acquired

It seems that every time you pick up a newspaper you read about another merger or acquisition. Chase Manhattan's acquisition of Chemical Bank was at that time the largest bank merger ever, and it resulted in the loss of thousands of jobs. AOL bought Time-Warner and more jobs were lost as the offices of its headquarters were consolidated. Your company could be next.

The people most likely to survive an acquisition are those who work for the acquiring company, but even that's not a sure thing. Federated Department Stores bought Macy's and closed several of its own stores.

Whenever a merger or acquisition occurs, employees of both groups are certain to be insecure and concerned. There's not much any supervisor or team leader can do until the dust settles, which often takes months or even years.

The following suggestions can give you and your group a better chance of survival:

◆ **Work harder, work smarter.** When Associated Finance acquired Guardian Loan, all of Guardian's employees were concerned. They were sure that the larger company would eliminate their jobs. Alberta, Guardian's credit manager, thought differently. She told her associates, "Our credit people are the best in the business. One reason they bought us was our excellent record in this area. They need us. It will take at least six months before Associated can make any changes here. Let's show them that we are essential to their success." And they did. When the reorganization finally took place, Associated merged several departments with its own, but the credit department was left intact.

◆ **Be prepared to do things differently.** Companies that acquire others install their own systems and procedures. Accept them without complaints. Neither you nor your associates should ever say, "We never used to do it that way." Work their way. If it requires you to learn new technology, learn it as soon as possible.

◆ **Be patient.** After you master the new company's methods and win the confidence of the new management, they will listen to your ideas for improvements and innovations.

> **Tactical Tools**
>
> When you deal with survivors of downsizing, mergers, or reorganizations, don't assume that things are the same as before. Take overt action to help your staff cope with their fears and stresses. Get your entire group involved in productive activities that not only keep them from brooding but also actively engage their minds and bodies.

When the Pressure Is On

Regardless of whether a company has downsized or reorganized because of an acquisition or another reason, you usually wind up with fewer people having to accomplish more work.

Suppose that a team of six people has been reduced to four but that the amount of work hasn't decreased. Work previously done at a leisurely pace must now be rushed. People who went home at 5 P.M. now work regularly until 7 or 8 P.M. Everyone feels the pressure. Morale is at a low.

How to motivate people who work longer hours and under constant pressure is the primary challenge manager's face, and there are no easy answers. Some managers counter complaints by telling their associates that they're lucky to have a job. This kind of negative motivation has only limited value.

By encouraging your staff to find short-cuts to better production, to eliminate unnecessary paperwork, and to come up with creative innovations, you can help them reduce some of the added burden.

Some companies have instituted stress reduction programs to help people cope with downsizing and reorganization. Let everyone know that, as business improves, temporary and, eventually, permanent staff members will be added to ease the workload.

> **Now Hear This**
>
> A survey of managerial and professional personnel by the U.S. Chamber of Commerce showed that the 40-hour work week is dead. Most respondents said that they work nine-hour days, another hour or more at home, and at least two hours on weekends.

When Wages Freeze

Suppose your company hasn't raised anyone's wages for three years. Your employees are unhappy and resist all your efforts to get them to produce more. You repeatedly hear the complaint, "Why should I knock myself out when they won't pay me more?"

Sanjay, a chief engineer at a chemical company, was tired of hearing this complaint. He had tried hard, but unsuccessfully, to get management to lift the freeze. At one of his department meetings he addressed the issue: "I know you haven't had a raise in three years. Neither have I, nor has my boss. You all know that business has been down during this time. After it improves, the freeze will end. Business is up this year, but not enough. Let's get to work so that we can do our part to make this a profitable company again."

This technique is one way to help staff members understand the problem—that it's one that can and will be overcome. (Of course it doesn't help if people read in the newspaper that the company CEO has just received a $1 million bonus.)

The Least You Need to Know

- By showing sincere interest in each of your associates, you establish a climate that's conducive to cooperation and team spirit.

- Provide positive reinforcement by seeking out and praising accomplishments instead of concentrating on faults that need correction.

- Encourage all members of the group or team to show appreciation for their co-workers through peer recognition programs.

- Put your appreciation in writing. Brief notes, letters of commendation, and certificates of achievement give long-term value to the act of praising.

- Create ongoing programs to recognize the achievements of both individuals and teams. Find original ways to keep these programs exciting and rewarding.

- Don't ignore your off-site employees. Recognize that they are an integral part of your team.

- You can often "remotivate" coasters by giving them new challenges.

- Survivors of downsizing need reassurance. Get them involved in productive projects that stimulate them and enable them to experience success.

Chapter 19

Retaining Good People

In This Chapter

- ◆ Why people leave their jobs
- ◆ Tips for preventing turnover

There are few things more draining to an organization—and more telling about the state of its culture—than the steady, systematic loss of highly effective and productive people. It is critical when employment is at a high peak and workers are hard to find. Nevertheless, even when unemployment rates are high and there are lots of people available, it is still very expensive, time consuming, and emotionally draining to lose good people and have to replace them. In this chapter, we will look at the reasons people leave and how to identify problems in your company so turnover can be reduced.

Keep Alert to Reasons for Turnover

There's nothing new about good people trying to improve their lot. Many outstanding people use periodic job changes as a key part of their career management strategy. The problems arise, however, when evidence of dissatisfaction among top workers seems to be the major recurrent reason for

Now Hear This

Good times don't wipe out "bad vibes" workers have about their jobs, says the Conference Board, a management research group in New York City. Even during the economic boom, strong stock market and high consumer confidence in the 1990s, less than 51 percent of Americans said they were happy with their jobs, down from 59 percent five years earlier.

high turnover rates. When that happens the results are almost always disrupting, if not severely damaging, to the organization.

Can you save these people before they take that drastic step that will separate them from the organization? Not always. It may be too late to make the changes that precipitated that individual's decision to leave. However, there are situations in which you can reach a dissatisfied employee and make changes that will encourage a change of mind. And even if that fails, you may learn what to do that will change the circumstances and prevent other good people from quitting.

Take Preemptive Action

Some companies have taken proactive steps to identify specific problems that an employee may have that might lead to voluntary separation. For example, when the HR manager of a multiunit, multistate financial institution accidentally found one of his key employees' resumés on an online job service, he met with her, learned why she was seeking a change, and was able to retain the employee. As a result, he assigned one of his staff to surf the major job-posting services seeking the bank's employees. This program, which he dubbed "salvaging," has resulted in four "saves" in the first six months and has provided critical information about the bank's human resources practices.

Another example is a retail chain in Illinois. At the annual performance review, the supervisor or team leader records on each employee's report what they say they want from the company over the next year that will help them meet their goals. Every month, the supervisor reviews these reports and determines what has and hasn't been done to meet these needs. This follow-through has led to greater productivity, higher morale, and a significant reduction in turnover.

The Chief Reasons People Quit

Let's look at some of the top reasons good people give for leaving their organizations.

Loss of Faith in Management

There seems little doubt that one of the big reasons good people leave their jobs is a gradual (and, alas, sometimes sudden) loss of faith in management.

Loss of faith in a boss or colleague is nothing new in business, or in life, for that matter. People disappoint. They exaggerate. They make mistakes. However, it isn't so much the fact that highly marketable people leave their jobs because they lose faith in management, but rather how quickly some of them come to the decision and how little patience they seem to show for any transgressions. This was demonstrated graphically after the Enron, Worldcom, and other scandals in 2002.

Good people know they have options and that they don't have to take as much nonsense or tolerate as much incompetence as they did in the past. Furthermore, good people have a good deal less patience today for behaviors they consider *shady* or *dishonest.* Today, people say they're more concerned with their reputations than they are their paychecks. They say they're worried about the *stigma* that could come from an association with a manager—or a firm—with a questionable history or reputation. They're just refusing to participate in things they find uncomfortable, even at the risk of losing their jobs.

Now Hear This

So much of what we call management consists of making it difficult for people to work.

—Peter Drucker, management consultant

Now Hear This

According to a report on Work Practices and Employee Loyalty made by Walker Information, in Indianapolis, Indiana, companies viewed as highly ethical by their employees are six times more likely to keep their staff. Nearly 80 percent of 2000 employees who questioned their bosses' integrity said they felt trapped at work or uncommitted and were likely to leave their jobs soon.

Feeling Unappreciated

Good people leave their jobs because they feel that their efforts and contributions are not appreciated enough. According to recent surveys, more than 80 percent of those who had made a decision to change jobs during the past year reported they did so, in part, out of a feeling that their contributions had gone largely unnoticed or were simply taken for granted by their superiors.

We often find managers who say they agree with these findings, but in truth do very little to send the kinds of signals that provide people with that sense of value. These

---

Tactical Tools

People really *do* need to feel they're appreciated and that what they're doing for their company is valuable and noteworthy. Managers and supervisors often assume that if employees are not criticized or reprimanded, they "know they're doing okay." Wrong! People need to be told that their work is good and is appreciated.

---

managers are often notorious for their high turnover rates and poor ratings when evaluated by their subordinates and peers in a 360 degree assessment (discussed in Chapter 20). They may say they care and that they appreciate the efforts of others, but the evidence seems to contradict it. They just don't seem to understand how important something so simple and so easy to do is.

William James, the great American psychologist, stated that the deepest urge in human nature is the craving to be appreciated. Yet, in our daily lives, we take so much for granted that we often forget to express our appreciation to others in our lives who make our successes possible and our daily lives more enjoyable. This is particularly true in the workplace.

Appreciation must be sincere. Phoniness is easily perceived. Insincerity cannot be disguised by fancy words. Your voice, your eyes, your body language reflects your true feelings. There is no reason to fake expressions of appreciation. Look for something specific that the employee has done that is worthy of praise and let it be known that it's appreciated. Supplementing your verbal comments with an occasional note of gratitude reinforces your appreciation and helps build a sense of loyalty.

Feeling Bored or Unchallenged

A sense of having "stagnated" at work is another major reason good people give for resigning. In fact, 67 percent of those responding to a recent survey listed it among the four leading reasons for their exit.

Organizations make a big mistake when they assume highly competent and well-compensated people are also happy with the routine of their jobs. The fact is, terrifically capable people get that way as a result of having searched for and accepted new challenges over the years. They're the type of people who relish change and thrive on new experiences.

Some jobs are basically boring, but any job can become boring when you do it over and over again, day after day, year after year. In many companies, jobs are enriched to minimize boredom. As pointed out in Chapter 16, by adding new functions and combining several simple tasks into a more challenging total activity, jobs can be made less boring.

Some additional ways to prevent jobs from becoming boring include the following:

- ◆ Reexamine all routine work that your group performs. Encourage all people who perform the work to suggest ways of making it more interesting.

- ◆ Switch things around. People performing routine work often get into a rut. They start out every day performing phase one, and then go to phase two and three, and so on. Unless it's essential that work be done in a predetermined order, suggest that they change the pattern. Start one day with phase six, and then go to phase three or seven or one. Breaking the routine alleviates boredom.

- ◆ Cross-train staff members to be able to perform a variety of jobs, so that they can move from one type of work to another.

- ◆ Encourage members to help associates—particularly new staff members—by becoming mentors to them.

A Highly Politicized Workplace

People also cite excessive workplace "politics" as a reason for leaving. Several surveys taken over the past year indicated that the level of trust in their management had deteriorated over the past two years; and that office politics and employee tensions had increased. The result, many claimed, is an environment less conducive to good work and good working relationships. This is a startling statistic and one that suggests any number of troubling trends.

Company politics has always been a factor contributing to high employee turnover, particularly in larger organizations where there is an ongoing rivalry among departments for higher budgets, better assignments, and favored positions. This is aggravated by competition for promotion, advancement, and control within the employee ranks.

> **Stop! Look! Listen!**
>
> Some executives encourage competition among employees on the mistaken notion that it will motivate each of the competitors for higher positions to be more creative and productive. Sometimes this does happen, but often the creativity is channeled into seeking ways to discredit rivals rather than promoting what is best for the company.

A few years ago the CEO of a major manufacturing company was nearing retirement and two of his senior vice presidents were under consideration to succeed him. The rivalry between them degenerated into a bitter conflict. Each man had his set of backers, who knew that if their man were selected, they would personally benefit by getting more power, status, and financial reward. The two years preceding the decision were fraught with rancor, "dirty tricks," and even sabotage. When one of the competitors was finally chosen, the unsuccessful candidate and several of his key supporters resigned. It took years for the company to recover.

Most company politics isn't as traumatic as this, but petty politics destroys morale, reduces productivity, and is a significant contributor to the loss of highly competent people, who may not be politically astute.

A More Lucrative Compensation Package

People have assumed for eons that the number one reason good people leave good firms is to accept a better compensation-related package. This is the case in a significant percentage of instances. As pointed out in Chapter 17, money is a motivator for many people, and people do leave for a better deal, especially when the package contains a large signing bonus and plenty of stock options. It's often just too much to resist.

Of course, to keep good people in your firm, the compensation package must be, at the least, in line with those of other companies in your industry and community. However, just paying more than others won't necessarily result in lower turnover. Money is important, but unless the corporate culture meets the needs of employees, money alone is unlikely to keep them from leaving.

Feeling Used Or "Exploited"

People who feel "used" or exploited by their companies don't hesitate to leave when the opportunity arises. In many cases, this feeling had developed after a downsizing, or other efforts to reduce costs or reassign work. A common complaint among employees is that they feel too much is being asked of them, and that work isn't being distributed in a fair and equitable way. According to one outstanding supervisor with more than 25 years of service at the same company, "Extra work just always seemed to gravitate toward those with a reputation for efficiency and an ability to get things done. It started to seem as though the more you did the more the company expected. I just got tired of making twice the effort as the other guy."

Sally's experience exemplifies another form of exploitation. She had been an auditor for a retail chain for six years and had built up a reputation for her ability to pinpoint errors in sales reports. She commented, "I just have one of those minds that focus on figures and when I scan a report, mistakes seem to just pop up. Twice during the last two years I worked there, I was by-passed for a promotion. When I asked why, I was told I was too valuable as an auditor. I told them that superiority in my present job should warrant a promotion, but the company ignored it. When it happened a third time, I quit."

Concern About the Future of the Firm

In addition to losing faith in one or more bosses, another frequent reason good people give for leaving their jobs is a declining faith in the performance and viability of the firm itself. This was particularly prevalent in a high percentage of dot.coms and other high-risk, new economy ventures when the dot.com boom collapsed. Many departing employees said that although they often liked the people they were working with and the nature of the work they were doing, these considerations were tempered by the doubts they had about the "survivability" of the firm. Interestingly, a majority of those involved in the *riskiest* situations (often a dot-com in dire need of capitalization) said a kind of transient mentality seemed to actually impart itself on the corporate culture.

A similar situation occurs when a company announces that it is closing a plant or even going out of business. Quite often, it's essential that they maintain a workforce to cover work in progress and fill customers' orders during the final stages. How can they retain workers who feel they should be out looking for new jobs and preparing for the future?

Many companies faced with this situation offer bonuses to workers who remain with the company until they are no longer needed. This works if the employee feels that getting the extra money makes up for the extra time it may take to find a new job. However, when jobs are scarce in the community or in the industry, many people choose to take what's available immediately rather than risk not getting a job later on.

When a major aircraft manufacturer in California acquired a former competitor in New York, they planned to close a good portion of the New York facility. It would take from six to nine months to accomplish this and they needed many key workers to remain for that period. Those workers who were asked to stay were given bonuses, plus promises of jobs in the California plant, if they wished to relocate. For those who chose not to relocate, the company retained an outplacement organization to try to place them with local firms who were willing to wait until they were released and to work with those who hadn't been placed until they found new positions. This resulted in a smooth transition.

Departure or Retirement of a Close Colleague

Although it's seldom mentioned as a leading factor in a decision to change jobs, organizational psychologists have known for a long time that the departure or retirement

Tactical Tools

When a key person leaves the company, counseling of the other members of his or her team by a psychologist or an executive coach may ease the transition and maintain morale and productivity.

of a trusted colleague can result in significant reductions in morale and enthusiasm among those remaining. The retirement or departure of a close colleague can stimulate a kind of grieving process in some people, and even lead to symptoms of depression. In some ways, it's akin to the feelings many people get when a close friend moves to another neighborhood, or, in more extreme cases, when a child goes off to college.

A More Flexible Benefits Package

Another top reason good people leave their jobs has to do with their company-sponsored benefits. As recently as just a few years ago it was very unusual to see a company venturing out too far beyond the standard fare in health and retirement packages. Today, it's not at all unusual to see people being offered all sorts of perks and conveniences specially customized to their individual lifestyles and preferences. As pointed out in Chapter 17, items like flextime, flex benefits, child care allowances, telecommuting, dress-down days, first-class airline travel, and generous stock options are far more common today than ever before.

Companies have recognized the need to get more creative in their packaging of benefits and have been forced to react to a shift in the wishes of workers in much the same way as they'd react to a shift in the wishes of customers.

Now Hear This

Percentages of surveyed "outstanding" employees who listed each item among the top four reasons for their resignations:

Loss of faith in management	74%
Feeling unappreciated	67%
Feeling bored or unchallenged	54%
A highly politicized workplace	50%
A more lucrative compensation package	50%
Feeling used or "exploited"	41%
Concern about the future of the firm	38%
Departure or retirement of a close colleague	30%
A more flexible benefits package	25%

(Source: Survey by The Leadership Capital Group, 2002)

Additional Reasons

In addition to the reasons expressed above, the following complaints were noted in the *separation interviews* conducted by the author for several clients.

◆ **Career stagnation.** Studies over the past few years have verified that most employees today don't expect to stay with the same company all of their lives. They'll change jobs if they feel it will help them meet their career goals.

Words to Work By

Separation interviews, also called exit interviews, are designed to probe for the real reasons people leave a job and to obtain from the employee information about the job or the company that may cause discontent.

It's not always possible for an employee's career goals and a company's needs to be congruent. However, in many cases accommodation can be made to bring them closer together.

Now Hear This

Comprehensive Insurance Co. kept one of its top people matching the employee's career goals with the company's needs.

Richard B. was hired as a trainee when he graduated from New York University in 1996 with a degree in accounting. Over the first few years of his tenure, he acquired experience in several departments, and four years later headed an underwriting team. He took advantage of the company's tuition reimbursement program and in 2001, achieved his MBA with a concentration on information technology. At his annual review that year, he expressed interest in moving into a division of the company in which his newly acquired training could be used. His boss pointed out that he was scheduled for a promotion in the underwriting department that could lead to a senior management position and persuaded Richard to accept the new job. Although he was successful in this advanced position, he wasn't happy. He planned to begin a search for a job in IT, but first he went to see the human resources manager, with whom he had established a personal friendship.

"Tom," he said, "I really like this company, but my real interest is in information technology. What should I do?" Tom pointed out that the company was planning to establish an e-marketing department. Although they were seeking people already experienced in that field, Tom persuaded the new department's manager to see Richard. The result: a transfer to the new department, where Richard has already contributed to its early successes.

Tactical Tools

Learn the career goals of your staff members and find ways to help them meet them in your company.

◆ **Unreasonable working hours.** Employees are often required to work longer hours than they really want to work. Sure, there are many workers who seek the opportunity to earn overtime pay, but others would prefer to put in fewer hours. And, when the employee is in a job category that doesn't mandate overtime pay, there is usually no added compensation for the extra hours.

Adding additional staff so overtime isn't needed, or making all overtime voluntary, are ideal solutions, but unfortunately they aren't always practical. Although not required by law to pay exempt workers for overtime work, some companies do pay them overtime bonuses. This often alleviates the objections to working the added hours, but it is expensive. Often, better planning and more efficient techniques can help overcome this problem.

◆ **Unpleasant working environment.** There's no question that a pleasant working environment is conducive to high morale and better productivity. But let's be realistic. There are many work places that by their very nature are dirty, noisy, or reek with unpleasant odors. Some of this may be alleviated. Dirty spaces can be spruced up by better waste control, a new paint job, or other forms of "beautification." Soundproofing or providing ear protectors such as those worn by workers in airports can sometimes reduce noise. Some chemical companies have found ways to minimize the bad odors that emanate from their processes.

A large financial institution, raised the morale of its staff (and reduced turnover) by replacing the traditional cubicles, which many employees considered like jail cells, with work stations in which several people were grouped as teams and the spaces separated by planters.

◆ **Lack of "state of the art" equipment.** A significant number of the employees complaints in the exit interviews concerned a company's use of inefficient or even obsolete equipment, such as outdated computers, laboratory equipment that was purchased more than 20 years ago, or manual personnel files instead of computerized systems to maintain employee records.

True, some workers are so accustomed to working "the old way," that they rebel at installing new equipment; but your most effective employees insist that they be provided with the best equipment available so they can keep at the cutting edge of their professions.

◆ **Bureaucratic bog down.** "It took weeks to get a decision. I had to go to three committees before I could even present my programs to management." Organizational red tape plagues many companies. Many successful organizations have reduced red tape by evaluating and redesigning their policies and procedures. Top people want results, and you won't keep them if bureaucratic stalling frustrates them.

◆ **Personal work preferences.** If an employee can work in the manner with which he or she is most comfortable, that person will be more productive. Some people prefer to work in collaborative teams; others prefer to be given specific directions; still others want the autonomy that goes with working alone. It's not possible to please everyone, but it pays to learn about the work-style preferences of employees and, where possible, to place them accordingly.

◆ **A bossy boss.** Over and over again in the exit interviews and in informal discussions with employees, people cited their boss as the reason for leaving. Even the word "boss" has a negative connotation. The adjective "bossy" is defined as "commanding, domineering, or overbearing." Sure, there are people who prefer to work for a boss who'll tell them what to do and how to do it, but most creative and productive people resent dominance and rebel against it.

◆ **Tolerating mediocre performance.** Employees also often complain about bosses who tolerate mediocre performance. Good, diligent workers resent co-workers who don't pull their own weight. When two top producers left the Brooklyn Distribution Center, an industrial tools wholesaler, last year, I conducted several exit interviews. One woman commented that she took her job seriously and put in long hours and produced over and above what was required. There were other workers in the department who put out minimum effort. In order to meet the department's quota, she had to work even harder to make up for what the slackers were not doing. When she complained to the department head, he shrugged it off with "That's the best they can do."

Another worker told a similar story. She went out of her way to produce quality work, even to the point of redoing sloppy work done by co-workers. She even volunteered to help them become more efficient, but was not supported by the department head. So long as everybody showed up for work each day, he was satisfied.

CAUTION

Stop! Look! Listen!

It's nice to be liked, but if your popularity is based on accepting mediocre work, the marginal workers will love you, but your best people will resent it and morale and productivity will suffer.

Preventive Maintenance

Supervisors and team leaders should make retaining top-level employees a high priority. It may take months or even years to recover from the loss of a key employee. Here are some suggestions:

- **Be alert.** If you wait until the dissatisfaction becomes overt, you've waited too long. You must know your staff members well enough to sense problems before they are expressed and take action to resolve them.

- **Re-recruit your best associates.** These people are the cornerstone of your team. Don't take them for granted. Make them feel important. Make a point to resell them on the company, the department, and their job. Spend as much time and effort on this as you would in recruiting a new staff member.

- **Incorporate your employees into the organizational culture.** Make them feel that they are an integral part of the company by giving them opportunity to express their ideas, to participate in decisions affecting their work and most importantly, build up their emotional commitment to their jobs.

The Least You Need to Know

- To reduce loss of key people, identify specific problems that an employee may have that might lead to voluntary separation and take steps to alleviate them.

- One major reason good people give for leaving their jobs is a sense that their efforts and contributions are not appreciated enough.

- Boredom and a sense of having "stagnated" at work is another major reason good people give for resigning.

- The compensation package must be, at the least, in line with those of other companies in your industry and community if you want to attract and retain good people.

- Most employees today don't expect to stay with the same company all of their lives. They'll change jobs if they feel it will help them meet their career goals.

- Employers need to focus on building relationships with their workers so these employees feel truly loyal to their organization and believe they are a valued part of the enterprise.

Part 6

Dealing With Employee Problems on the Job

You have a good group in place, and all its members are carrying their weight—well, maybe not everyone. You know that some of your co-workers can do better. They're meeting their performance standards, but just barely. Performance review time is approaching, so here's your chance to shape them up. There's Burt, who seems to be on the verge of burnout; Ellen, who is so sensitive you're afraid to correct her errors; Stacey, who's always finding something to gripe about; and then there's that new pro-grammer, whom you suspect has a drinking problem. To keep your team functioning effectively, you need to counsel and help them.

This part of the book provides tips and techniques to help you overcome these challenges and maintain a top performing team.

Chapter 20

Making Performance Reviews More Meaningful

In This Chapter

- ◆ Setting performance standards
- ◆ Completing a formal performance appraisal
- ◆ Deciding whether to measure by traits or by results
- ◆ Conducting effective appraisal interviews
- ◆ When your performance is evaluated

"How am I doing?" you ask your boss. Just as you want to know what your bosses think of your work, your staff members are concerned about your opinion of their work. Most companies have periodic (usually annual) employee appraisals, but supervisors shouldn't wait for this formal review. Between appraisal sessions, you should talk to your associates regularly about their performance and make it an ongoing part of your coaching.

This chapter discusses how to set performance standards that are meaningful to your employees and describes some of the techniques for measuring performance. You'll also learn how to conduct a formal appraisal interview.

Setting Performance Standards

All employees should know just what's expected of them on the job. Many companies develop and incorporate *performance standards* at the time they create a job description. In other companies, the job evolves as standards are established.

Words to Work By

Performance standards define the results that are expected from a person performing a job. For performance standards to be meaningful, all people doing that job should know and accept these standards. Employee participation in the establishment of performance standards is one way to ensure this understanding.

In routine jobs, the key factors of performance standards involve quantity (how much should be produced per hour or per day) and quality (what level of quality is acceptable). As jobs become more complex, these standards aren't an adequate way to measure performance. Ideas and innovations that are conceived in creative jobs cannot be quantified, and quality may be difficult to measure. This situation doesn't mean that you can't have performance standards for these jobs, but it does require a different approach, such as the results-oriented evaluation system described later in this chapter.

Establishing Criteria for Performance Standards

Performance standards are usually based on the experiences of satisfactory workers who have done that type of work over a length of time. Whether the standards cover quality or quantity of the work, or other aspects of the job, they should meet these criteria:

◆ **Be specific.** Every person doing a job should know exactly what he or she is expected to do.

◆ **Be measurable.** The company should have a touchstone against which performance can be measured. Measuring performance is easy when a standard is quantifiable; it's more difficult (but not impossible) when it isn't quantifiable. When a numerical measurement isn't feasible, some of the criteria may include timely completion of assignments, introduction of new concepts, or contribution to team activities.

◆ **Be realistic.** Unless standards are attainable, people consider them unfair and resist working toward them.

Let Them Evaluate Their Own Performance

When all team members know what's expected of them and against which standards they'll be measured, self-evaluation becomes almost automatic. Employees don't have to wait for their team leader to tell them that they're below standard or behind schedule—they see that for themselves and can take corrective action immediately.

Self-evaluation makes a supervisor's job easier. Like a good coach, he helps keep the staff aware of the standards and provides support and encouragement to stay on target.

Now Hear This _____

W. Edwards Deming, the father of the quality movement, was strongly opposed to performance reviews. He believed that, in most companies, performance was equated with quantity at the sacrifice of quality. This was the case for a long time, but quality standards today are given equal or greater weight in evaluations.

Conducting Formal Performance Appraisals

Even if team members know the performance standards and can measure their own performance, and if team leaders reinforce this process with ongoing discussions about performance, there's still a need for formal appraisals. Most formal appraisals are conducted annually. Many managers add an informal appraisal semiannually or quarterly as a means of keeping employees aware of their progress.

This list describes some of the reasons that formal appraisals are important:

◆ They provide a framework for discussing a team member's overall work record. The team leader can use this meeting to recognize an employee for past successes and provide suggestions for even greater contributions.

◆ They become more objective and enable team leaders to compare all members of the team against the same criteria.

◆ They provide helpful data for determining what type of additional training team members need.

◆ In many companies, they're the primary factor in determining salary increases and bonuses.

Tactical Tools

When you rate your team members, don't be overly influenced by their most recent behavior. Employees know that it's rating time, and they'll be as good as a kid just before Christmas. Keep a running log of their behavior during the entire year.

♦ Their formality causes them to be taken more seriously than informal comments about performance.

♦ They can be used as a vehicle for goal setting, career planning, and personal growth.

Examining the Downside of Formal Appraisals

Formal appraisals have some inherent problems, a few of which are ...

♦ They can be stressful for both supervisors and staff members.

♦ They make some supervisors so uncomfortable about making associates unhappy that they overrate their performance.

♦ Many are inadequate, cumbersome, or poorly designed, which creates more problems than solutions.

♦ In some appraisals, good workers are underrated because their supervisors are afraid that staff members might become competitors.

Now Hear This

At Dun & Bradstreet seminars, supervisors were asked what they thought were the worst aspects of their jobs. The worst was having to fire people; a close second was conducting formal appraisal interviews.

A properly managed performance appraisal can be a highly stimulating experience for both team member and team leader. To make it most effective, don't treat it as a confrontation. Treat it instead as a meaningful two-way exchange that leads to an employee's commitment to reach out for improvement and set and implement goals for the coming year that will lead to a more productive and satisfying work experience.

Choosing the Best System for You

Your company may have in place an appraisal system that you are obligated to use. It may be helpful, however, to use aspects of other appraisal methods in addition to the method formally requested by your company. Many companies use an appraisal system that combines aspects of all the methods described in the following sections.

Check the Box: The Trait-Based System

You've been rated by them. You've used them to rate others. The most common evaluation system is the "trait" format, in which a series of traits are listed in the left margin, and each is measured against a scale from unsatisfactory to excellent (see the following figure):

Trait-Based Appraisal Worksheet					
	Excellent (5 points)	Very Good (4 points)	Average (3 points)	Needs Improvement (2 points)	Unsatisfactory (1 point)
Quantity of work					
Job knowledge					
Dependability					
Ability to take instruction					
Initiative					
Creativity					
Cooperation					

This system seems on the surface to be simple to administer and easy to understand, but it's loaded with problems:

◆ **A central tendency.** Rather than carefully evaluate each trait, it's much easier to rate a trait as average or close to average (the central rating).

◆ **The "halo effect."** Some managers believe that one trait is so impressive they rate all traits highly. Its opposite is the "pitchfork effect."

◆ **Personal biases.** Managers are human, and humans have personal biases for and against other people. These biases can influence any type of rating, but the trait system is particularly vulnerable.

◆ **Latest behavior.** It's easy to remember what employees have done during the past few months, but managers tend to forget what they did in the first part of a rating period.

Some companies encourage the use of the bell curve in rating employees. The bell curve concept is based on the assumption that in a large population most people will fall in the average (middle) category, a smaller number in each of the poorer-than-average and better-than-average categories, and a still smaller number in the highest and lowest categories.

The trouble with the use of the bell curve in employee evaluations is that small groups are unlikely to have this type of distribution—and it may work unfairly against top- and bottom-level workers.

Suppose Carla is a genius who works in a department in which everyone is a genius. Carla is the lowest level genius in the group, however. In a bell curve for that group, she would be rated as "poor." In any other group, she probably would be rated "superior." Or suppose that Harold's work is barely satisfactory but that his entire group is performing below average. Compared with the other employees, he's the best. If you use a bell curve, you have to rate him "superior."

Making the Trait-Based System More Effective

The best way to overcome deficiencies in the trait system is to replace them with a results-oriented system (described later in this chapter). If your company does use the trait method, here are some suggestions to help make it more equitable:

- ◆ **Clarify standards.** Every manager and team leader should be carefully informed about the meaning of each category and the definition of each trait. Understanding quantity and quality is relatively easy. But what is "dependability"? How do you measure "initiative," "creativity," and other intangibles?

  By using discussions, role-playing, and case studies, you can develop standards that everyone understands and uses.

- ◆ **Establish criteria for ratings.** It's easy to identify superior and unsatisfactory employees, but it's tougher to differentiate among people in the middle three categories.

- ◆ **Keep a running log of associates' performance throughout the year.** You don't have to record average performance, but do note anything special that each member has accomplished or failed to accomplish. Some notes on the positive side may say, for example, "Exceeded quota by 20 percent," "Completed project two days before deadline," or "Made a suggestion that cut by a third the time required for a job." Notes on the negative side might say, "Had to redo report because of major errors" or "Was reprimanded for extending lunch hour three days this month."

- ◆ **Make an effort to be aware of your personal biases and to overcome them.**

- ◆ **Have specific examples of exceptional and unsatisfactory performance and behavior to back up your evaluation.**

Measuring Results: A More Meaningful System

Rather than rate team members on the basis of an opinion about their various traits, in this appraisal system the people who do the rating focus on the attainment of specific results. Results-based ratings can be used in any situation in which results are measurable. This system is obviously easier to use when quantifiable factors are involved (such as sales volume or production units), but it's also useful in such intangible areas as attaining specific goals in management development, reaching personal goals, and making collaborative efforts.

In a results-oriented evaluation system, the people who do the evaluating don't have to rely on their judgment of abstract traits, but instead can focus on what was expected from team members and how closely they met these expectations. The expectations are agreed on at the beginning of a period, and measured at the end of that period. At that time, new goals are developed to be measured at the end of the following period.

Here's how this system works:

♦ For every job, the team leader and the people doing the job agree on the *KRAs (key results areas)* for that job. Employees must accomplish results in these areas to meet the team's goals.

♦ The team leader and the team member establish the results that are expected from the employee in each of the KRAs.

Words to Work By

A **KRA (key results area)** is an aspect of a job on which employees must concentrate time and attention to ensure that they achieve the goals for that job.

♦ During a formal review, the results an employee attained in each of the KRAs are measured against what was expected.

♦ A numerical scale is used in some organizations to rate employees on how closely they come to reaching their goals. In others, no grades are given. Instead, a narrative report is compiled to summarize what has been accomplished and to comment on its significance.

♦ Some companies request that staff members submit monthly progress reports compiled in the same format as the annual review. This technique enables both the staff member and the leader to monitor progress. By studying the monthly reports, the annual review is more easily compiled and discussed.

Following is a sample form for a results-oriented evaluation.

Results-Oriented Evaluation

Team member: _____

Date: _____

Job: Tax accountant

Results expected	**Results achieved**
Key Results Area 1	Prepare federal, state, and local tax returns on a timely basis
_____	_____
_____	_____
_____	_____
Key Results Area 2	Advise management of changes in and administrative interpretations of tax laws
_____	_____
_____	_____
_____	_____
Key Results Area 3	Study management policies and report on their tax ramifications
_____	_____
_____	_____
_____	_____

Pros and Cons of Appraisal by Results

Although results-oriented evaluations can be more meaningful than trait systems, they're not free of problems:

◆ **Set reasonable goals.** Unless you and the team member take an objective view of what he or she should accomplish, you may set unrealistic expectations. The danger is that you may set standards so low employees attain them with little effort, or that you set them so high employees have little chance of attaining them.

◆ **Not all goals are equal in importance.** You should consider the value of the expectation in comparison to the overall goals of the team and the company.

◆ **Intangible goals are more difficult to measure.** Even intangible factors, however, have tangible phases that can be identified. For example, rather than indicate that a goal is to "improve employee morale," specify it in terms that are measurable, such as "reduce turnover by X percent" or "decrease the number of grievances by Y percent." Rather than state a goal as "Develop a new health insurance plan," break it into phases, such as "Complete study of proposed plans by October 31" or "Submit recommendations by December 15."

Collaborative Evaluation

To make the results-oriented format even more meaningful, use the *joint supervisor/ associate* model. If performance evaluations are based on the arbitrary opinion of a supervisor, they serve only part of the real value that reviews can provide. Such a model provides a formal evaluation for the purpose of raises or promotions and enables you to tell employees how to improve performance, but it doesn't involve team or staff members in the process.

A joint review can do this more effectively. The joint supervisor/associate review is particularly useful for evaluating creative jobs such as research and development or jobs in the arts, where teams are most effective. Team members and their leaders collaborate on the standards that are expected, build in the flexibility to accommodate the special circumstances under which they are working, and agree on the criteria that will be used in evaluating the work.

The team member and team leader then complete the evaluation form. The KRAs and the "results expected" items are agreed on in advance (usually during the preceding review). The team member and the leader independently indicate the "results achieved."

> **Words to Work By**
>
> In a **joint supervisor/ associate** evaluation, sometimes called a collaborative evaluation, a staff member evaluates his or her own performance, and the team leader or supervisor also evaluates it. The final report results from a collaborative discussion between the two of them.

> **Stop! Look! Listen!**
>
> If a team or staff member in evaluating his or her own performance, gives themselves a significantly higher rating than you do, be particularly sensitive in the discussion so that it doesn't degenerate into a confrontation. Use specific examples rather than statements of opinion to make your points.

At the appraisal interview (described later in this chapter), the supervisor or team leader and the associate discuss the comments on the form. During this session, the appraisal begins to move from a report card to a plan of action for growth and team-work.

Many companies that don't use joint evaluations ask employees to evaluate their own performance before meeting with their supervisor or team leader. They complete a copy of the appraisal form. At the meeting, similarities and differences in the ratings are discussed, and adjustments in the ratings resulting from the discussions are reflected in the formal evaluation that's filed with the human resources department. If the employee still disagrees with the evaluation after the discussion, in some companies a rebuttal may be written, which is filed along with the supervisor's report.

Benefits of the Collaborative Review

A collaborative review of performance has the following advantages:

- Gives staff members the opportunity to make a formal appraisal of their own work in a systematic manner.

- Allows for a thorough discussion between the supervisor or team leader and the associate about their different perceptions of expectations and results achieved.

- Enables a supervisor or team leader to see areas in which he or she may have failed in developing an associate's potential.

- Helps the associate and the team leader or supervisor to identify problem areas that might easily be overlooked on a day-to-day basis.

- Pinpoints areas in which employees need improvement and in which they need additional training.

- Gives an opportunity to discuss areas in which an associate can become even more valuable to his or her group.

- Provides a base on which realistic goals for the next period can be discussed and mutually agreed on.

- Helps each person measure performance and progress against his or her own career goals and serves as a guide in determining the appropriate steps to move forward.

The Nuts and Bolts of the Appraisal Interview

Regardless of whether you have evaluated employees by the trait method or the results method and whether they have made a self-evaluation, the most important facet of the appraisal process is the face-to-face discussion of the evaluation.

To make this interview most valuable, you should carefully plan it and systematically carry it out.

Prepare and Plan Your Approach

Before sitting down with an associate to discuss a performance appraisal, study the evaluation. Make a list of all aspects you want to discuss—not just those that need improvement but also those in which the employee did good work. Study previous appraisals, and note improvements that have been made since the preceding one. Prepare the questions you want to ask about past actions, steps to be taken for improvement, future goals, and how the person plans to reach them.

Reflect on your experiences in dealing with this person. Have there been any special behavioral problems? Any problems that have affected his work? Any strong, positive assets you want to nurture? Any special points you want to discuss?

Discussing Performance with Your Associate

After you have made the employee feel at ease, point out the reasons for the appraisal meeting. Say something like this: "As you know, each year we review what has been accomplished during the preceding year and discuss what we can do together in the following year."

Point out the areas of the job in which that person has met standards, and particularly the areas in which they have done especially good work. By giving specific examples of these achievements, you let the associate know you're aware of his or her positive qualities.

Because salary adjustment is usually based on overall performance, employees should be made aware that your praise of one or a few accomplishments isn't a guarantee of a raise. You might say, "The way you handled the *XYZ* account shows that you're making great progress. Keep up the good work." By saying it this way, you show that you're aware of the progress, but that there's still a ways to go. Rather than interpret the praise as "Wow, I'm good—this means a big raise," the reaction is, "I'm doing fine, but I'm not there yet."

Words to Work By

The word **interview** is derived from **inter** (which means "between") and **view** (which means "look"). An interview is a "look" at a situation "between" the parties involved. An appraisal interview isn't the supervisor telling the associate, "This is what you did well, and that is what you did poorly"—it's a two-way discussion about performance.

Encourage associates to comment. Listen attentively, then discuss the aspects of performance or behavior that didn't meet standards. Be specific. It's much more effective to give a few examples where expectations haven't been met than to just say, "Your work isn't up to snuff." Ask the employee what he or she plans to do to meet standards and how you can assist him or her to achieve them.

If employees' problems aren't related to performance, but rather to behavior, provide examples: "During the past year, I've spoken to you several times about your tardiness. You're a good worker, and your opportunities in this company would be much greater if you could only get here on time." Try to obtain a commitment and a plan of action to overcome this fault.

Making Criticism Constructive

Many managers find it difficult to give criticism. Here are some guidelines to help deal with this sensitive area:

- ◆ Begin with a positive approach by asking the staff member to assess the successes achieved and the steps taken to achieve those successes.

Tactical Tools

Most people are uneasy about appraisal interviews. Allay these fears by making some positive comments when you schedule an interview. You can say, "I've scheduled your appraisal interview for 2:30 on Wednesday. I want to talk about your accomplishments this year and discuss our plans for next year."

- ◆ Encourage her to talk about projects that didn't succeed and what caused the failure.

- ◆ Ask what might have been done to avoid the mistakes made.

- ◆ Contribute your suggestions about how the matter could have been done more effectively.

- ◆ Ask what training or help you can provide.

- ◆ Agree on the steps the associate will take to ensure better performance on future assignments.

Soliciting Employee's Comments

Throughout interviews, encourage associates to comment on or make suggestions about every aspect of the review. Of course, they may have excuses or alibis. Listen empathetically—you may learn about some factors that have inhibited optimum performance. There may be factors within the company that keep an employee from performing adequately. For example, you may find out that someone has an older-model computer that has started "crashing" several times a day ever since the company upgraded software. You may not have been aware that this recurring problem was affecting the person's job performance. With this new information, you can take steps to correct the situation by budgeting for a computer upgrade. By giving the person the opportunity to express his or her reasons or arguments, you can take steps to correct the situation.

Even if the excuses are superficial and self-serving, allowing them to be voiced clears the air. Then you both can be prepared to face real situations and come up with viable ideas.

There are instances when the poor performance may be the result of serious personal problems such as a dying parent, a sick child, marital discord, or psychological disturbances. In such cases, the supervisor may tolerate a short-term decline in productivity. If it persists, refer the employee to the company's employee assistance program, if available (see Chapter 22) or suggest professional assistance.

Reviewing Last Year's Goals and Setting Next Year's

If the preceding year's goals were met, congratulate the associate. Talk about the steps that were taken to meet goals and what was learned from this experience. If not all the goals were met, discuss any problems and the steps that might now be taken to overcome them.

An appraisal interview isn't just a review of the past—it's also a plan for the future. Ask the question, "What do you want to accomplish during the next 12 months?" The answer might include production goals, quality improvement, behavioral changes, and plans for advancement.

In addition to goals directly related to work, a staff members' future plans may include personal career development plans (such as obtaining additional training on the job or in school), participation in trade or professional societies, and other off-job activities that can enhance a career. Be supportive of these types of goals, and point out what your company can do to help, such as providing tuition reimbursement. However, don't make promises for advancement or career growth you can't deliver.

Have staff members write down each of their goals, and indicate next to them what they plan to do to achieve them. Give one copy to the staff member, and keep one with the performance appraisal form. You can use it as part of the appraisal interview the following year.

Conclude with a Summary and an Action Plan

At the end of an interview, ask the associate to summarize the discussion. Make sure that the person fully understands the positive and negative aspects of her performance and behavior, plans and goals for the next review period, and any other pertinent matters. Keep a written record of these points.

In many companies, employees who disagree with an evaluation are given the opportunity to write a rebuttal to be attached to the appraisal. When salary adjustments are based on ratings, some organizations provide a procedure for appealing a review.

End the interview on a positive note, by saying, "Overall, you've made good progress this year. I'm confident that you'll continue to do good work." On the other hand, if the overall work has not been satisfactory, encourage the employee to improve by noting what steps you will take to help him or her get back on track.

In the case of workers who have failed to make progress over time and this review is a prelude to termination, explain what they must do to retain the job, and the specified time frame. More on how to terminate for poor performance can be found in Chapter 24.

Recording the Review

In most companies the appraisal form is sent to the human resources department to be placed in the employee's personnel file. Some companies require that a copy be sent to the next level of management—the person to whom the supervisor or team leader reports.

Even if it's not a formal practice in your company, it's a good idea to give a copy of the appraisal to the staff member. It serves as a reminder of what was discussed at the appraisal interview and can be referred to during the year. And, as mentioned, if it includes goals the employee and you have agreed on for the year, the employee can reread it from time to time to keep motivated.

Ten Points to Remember When Reviewing Performance

1. Know exactly what you want to achieve. Let your employees know what is expected of them.

2. Keep a record of employee performance from which to cite specific examples.

3. Discuss the written evaluation with the employee.

4. Listen to the employee's comments, then ask questions to stimulate thought.

5. Focus on the individual. Do not compare him with other members of the group.

6. Show that you care about employees' performance and their careers.

7. Reinforce good behavior. Be specific in your criticism. Give examples from their performance record. Ask them how they can do even better. Add your own suggestions.

8. Focus on the behavior, not on the person.

9. Don't be afraid to give honest criticism. Most employees want to know where they stand and how to improve.

10. Help each person to set personal goals that are congruent with the goals of the group—and the company—and to develop a plan of action to reach those goals.

> **Tactical Tools**
>
> In the evaluation interview, concentrate on the work, not on the person. Never say, "You were no good." Say instead, "Your work didn't meet standards."

The 360° Assessment

Multilevel assessments have become an increasingly popular approach, used to identify how a manager is viewed by his or her bosses, peers, subordinates, and even outsiders (for example, vendors and customers). Usually referred to as 360° assessments, such reviews have been adopted by companies like AT&T, IBM, and other Fortune 500 corporations.

People don't see themselves as others see them. We perceive our actions as rational, our ideas as solid, our decisions as meaningful. Traditionally, performance is evaluated only by one's own manager. This does give us insight into how our work is perceived by that person, but she isn't the only person with whom we interact.

Even more complex is the evaluation of senior managers, who frequently aren't evaluated at all. When these executives are assessed by peers and subordinates, they may learn things about their management style that they weren't aware of. Many are shocked to find out how people perceive them and, as a result, take steps to change their management styles.

Despite the advantages of multilevel assessments, there are also potential drawbacks. Feedback can hurt. Evaluators aren't always nice or positive. Some people see their role as assessor as an opportunity to criticize others' behavior on the job.

Words to Work By

Multilevel or 360° assessments identify how a manager's bosses, peers, subordinates, and even outsiders such as vendors and customers view him or her.

Another flaw concerns conflicting opinions. Who decides who is right? Or what if an appraisal is biased? If the evaluator does not like the person being evaluated, the responses might be skewed negatively; if the person being evaluated is a friend, the evaluation might be skewed positively. Often, people rating senior executives fear the consequences of being completely truthful.

In order to ensure that the 360° assessment has a better chance of producing a change, follow these suggestions:

♦ Keep the appraisals anonymous and confidential.

♦ To have sufficient knowledge of the person being rated, the appraisers should have worked with the person being appraised for at least six months.

♦ Appraisers should give written comments as well as numerical ratings. This enables their evaluations to be more specific and meaningful.

♦ To avoid "survey fatigue," don't use 360° assessments on too many employees at one time.

Turning the Tables: When Your Boss Reviews Your Performance

Performance reviews aren't limited to you assessing your staff. Your boss also evaluates your own performance. Now it's you sitting in the hot seat.

Even though you may have undergone many such reviews in your career, it's always a bit disquieting to be in that spot. You feel like a kid sitting in the school principal's office. You may even feel jittery and ill at ease, even though you have a good relationship with your boss. Maybe you're scared, especially if you and your boss have a shaky relationship.

Most people have these kinds of reactions even when they know they have done good work. It's human nature to fear such an important meeting. So much depends on it:

your immediate future; whether or not you'll get a raise; the opinion your boss has of your potential. And for sure the boss will have something negative to say.

Here are some tips to help you handle this situation:

- ◆ **Review your own performance.** Whether or not your company requires employees to make self-evaluations, do it. Take a blank copy of the review form and fill it out. This will allow you to think about your performance in the same way your boss does.

- ◆ **List your accomplishments.** Include all the special things you did over the past year to contribute to the success of the department. Give specifics, such as how much you exceeded quotas, the amount of money one of your suggestions saved the company, tough problems you solved, and so on.

- ◆ **Consider your deficiencies.** None of us is perfect. You probably did some things that didn't work out and have areas in which you know you can do better. Your supervisor is likely to bring this up at the review. Instead of thinking up excuses, point out what you have already done or what you plan to do to improve your skills in those areas.

- ◆ **At the interview, listen attentively.** Do not interrupt except to ask clarifying questions. Under no circumstances should you disagree or try to rebut a point. Let the supervisor finish before you make any comments.

- ◆ **Be constructive.** Now is the chance to make your rebuttal. If you have carefully prepared a list of accomplishments and are cognizant of your deficiencies, you are ready to make your points. Start by thanking your supervisor for his or her support over the past year, then say: "I understand what you have told me and I appreciate your frankness. However, there are certain accomplishments of which I am particularly proud and for which you complimented me at the time, which you may not have taken into consideration in the review." Then enumerate the items. If the supervisor focused on some of your deficiencies, don't make excuses for them. Instead, talk about what you are doing to overcome them. Suggest that before the evaluation is made final, these be considered.

- ◆ **Set goals for the future.** If you had set goals for this year at last year's review, discuss how close you came to reaching them. If, during the year, they changed, discuss the circumstances. Now, discuss your goals for the ensuing year. Get your boss's agreement that these are worthwhile goals and then commit yourself to attain them.

The Least You Need to Know

- For every job, set performance standards that are clearly understood and accepted by those who will perform the job.

- When people know what is expected of them, they can monitor their own performance on an ongoing basis.

- If you use the trait method to evaluate your staff members, be careful to avoid the dangers of central tendency, the halo and pitchfork effects, personal biases, and an emphasis on most recent behavior.

- Results-oriented evaluations measure actual performance against predetermined expectations.

- A joint supervisor/associate evaluation enables both parties to evaluate performance and agree on what can be done to reinforce strengths and build up weaknesses.

- An evaluation interview should be an interchange between you and your staff member in which you openly discuss accomplishments, areas for improvement, and goals established for the next review period.

- Don't fear the performance review. It can be a beneficial and worthwhile experience. You can make it even more valuable to yourself by going into the review prepared to handle it in a constructive manner.

Chapter 21

Dealing With Problem Employees

In This Chapter

- ◆ Helping people who don't like themselves
- ◆ Dealing with sensitive, temperamental, and negative people
- ◆ Avoiding stress and burnout
- ◆ Confronting alcohol and drug abuse problems
- ◆ When the problems are not with your staff, but with peers
- ◆ Dealing with the boss's relatives
- ◆ Violence in the workplace

Your group is made up of people—human beings—who bring to their jobs skills, intelligence, and creativity. But people also have idiosyncrasies, attitudes, moods, and problems—and they bring those things to the job, too. One of the great challenges of being a leader lies in recognizing and dealing with these types of problems so that your department will run smoothly.

Some of the more common problems that supervisors and team leaders must deal with are discussed in this chapter. Among them are helping build up team members' self-confidence so that they'll become better contributors to your team's efforts, overcoming negative thinking, and dealing with sensitive and temperamental people.

You'll also learn how to cope with associates who are under stress and those who burn out. In addition, this chapter explores what can be done if team members have AIDS or are facing alcohol and drug abuse.

Building Up Low Self-Esteem

Most people recognize the importance of *self-esteem.* In one Gallup-Newsweek poll, 89 percent of respondents said that self-esteem was the primary factor that motivated them to work harder to succeed. Sixty-three percent said that spending time and effort to develop self-esteem was a worthwhile endeavor.

> **Words to Work By**
>
> **Self-esteem** refers to the way you feel about yourself—it's based on the perceptions you have about yourself. If you think of yourself as a success, you will be a success; if you think of yourself as second rate, you will always be second rate—unless you change your self-perception. And it *can* be done.

Consider the phrase "developing self-esteem." Many people who have had a low opinion of themselves have been able to overcome it by making a commitment to make a change. Sometimes they seek professional help, but often they do it through self-determination: They rewrite the script on which they base their life. As a leader, you're in a position to help such people develop self-esteem.

People with low self-esteem show it in the way they talk about themselves. They're more likely to complain about their failures than to brag about successes. They rarely express opinions that differ from those of other staff members, and when they do, they preface it with an apology. When pressed to express their thoughts or ideas, they start their answers with, "I'm not sure about this" or "I'm probably wrong, but ...." They never volunteer to lead a discussion, and they take charge of a project only when the leader assigns it, and then they express doubts about their ability to do it properly.

A person's low self-esteem (or worse, self-loathing) unfortunately may have deep psychological roots that stem from childhood. Parents may instill this trait in their children by being overly demanding. For example, if Jason gets a test score of 90 percent and his parents berate him for not getting 100 percent, or if Sarah is a talented pianist but her parents deride her playing because she's not a child prodigy.

Jason and Sarah are likely to write scripts for themselves as failures, doomed always to be inadequate. People whose scripts are based on parental belittlement probably need professional assistance to overcome it.

However, as a manager, you can help by focusing on successes, not on failures. Most people don't loathe themselves, but they may have temporary self-esteem slumps and need bolstering. If they don't deal with those slumps, more serious consequences can occur. Most people don't need professional care; they can do it themselves.

Focusing on Success, Not on Failure

Loss of self-esteem stems from failure. All of us have failures and successes in our jobs and in our lives. By focusing on failure, self-esteem deteriorates. Concentrate instead on the successes you have achieved.

One technique involves keeping a success file (see Chapter 18). Enter in this file any accomplishments you're especially proud of—things for which you've been commended. These things prove that you've succeeded in the past and serve as your assurance that you can succeed again.

Esteem-Building Suggestions

In addition to maintaining success files, you can help associates build self-esteem in the following ways:

♦ Give them positive reinforcement for every achievement, and praise for progress made in their work. Equally important, be positive when they come up with a good idea or make meaningful contributions to team discussions and activities. People with low self-esteem need to be continually reminded that you, the team leader, respect them and have confidence in them.

♦ Give them assignments you know they can handle, and provide added training, coaching, and support to ensure that they'll succeed. The taste of success is a surefire way to build self-esteem.

♦ Suggest that they take courses designed to build self-confidence, such as the Dale Carnegie Course or assertiveness training programs. Provide them with inspirational tapes or books.

> **Tactical Tools**
>
> Keep a success file for your team or group. Enter in it the special achievements of each of the members and of the team or group as a whole. Encourage each associate to keep a personal success log. When things don't go well or when you and any one of them are feeling low, have everyone reread the file.

If, despite these efforts, a person doesn't become more self-confident, professional help may be necessary. Suggest that he see a counselor in your employee assistance program (see Chapter 22).

Dealing with Sensitive Sam, Temperamental Terry, Negative Nell, and Others

You undoubtedly have some of these people in your group. Every team leader or supervisor does. They can make your life miserable or make it an ever-changing challenge. You can't ignore these folks—you have to deal with them, so this section gives you some suggestions.

Sensing the Over-Sensitive

No one likes to be criticized, but most people can accept constructive criticism. Some people resent any criticism, though. Whenever you make even the slightest criticism of their work, they pout and get defensive and accuse you of picking on them.

Be gentle with them. Be diplomatic. Begin by praising the parts of assignments that they have done well. Then make some suggestions about how they can do better in unsatisfactory areas.

Kathy's fear of being criticized has made her overly cautious in all areas of her work. Rather than risk a slight error, she checks, double-checks, and then rechecks everything she does. This process may minimize her exposure to criticism, but it's so time-consuming that it slows down her entire team. Worse, she stalls in making decisions, claiming that she needs more information. Even after she gets the information, she passes the buck to someone else.

If members of your group or team behave as Kathy does, follow these guidelines to help them overcome their fears:

Stop! Look! Listen!

Don't praise sensitive people *only* as a prelude to criticism. They may have low self-esteem and, therefore, need a great deal of positive reinforcement.

- Assure them that, because of their excellent knowledge in their field, their work is usually correct the first time and doesn't have to be checked repeatedly.

- Point out that occasional errors are normal and that they can be caught and corrected later without reflecting on the ability of the person who made the errors.

- If you agree that people need more information before making a decision, guide them toward resources to help them obtain it. If you feel that they have adequate information, insist that they make prompt decisions.

- If associates ask you what to do, tell them that it's their decision and to make it quickly.

In most cases, overly sensitive people have the expertise and do make good decisions. They may need your reassurance to help convert their thinking into action.

Tampering with Temper Tantrums

Terry is a good worker, but from time to time he loses his temper and hollers and screams at his co-workers and even at you. He calms down quickly, but his behavior affects the work of your entire team, and it takes a while to get back to normal performance. You've spoken to Terry about his temper several times, but it hasn't helped.

It isn't easy to work in an environment in which people holler and scream, particularly if you're the target. Because the victims of a tirade may be unable to work at full capacity for several hours afterward, this situation cannot be tolerated.

Here are some suggestions for dealing with someone who has temper tantrums:

- After the person calms down, have a heart-to-heart talk. Point out that you understand that it's not always easy for someone to control his or her temper but that such tantrums aren't acceptable in the workplace.

- If another outburst occurs, send the person out of the room until he or she can calm down. Let the person know that the next offense will lead to disciplinary action.

- Recommend the old adage, "Count to 10 before opening your mouth."

- If you have an employee assistance program (see Chapter 22), suggest that the team member see one of its counselors.

Tactical Tools

If the person you're criticizing begins to cry or throw a tantrum, walk out! Say you'll return after he or she calms down. Wait 10 minutes, then try again. Assure the person that this isn't a personal attack but a means of correcting a situation. *Note:* Don't conduct these types of meetings in your office. It's not a good idea to leave an upset person alone in your office—use a conference room instead.

Negating Negativity

Almost every organization has a Negative Nell or Ned. Whenever you're for something, they're against it. They always have a reason that what you want to accomplish just can't be done. They can tear down your team with pessimism.

Stop! Look! Listen!

In dealing with negative people, acknowledge their arguments and persuade them to work with you to overcome their perceived problems so that the project can move along. Make the person part of the solution rather than an additional problem.

The reasons for an employee's negativity vary. It may stem from some real or perceived past mistreatment by your company. If that's the case, look into the matter. If the person has justifiable reasons for being negative, try to persuade him that the past is past and to look to the future. If misconceptions are involved, try to clear them up.

Negativity is often rooted in long-term personality factors that are beyond the ability of any team leader to overcome. In that case, professional help is necessary.

Let's look at some of the problems negative people cause:

♦ **Resistance to change.** Even people with a positive attitude are reluctant to change. It's comfortable to keep doing things the way they've always done them. Positive thinking people can be persuaded to change by presenting logical arguments. Negative people resist change just for the sake of resisting. No argument ever helps. They often do everything they can to sabotage a situation so that the new methods won't work and they can say, "I told you so."

♦ **Impact on team morale.** Just as one rotten apple can spoil a whole barrel, one negative person can destroy the entire team's morale. Because the negativism spreads from one person to another, it's tough to maintain team spirit under these circumstances.

When you present new ideas to negative people, get them to express their objections openly. Tell them, "You bring up some good points, and I appreciate them. As we move into this new program, let's carefully watch for those problems. We must give this new concept a try. Work with me on it, and together we'll iron out the kinks."

Negative Personalities

Opal exudes negativity. It's not what she says—it's how she acts. She takes any suggestion as a personal affront and takes on any new assignment with such reluctance and annoyance that she turns everyone off.

People such as Opal often don't realize how they come across to others. They probably act this way in their personal lives as well as on the job. They're the type of people who don't get along with their families, have few friends, and are forever the dissenters. Have a heart-to-heart talk with these people to let them know how their attitude affects your team's morale. Amazingly, many negative thinking people have no idea that their behavior is disruptive to others. You might suggest that they enroll in a personal improvement program.

Playing "Gotcha"

Have you ever worked with an associate whose greatest joy in life is to catch other people—especially you—making an error?

People who play this game are trying to show their superiority. Because they usually have no original ideas or constructive suggestions, they get their kicks from catching other people's errors, particularly their boss's. They try to embarrass you and make you uncomfortable. Don't give them that satisfaction. Make a joke about it ("What a blooper!"), or smile and say "Thanks for calling it to my attention before it caused real problems." If Gotchamongers see that you're not riled by their game, they'll stop and try to get their kicks elsewhere.

Working with Unhappy People

There's likely to be at least one unhappy person in your group. We all experience periods when things go wrong at home or on the job—and it affects the way we do our work and how we interact with other staff members. Supervisors should be alert to these situations and take the time to chat with the person. Giving a person the opportunity to talk about a problem often alleviates the tension. Even if the problem isn't solved, it clears the air and enables the associate to function normally.

Some people, however, will always be unhappy about something. They often aren't satisfied with work assignments. Even when you comply with their requests and accommodate their complaints, they're not satisfied. They display their unhappiness by being negative. If someone's request for a change in scheduling a vacation is denied, for example, that person may get angry and let it show both overtly and subtly in his attitude.

Although you can never make everyone happy, you should try to. Rebuilding the morale of people who believe that they've been treated unfairly takes tact and patience. Managers can avoid some unfair situations by making sure—at the time a decision is made—to explain the reasons behind the decision. In the vacation example, you could explain that your company sets up the vacation schedule months in advance and that two other employees are taking their vacations at the same time. Then make it clear that your group can't spare the employee that week. You may even suggest that the unhappy person try to find another staff member who will trade vacation time.

If this technique doesn't satisfy your associate, have a heart-to-heart talk with the person. Point out how constant griping and a negative attitude affect other staff members. Make reassurances that the person is a valuable member of your team and that it's not always possible to get everything we want. Encourage the person to be mature—to accept disappointments and go on with life.

Words to Work By

Dr. Hans Selye defines **distress**, or **bad stress**, as the chronic state of anxiety caused by unremitting pressures of job, personal, or societal problems.

Now Hear This

No matter how much pressure you feel at work, if you could find ways to relax for at least five minutes every hour, you'd be more productive.

—Dr. Joyce Brothers

Addressing Stress and Burnout

All jobs have their share of stress. If they didn't, they would quickly become boring. It's when *stress* becomes *distress* that problems occur. The stress may show up in the way employees' behavior has changed. People who had always been patient become impatient. Calm people may become tense. Associates who have always been cooperative rebel. All these signs show up when people are under stress. Some people under stress may show physical symptoms or complain that they have trouble falling asleep or in sleeping through the night. They're often tired all the time—even if they do get a good rest. They may have stomach pains, a fast heartbeat, or frequent headaches.

"I'm So Tired I Can't Think Straight!"

Rest can cure physical fatigue, but most people are more likely to be mentally, not physically, fatigued on the job. If your people work with computers or in other mentally strenuous jobs, remind them that physical exercise can alleviate fatigue and stress. Suggest that they take a lunchtime walk, go swimming or jogging, or participate in a sport after work. Some companies have exercise rooms in which employees can use a stationary bike or a weight machine during their lunch hour. People who have a regular regimen are less likely to become mentally fatigued.

Burnout

People are not light bulbs. A light bulb shines brightly and suddenly—poof! It burns out. People burn out slowly and often imperceptibly. Although some burnouts result in physical breakdowns such as a heart attack or ulcers, most are psychological. Team members lose enthusiasm, energy, and motivation, and it shows up in many ways. They hate their job, can't stand co-workers, distrust the team leader, and dread coming to work each morning.

Burnout can be caused by too much stress, but that's not the only cause. It can also be a result of frustration: Promises made weren't kept or an employee was passed over for an expected promotion or salary increase. Some leaders and managers burn out because of the pressures of having to make decisions that, if made poorly, can cause catastrophic problems. Others just burn out from having to work excessively long hours or do unrewarding work.

Stop! Look! Listen!

If a person is constantly fatigued from work, suggest that she see a physician for a thorough medical examination and for suggestions to relieve fatigue and stress.

Often the only means of helping someone recover from burnout is to suggest professional help. There are some things you can do, however, to help put a burned-out associate on the road to recovery:

- **Be a supportive person.** Demonstrate your sincere interest by encouraging the person to talk about and assess her concerns and put them into perspective.

- **Consider changing job functions.** Assigning different activities and responsibilities or transferring the person to another department changes the climate in which she works and provides new outlets that may stimulate motivation.

- **Give the person an opportunity to acquire new skills.** This not only helps him focus on learning rather than on the matters that led to the burnout but also makes the person more valuable to your company.

If, despite your efforts, the employee doesn't improve, strongly suggest professional counseling.

Plowing into Pressure

When pressure on a job becomes so great that employees get close to breaking down, encourage them to follow these suggestions:

◆ **Take a break.** If possible, get away from your workplace—get out of the building. If you work in a city, take a walk around the block. If you work in an industrial park, walk around the parking lot. If the weather is bad, walk around inside the building. In 10 or 15 minutes, you'll feel the stress dissolve and be able to face your job with renewed energy.

◆ **Exercise.** If you work in a crowded office, it's obviously not expedient to get up in the middle of the room and do jumping jacks or push-ups, but you can choose from several relaxation exercises without being obtrusive. Books and videotapes are available to show you how. If your company has an exercise room, get on the treadmill for five minutes (not enough to work up a sweat, but enough to relax your mind).

◆ **Change your pace.** Most people work on more than one project at a time. If the pressures are too great on your current project, stop for a while and work on another one. When you return to your original assignment, it will go much more smoothly.

When There's Too Darn Much Work to Do

Your staff has survived downsizing and reorganization. You now have fewer members, and each of them is working longer and harder. Your boss is piling more and more work on you, and your group just can't handle it. Because there's a limit to any group's time and energy, you decide that you have to speak to your boss.

Tactical Tools
Learn to say "no." When you're asked to take on a special assignment that won't help you meet your goals, decline diplomatically. Explain that you realize it's an important project but that you're already involved with several high-priority assignments and, as much as you want to help, you just can't.

Before you approach your manager, thoroughly analyze the jobs your group is doing. Indicate how much time staff members devote to each project, and determine each project's importance to the accomplishment of your department's goals. Reexamine your boss's priorities. Decide with your associates what they can do to work smarter rather than harder.

If you still feel after this analysis that your team has more work than it can handle effectively, meet with your boss to review its results and try to reorder your team's priorities. Your boss may agree to defer certain time-consuming jobs because others are more important; reassign some jobs to other groups; or authorize additional personnel.

Don't let other managers push your team around. Sometimes pressure comes from other teams or departments with whom you're collaborating. You and the leader of the other team should try to work out a schedule that alleviates the pressure. If you can't agree, take it up with the manager who supervises both teams.

Sometimes the pressure results from you or members of the group volunteering for special projects. Learn to say "no." Keep associates aware of your priorities, and point out that it's not an indicator of laziness or unwillingness to cooperate if they reject requests to volunteer for special projects outside the group's activities.

Managing Stress

Although some physicians treat stress with tranquilizers and other medication, unless you're under extreme pressure, you can take other steps to help manage your own stress:

- **Keep in tiptop shape.** Watch your diet, and engage in a regular exercise program.

- **Learn to relax.** Participate in deep meditation or programmed relaxation exercises. Be sure to reserve time to spend alone.

- **Learn to love yourself.** People with high self-esteem are less likely to be adversely affected by pressure from others.

- **Explore your spirituality.** Whatever your religion, spiritual experience can guide you toward peace of mind.

- **Keep learning.** The experience of ongoing learning keeps you alert, open-minded, and stimulated.

- **Develop a support team.** Avoid major stress by having friends and family members available to back you up when things don't go well.

- **Accept only commitments that are important to you.** Politely turn down other projects that drain your time and energy.

- **Seek new ways of using your creativity.** By rethinking the way you perform routine tasks, you make them less boring and stressful. By developing creative approaches to new assignments, you make them less stressful to handle.

- **Welcome changes.** Consider them new challenges rather than threats to the status quo.

- **Replace negative images in your mind with positive ones.**

Dealing With Alcohol and Drug Problems

Suppose one of your associates seems to have an alcohol problem. You've never seen the person drink or come to work drunk, but you often smell alcohol on the person's breath. He is frequently absent, especially on Mondays.

You can't ignore this situation. Speak to him about it, and prepare to hear all sorts of denials: "Me, drink? Only socially." Or, "Alcohol breath? It's cough medicine."

Stop! Look! Listen!

If you send drunk people home, don't let them drive. If they get into an accident, you or your company may share liability. Don't ask another employee to drive the person home. Call a taxi.

Rather than talk about a drinking problem, talk about job performance, absence from work, and other job-related matters. Inform him that if the situation continues, you'll have to take disciplinary action.

If he continues this behavior pattern, bring up your concern about the drinking and suggest—or insist on—counseling.

Discussing Alcohol Problems

It isn't easy to discuss such a sensitive and personal matter as an alcohol problem. The U.S. Department of Health and Human Services suggests the following approach, in its pamphlet "Supervisor's Guide on Alcohol Abuse":

♦ **Don't apologize for discussing the matter.** Make it clear that job performance is involved.

♦ **Encourage the employee to explain why work performance, behavior, or attendance is deteriorating.** This approach may provide an opportunity to discuss the use of alcohol.

♦ **Don't discuss a person's right to drink or make a moral issue of it.** Alcoholism is a disease that, left untreated, can lead to many more serious illnesses.

♦ **Don't suggest that he or she use moderation or change drinking habits.** According to Alcoholics Anonymous, alcoholics cannot change their drinking habits without help. But it's up to them to make the decision to stop drinking and take steps to get that help.

♦ **Don't be distracted by excuses for drinking.** The problem as far as you're concerned is the drinking itself—and how it affects work, behavior, and attendance on the job.

◆ **Remember that alcoholics, like any other sick people, should be given the opportunity for treatment and rehabilitation.**

◆ **Emphasize that your primary concern is the associate's work performance.** Point out that if his or her behavior doesn't improve, you'll have to take disciplinary action, including suspension or discharge.

◆ **Point out that the decision to seek assistance is the associate's responsibility.**

If your company has an employee assistance program (see Chapter 22), describe it and strongly recommend that it be used.

Preventing Drinking and Drug Use on the Job

In most companies, showing up at work drunk or drinking on the job is a punishable offense. However, it's not always easy to prove that a person is drunk. Appearing to be drunk isn't enough. Even a police officer cannot arrest a suspect for driving while intoxicated, unless he or she substantiates the claim with a breath or blood test.

If one of your employees seems to be drunk, your safest course is to send the person to your medical department for testing. If that's not possible, you must take direct action. Don't allow the person to work—send them home. The next day, discuss the situation and point out that if it occurs again, you'll take disciplinary action. Also, make sure to suggest counseling.

Although drug use on the job has increased, it isn't nearly as common as drinking. Treat drug users in the same way you deal with drinkers. Because drug use (and particularly the sale of drugs) is illegal, however, you should consult your attorney about the best ways to handle this situation.

Testing for the use of drugs is becoming an increasingly routine practice in many companies. A survey of more than 3,500 companies showed that 48 percent test job applicants and 43 percent periodically test employees. Although some companies do conduct random drug tests, most of them test employees only when they suspect drug use.

> **Tactical Tools**
>
> To prevent any misunderstandings or ambiguities, every company should have a formal policy prohibiting drinking on company premises or during working hours. This policy should be in writing and reviewed periodically with all employees. Restrictions should specifically include beer and wine in addition to "hard" liquor.

> **CAUTION**
>
> **Stop! Look! Listen!**
>
> The ADA (Americans with Disabilities Act) includes alcoholism and drug addiction as disabilities (see Chapter 7).

HIV/AIDS in the Workplace

Despite all the articles and TV programs that make clear that HIV is spread primarily through semen and blood, many people still have an unreasonable fear of even casual contact with a person who has the virus.

Now Hear This

You can obtain literature about HIV/AIDS and information about awareness programs from your local health department or from the CDC National AIDS Clearing House at 1-800-458-5231.

When it becomes known that an employee of a company has HIV or AIDS, many co-workers refuse to work with that person. If the person with AIDS is on your team or works in conjunction with it, this attitude can disrupt your team's activities.

To avoid these situations, companies have instituted programs to inform employees of the true facts about the virus and the disease. HIV/AIDS-awareness programs include videos, pamphlets, articles in the company newspaper, and talks to employees by doctors.

"It's Not My Staff—It's My Peers"

You get along fine with your boss. You and your staff members have a great relationship. But you keep running into conflicts and problems with one or more of your peers—other team leaders or staff managers. Why?

There could be dozens of reasons. First look into yourself. Is it you or them who cause the problem? It's not easy to be introspective, but try to be honest with yourself. If you don't get along with many people, it may be something that you are doing or thinking that causes it. You may be stubborn and insist on doing things your way. You may come across as arrogant or domineering and you are not aware of it. So evaluate yourself. Ask friends or associates to help you with this.

On the other hand, if you get along fine with most people but have problems with one or a few, the difficulties are more likely their fault. Look for the cause if you can. Maybe they're the kind of people who can't get along with anyone. Maybe their goals and agenda differ from yours. Here are a couple of explanations:

◆ **Competition:** The other person may look upon you as a competitor for advancement in the company and consciously or subconsciously fears cooperating with you.

◆ **Jealousy:** He or she resents your position or accomplishments.

There isn't much you can do about your peers' personality problems. These people need professional help. They rarely succeed in their jobs and unless they are experts in a hard-to-replace technical job, they won't be around for long.

As for problems stemming from competition or jealousy, you can deal with them diplomatically. Remember you need to gain the cooperation of even competitive or jealous people to accomplish any project in which both of you are collaborating.

Don't Command Them—Sell Them Instead

Follow the principles of good salesmanship when you deal with peers who are reluctant to cooperate.

1. **Gain their attention.** When presenting an idea they might resist, make a comment that will get them to sit up and take notice. Everybody likes compliments. So compliment them on something they accomplished that you truly admired. You now have their attention.

2. **Ask questions.** Find out what excites the other person about the situation. Instead of presenting your idea, ask questions. Listen to their responses. Most people are so anxious to "sell" their ideas that they don't fully listen to what the "buyer" really wants. Don't presuppose that his interests are identical to yours. You may want to emphasize the cost savings your idea will engender, but your colleague may be much more excited about the creative potential it provides. You won't know this unless you listen.

3. **Present evidence.** Develop considerable evidence to back up the ideas you want to sell. Once you learn what the other person really wants, you can tailor your evidence to that person's desires.

4. **Be prepared to deal with objections.** If you have had previous dealings with that person, you may anticipate what objections may be raised and be ready to counter them. Your questions will uncover others. Learning the objections is the best way to know where the real problems lie.

5. **Close the sale.** Get the other person to agree to a plan of action that you both feel will get the job done. Ask her to summarize it so you are sure that there is a clear understanding.

Dealing With the Boss's Relatives

Have you ever worked for a company in which the boss placed his relatives in key positions? Well, sometimes these men and women are real contributors, but often they are incompetent or worse. Some business owners do feel an obligation to hire relatives, even when they know they are incompetent, but smart managers place them in positions where they can do minimal harm.

I've seen silly sons, dim-witted daughters, brazen brothers, nutty nephews, crazy cousins, and incompetent in-laws in positions that they handled poorly and, even worse, that led them to derail the good work of competent staff members.

> **Words to Work By**
>
> *The Einstein Theory of Advancement:* Relativity. If you're a relative of the boss, you get the promotion.

In one company, the boss's brother had only one agenda—to keep costs down. He had veto power over all purchases and never approved anything that wasn't, in his opinion, absolutely necessary. If a clerk wanted a pencil, he had to show that the stub of the one he was using was less than two inches long. To obtain approval of major expenditures, people always had to go over his head to the boss.

In another company, the boss's daughter held a variety of jobs. She not only messed up the jobs but also would cry on her daddy's shoulder if her supervisors criticized her. Rather than lose some of his top producers, the boss transferred her to another department—where, of course, the same thing occurred.

What can you do when faced with this nepotism? Here are some suggestions:

- **Make an honest effort to smooth the relationship.** Be diplomatic. Be patient. Try to persuade the relative to see things your way. Let her think that what you want is really her idea.

- **If that fails, have a heart-to-heart talk with the boss.** Let him or her know what the specific problems are and suggest solutions that are in the best interest of the company.

- **Find ways to bypass the relative.** For example, in dealing with the penny-pinching brother, sell the boss on the value of your idea before you even bring it up to the brother.

- **Be prepared to defend your stand.** The boss may favor relatives, but the success of the business comes first. Have the pertinent facts and figures to back you up.

- **Last resort: Draw the line** (not to be used unless you are confident that you'll win). Point out that unless the relative ceases to interfere, you cannot do the job you have been assigned to do. This may be interpreted as an ultimatum, and it may force you to quit if not accepted. However, if the boss is objective about it, you may win your point.

Workplace Violence—A Growing Menace

Workplace violence is the second leading cause of death in the workplace. Three people in America are murdered on the job every working day. Although the rate of homicides has decreased in recent years, the rate of violent assaults has increased. Reasons that workplace violence occurs for many reasons, including the following:

- **Economic.** Corporate downsizing and layoffs cause unrest in the company.

- **Societal.** Drugs, alcohol, availability of guns, fractured families.

- **Psychological.** Personal breakdowns of individuals due to serious problems in their lives.

- **Organizational culture.** Over-stressed work force; pressure of the job.

- **Workplace climate.** Some workplace environments have the seeds of violence built into them—just waiting for a chance to explode. Some of these are:

    - Authoritarian management style

    - Unpredictable supervisory methods

    - Undervalued work and dignity of people

    - High degree of secrecy (not sharing information)

    - Disproportionate discipline

    - Bias against and favoritism toward some employees

    - Strained labor/management relations

In recent years, post offices have drawn much public scrutiny for seeming to breed workplace violence. The actual incidence of such violent acts at post offices, however, is well below average. As a matter of fact, the U.S. Postal Service has taken special steps to provide a safe working environment for its employees.

A six-step procedure, emulated by many private sector companies, has been established to strategize prevention of violence in the postal service:

- **Selection.** Hire the right people for the right job in the first place. By carefully selecting and placing new employees, you greatly minimize the risk of their ever becoming discontent.

- **Security.** Ensure appropriate safeguards for people and property.

- **Communication of policy.** The policies of appropriate behavior on the job should be clearly established and communicated to all employees at all levels of the organization. Employees should fully understand what constitutes acceptable and unacceptable behavior. In addition, management should reinforce its policy: All employees should be aware of the penalties of violation.

- **Environment and culture.** Create a work environment and maintain a climate that is perceived as fair and free of unlawful and inappropriate behaviors.

- **Establishment of resources.** Ensure that managers, supervisors, and employees are aware of the available resources to assist them in dealing with the problems of work and daily living. Employee assistance programs should be set up and be easily accessible to all employees.

- **Separation.** When separation is necessary, the process should be handled professionally. Managers should assess the possibility of inappropriate behavior or potential violence and confer with specially trained people to figure out how to handle the situation.

Before a worker is ever handed a pink slip, the service should make sure the employee receives a threat assessment interview to assess any inappropriate behavior and/or potentially violent circumstances. If applicable, call in a union representative to outline the reasons termination is necessary. Often, they will agree and will explain to the worker why they will not represent them in a protest of the firing.

> **Tactical Tools**
>
> Prevent trouble by rapid redress of disputes:
>
> **R**esolve
> **E**mployment
> **D**isputes
> **R**each
> **E**quitable
> **S**olutions
> **S**wiftly

In addition, company-paid career counseling sessions can go a long way in creating goodwill and a peaceful parting. Follow-up security by an outside firm can also be helpful.

Workplace violence awareness programs have been instituted for postal service managers, supervisors, and union leaders. These programs provide individuals with the skills and techniques that foster professional interactions with employees.

The Least You Need to Know

♦ Build up your staff members' self-esteem by helping them to focus on their successes—not on their failures.

♦ When you discuss an associate's work and she is sensitive, be gentle, tactful, and positive.

♦ When you present new concepts to negative people, let them express their reservations and then get them to help develop solutions.

♦ Help your group (and yourself) alleviate mental fatigue by following a regimen of physical activity before, after, and even during working hours.

♦ When employees are overcome by the pressures of the job, suggest that they take a walk, do relaxation exercises, or shift to a different project. The tension will ease, their minds will clear, and they'll work more effectively.

♦ If an employee has an alcohol or drug abuse problem, don't ignore it. Discuss how it affects that person's work and the work of your entire team. Suggest counseling (if necessary, insist on it).

♦ The best way to deal with problems with peers is to use diplomacy and salesmanship to persuade the person to your way of thinking.

♦ To minimize the risks of violence in the workplace, develop a program to sensitize supervisors and workers to identify and deal with potential problems.

22

The Manager as a Counselor

In This Chapter

- ◆ Handling gripes, complaints, and grievances
- ◆ Resolving conflicts
- ◆ Understanding the counseling process
- ◆ Working with employee assistance programs

Whether your group is organized in the supervisor/employee mode or as a team, it takes the coordinated effort of all members to keep it operating at optimum capacity. It takes only one member of the group who isn't functioning effectively to prevent it from achieving its objectives. As the manager, you are the coach. You must identify problems in their early stages and correct the situation before it mushrooms into a major problem. Your tool: counseling.

Counseling is a means of helping troubled associates overcome barriers to good performance. By careful listening, open discussion, and sound advice, a counselor helps identify problems, clarify misunderstandings, and plan solutions.

When a supervisor or team leader "counsels" an associate, it's more analogous to a coach of an athletic team counseling a player than to a psychotherapist counseling a patient. Trained specialists should do professional counseling, and, as you will learn in this chapter, sometimes referrals to these specialists are necessary.

Handling Gripes and Grievances

Sometimes you see a problem; sometimes you don't. You find out only when someone complains. A complaint may be your first hint of an impending problem, a reminder of an ongoing situation that hasn't been attended to, or it may just be one of your associates letting off steam. Nevertheless, you don't know until you check it out. This section addresses how you can best work through gripes and grievances with your team members.

Dealing with Chronic Complainers

You know your people. Some of them are always complaining. They gripe about the temperature in the room. They gripe about the work they're assigned. They gripe about everything you tell them. You've heard these same complaints over and over again.

Stop! Look! Listen!

As tempting as it may be to threaten to fire uncooperative employees, don't do it unless you really can carry it out. Most union contracts make the process for firing employees complex. Sometimes company policies, EEO implications, or other factors restrict these actions.

These types of people work in every company. They get their kicks from complaining. Sometimes they do have legitimate complaints, of course, so you can't just automatically ignore them. You have to listen—and that can be time-consuming and annoying.

One way to minimize this kind of griping is to pay more attention to the people who complain. The reason for the complaints is often their desire to be the center of attention. By talking to them, asking their opinions, and praising their good work, you satisfy their need for attention and give them less reason to gripe.

Checking Out Complaints

Most complaints are signals to you that shouldn't be ignored. Even if a complaint seems to have no validity, check it out anyway. You don't always have all the information, and you may discover facets of the situation you weren't aware of.

Follow these steps to find out what's going on:

1. **Listen.** Even if a complaint seems to be unfounded, in the mind of the complainant it's a serious matter.

2. **Investigate.** Take nothing for granted. Look at the record, and talk to others who know about the situation.

3. **Report back.** If the gripe is unfounded, explain your reasoning to the complainant. If it *is* substantiated, explain what you will do to correct it.

4. **Take action.** Do what must be done to correct the problem.

> **Words to Work By**
>
> A **gripe** is an informal complaint. A **grievance** is a formal complaint, usually based on the violation of a union contract or formal company policy.

What Happens When You Don't Have the Authority to Correct a Problem

Suppose a complainer is correct: Your investigation verifies that the complaint is justified, but you can't do anything about it. Find out who can. Bring the situation to the attention of your boss or whoever can adjust it.

Diana, a team leader, was frustrated. When she described to her boss, Charles, a problem her team members were having, he promised to rectify it but never did.

Diana's reminders were rebuffed. She was concerned about not only having to continue to work with this unsatisfactory situation but also losing the respect of her team members. She discussed the situation with Elizabeth, a manager who had been her mentor earlier in her career.

Elizabeth's advice: "Let Charles know how important it is to your team to have someone listen to their complaints and consider them seriously. Remind Charles that you deal with every problem over which you have authority, but that this one is out of your jurisdiction. Point out that you screen all complaints and don't pass on the ones that aren't justified. If there's a reason that action has not or cannot be taken, you want to know so that you can pass on the information to your team. Tell him that they're reasonable people who understand that they can't get everything they want, but that they expect that their complaints will be taken seriously. Then let your associates know what action you're taking and what results from it."

Filing Formal Grievances

When a company has a union contract, the procedures for handling grievances are clearly outlined. Companies that don't have union agreements often set up their own procedures for dealing with employee grievances.

Here's a typical four-step approach:

1. The person making the complaint discusses it with his or her immediate supervisor or team leader. Every attempt to resolve the problem should be made at this level.

CAUTION

Stop! Look! Listen!

If no complaints are called to the management's attention, it doesn't necessarily mean that there aren't any. It may mean that communication is blocked. If no one attends to grievances and gripes, they fester in the minds of the aggrieved and burst out sooner or later in low morale. Keep those channels open.

2. If no settlement is reached, the individual should be given an opportunity to bring the problem to the next level of management without fear of reprisal.

3. If the complaint is still unresolved, it may go to the general manager or a specially appointed manager (often the human resources director). An agreement is usually reached during this stage.

4. Although arbitration is rare in a nonunion environment, management in some companies provides for a mutually agreed upon third party to be available if the company and the aggrieved person cannot work out their problem.

As the immediate supervisor or team leader, you play the key role in this process. You should make every effort to resolve grievances without having to go beyond step 1. Grievance procedures take time and energy that would be better spent doing your team's primary work. To help you deal with a grievance systematically, use the following sample grievance worksheet.

Grievance Worksheet

Complainant: _____   Date: _____

Team leader:_____

Grievance: _____

_____

_____

_____

Report of investigation: _____

_____

_____

_____

If justified, action taken: _____

_____

_____

If not justified, reason: _____

_____

_____

Date reported to complainant: _____

Complainant's comments: _____

_____

_____

Team leader's comments: _____

_____

_____

Preventing Grievances

Dealing with grievances is time-consuming and takes you away from more productive work. This section provides some suggestions for preventing grievances from developing on your team:

◆ Regularly let all staff members know how they're doing. People want feedback on not only their failures but also their successes.

◆ Encourage associates to participate in all aspects of planning and performing the work.

◆ Listen to their ideas.

◆ Make only promises that you know you can keep.

◆ Be alert to minor irritations and trivial problems so that you can correct them before they become serious dissatisfactions.

◆ Resolve problems as soon as possible.

Resolving Conflicts Within Your Group

Two types of conflicts occur when people work together. One is tangible (a disagreement about a project, for example), and the other is intangible (two people just don't like each other, for example, and can't get along). In this section, you'll learn some techniques for managing both types of conflicts.

Suppose you give an assignment to two of your staff members, Ken and Barbie. They discuss the project and cannot agree about how it should be pursued. They both come back to you to resolve the problem.

You can use one of two approaches: *arbitrate* or *mediate*.

Words to Work By

In **arbitration**, both parties present their side of a problem and an arbitrator decides what should be done. In **mediation**, both parties present their side of a problem and a mediator works with them to reach a mutually satisfactory solution.

Mediating Disagreements

Mediation is the preferred approach because it's more likely to result in a win-win compromise. The most negative effect of using mediation is that it's time-consuming (and you often don't have much time to solve a problem).

Suppose you have chosen to mediate the disagreement between Ken and Barbie. To make a mediated conflict resolution work, all parties involved must be fully aware of the procedure to be followed. *Unless all parties have a clear understanding of the approach, it cannot succeed.*

First, Barbie tells how she views the situation. You might think that the next step is for Ken to state his side—but it isn't. Instead, Ken is asked to state Barbie's view as he understands it.

The reason for this step is that when the first party explains his view to the other party, the other person typically only partly listens. That person may be thinking about what he or she plans to say and how to rebut the argument. By being aware of having to repeat the first person's views, that person becomes aware of having to listen carefully.

In addition, by having the second person repeat the first person's side of the story, any areas of misunderstanding can be clarified before the second person presents her views. It's amazing how often these types of misunderstandings cause conflicts. The same process is then followed with the second person stating his or her views.

During this discussion, you (as the mediator) take notes. After each person presents his views, you review your notes with the participants. You might say, "As I view this, you both agree on 80 percent of the project. Now let's list the areas in which you disagree." Most disputes have many more areas of agreement than disagreement. By identifying these areas, you can focus on matters that must be resolved and tackle them one at a time.

Because you don't have an unlimited amount of time, you must set a time limit on these meetings. Suppose you've set aside two hours for the first meeting. At the end of the specified time, you still have several more items to discuss. Set up another meeting for that purpose. Suggest that the participants meet in the interim without you to work on some of the problems. Often, after a climate of compromise is established, a large number of issues can be resolved without your presence.

Now the next meeting is scheduled for one hour, and more problems are resolved. If the project must get under way, this may be all the time you have. If some unresolved problems still exist, you have to change your role from mediator to arbitrator and make the decisions.

Time to Arbitrate

The following five steps can help you arbitrate a conflict, if you choose to deal with it in that way:

Tactical Tools

In explaining why you made a decision, treat your associates as adults. It's childish to say, "I'm the boss, and this is what I've decided." Let all concerned know the reason behind decisions, and clarify misunderstandings before implementing a decision.

1. **Get the facts.** Listen carefully to both sides. Investigate on your own to get additional information. Don't limit yourself to "hard facts." Learn about underlying feelings and emotions.

2. **Evaluate the facts.**

3. **Study the alternatives.** Are the solutions suggested by the two parties the only possible choices? Can compromises be made? Is a different resolution possible?

4. **Make a decision.**

5. **Notify the two parties of your decision.** Make sure that they fully understand it. If necessary, "sell" it to them so that they will agree and be committed to implementing it.

When Team Members Can't Get Along

If two people in your team or group dislike each other so much that it affects their work, you have to do something about it. First find out why the two people dislike each other. This type of animosity often stems from a past bitter conflict. In the rough and tumble of competition for advancement in many organizations, some people stab others in the back to gain an advantage. It's unlikely that you'll ever be able to get them to work together in harmony, however, because a deep-seated antagonism taints their every contact with each other.

If at all possible, transfer one or both parties to different departments that have little contact with each other. That option isn't always feasible because you need the skills and experience they possess, or there may not be any other departments in which they can use their skills. You have to take steps to overcome this situation.

Speak to each person. If your attempts to persuade them to cooperate fail, lay down the law: "If this team is to succeed, all its members must work together. What happened in the past is past. Write it off. I'm not asking you to like each other. I don't care if you never associate with each other off the job. I'm demanding that you work together to meet our goals." If necessary, follow up this directive with disciplinary action.

Often the reason for the dislike isn't based on any specific factor. It happens to all of us: You meet a person and something about him or her turns you off and you immediately dislike that person.

Suppose you introduce your new team member, Jack, to Rachel. Rachel's first reaction is, "I don't like him," and it carries over into their working relationship.

Psychologists say that this reaction occurs because something about this person subconsciously reminds the other of some unpleasant past experience. Something about Jack (his haircut, the manner in which he speaks, a mole on his left cheek) reminds Rachel of a third grade bully who made life miserable for her way back then—and she hates him. These factors, called minimal cues, trigger long forgotten subconscious memories that still influence our reactions to people.

When you notice that team members have an unexplainable dislike for other members, tell them about minimal cues. Help them understand that their reactions are normal, but that it's important not to let these reactions influence their attitudes toward other people. Awareness of the psychology underlying this feeling will help overcome a person's irrational attitude.

> **CAUTION**
>
> **Stop! Look! Listen!**
>
> Don't give advice about serious personal matters. You're not a trained psychologist. Listen! Help put the problem into perspective. Provide or suggest sources for additional information. Help associates clarify a situation and come to their own conclusions.

"I'm Not Dear Abby"

In addition to counseling about employee performance, alcoholism and drugs, and work-related gripes and grievances, supervisors may be called upon to counsel their associates about personal matters that may affect their work.

All of us have personal problems. We worry about our health, about our families, and about money. We always have something to worry about. People carry their worries with them into the workplace, and worries do affect their work.

You may be reluctant to pry into an associate's personal life—and many people resent prying. Sometimes, however, it's necessary. It's much easier if you and your associates have good personal relationships and if you've always shown interest in the members as individuals. Counseling is a natural follow-through on your usual interest.

If you have this type of relationship, begin the discussion by commenting about job-related matters. Ask a question about the project that's involved, for example. It may lead into a discussion of the problems the person is having with the project, which may be caused by personal matters.

Be an empathetic listener. Your role as counselor is to give team members an opportunity to unload their problems. Encourage them by asking questions. Don't criticize, argue a point, or make a judgment. Act as a sounding board to help release the pressures that are causing the problem. Help the person clarify the situation so that the solution will be easier to reach.

> **Tactical Tools**
>
> When you have to work with someone you dislike, make an effort to find something you *can* like about the person: job skills, sense of humor, or a personality trait, for example. Focus on the good point(s). You'll soon forget the intangible factor that generated your dislike.

Counseling isn't a cure-all. There are many areas in which you just can't help. When a problem is one you can help by just talking it out, your intervention can be useful. Don't lose patience or give up too easily. Often, more than one session is necessary to build a sense of trust and to get a team member to open up.

Knowing What to Do When Talking Doesn't Help

When job problems are caused by alcoholism or drug addiction, there's little you can do other than encourage or even insist on appropriate programs (refer to Chapter 21). When the real cause stems from deep-seated emotional factors, professional help is necessary.

You may be reluctant or even embarrassed to suggest that a team member see a professional counselor. Many people take umbrage at this suggestion: "Do you think I'm nuts?" Point out that going to a professional counselor is now as accepted as going to a medical doctor. Young people are exposed to counseling beginning in elementary school. The most frequently given advice offered by Dear Abby, Dr. Joyce Brothers, and other advice columnists is to seek counseling when faced with serious problems.

> **Stop! Look! Listen!**
>
> When you refer someone for professional help, avoid using the terms "psychiatrist," "psychologist," or "therapist"— they have negative connotations to most people. Tell a troubled person that he or she might benefit from seeing a *counselor* who specializes in a particular area. Back up your advice by explaining how counseling has helped other people.

Not all problems that require professional assistance are psychological. They may be caused by a medical condition or serious financial troubles. Often they're marital or family situations.

If your company has an employee assistance program (discussed in the following section), making a referral to it immediately relieves you of the burden of suggesting specific counseling (see the following section). If not, your human resources department may help provide referrals. You may find it helpful to research the available sources of help in your community:

◆ **Medical doctors:** If a company doesn't have its own medical department or HMO, or if an employee doesn't have a primary care physician, local hospitals or medical societies can provide a list of qualified physicians.

◆ **Psychiatrists:** These M.D.s deal with serious psychological disorders.

◆ **Psychologists or psychotherapists:** These specialists usually have a degree in psychology or social work and can handle most of the usual emotional problems people face.

◆ **Marriage counselors and family therapists:** These professionals deal with marital problems, difficulties with children, and related matters.

Obtain from your local family service association or mental health association the names of qualified psychologists, psychiatrists, or marriage and family therapists in your area.

◆ **Financial counselors:** These people help others work out payment plans with creditors, develop budgets, and live within their income. Your bank or credit union can provide referrals.

Employee Assistance Programs (EAPs)

An employee assistance program, or EAP, is a company-sponsored counseling service. Many companies have instituted these programs to help employees deal with personal problems that interfere with productivity. The counselors aren't company employees, but instead are outside experts retained on an as-needed basis. Initiating the use of the EAP can be done in two ways, which are discussed in this section.

Sometimes an employee takes the initiative in contacting the company's EAP. The company informs its employees about the program through e-mail, bulletins, announcements in the company newspaper, meetings, and letters to their homes. Often a hotline telephone number is provided.

Gerty believes that she needs help. Constant squabbling with her teenage daughter has made her tense, angry, and frustrated. In a brief telephone interview with her company's EAP, the screening counselor identifies Gerty's problem and refers her to a family counselor. Gerty makes her own appointment on her own time (not during working hours—EAPs are not an excuse for taking time off the job). Because the entire procedure is confidential, no report is made to the company about the counseling (in most cases, not even the names of people who undertake counseling are divulged).

Another way to start the process is by having a supervisor take the initiative to contact the EAP. Suppose the work performance of one of your top performers has recently declined. You often see him sitting idly at his desk, his thoughts obviously far from his job. You ask him what's going on, but he shrugs off your question by saying, "I'm okay—just tired."

Now Hear This

EAPs aren't new. They began in the 1940s as alcohol rehabilitation programs. People who couldn't perform their job duties because of a drinking problem were usually fired. Companies that often had invested large amounts of money in developing employees' skills started these programs to protect their large investments.

After several conversations, he finally tells you about a family problem, and you suggest that he contact your company's EAP.

Even though you've made the referral and the employee has followed through, don't expect progress reports. From now on, the matter is handled confidentially. Your feedback comes from seeing improvement in the employee's work as the counseling helps with the problem.

Employee assistance programs are expensive to maintain, but organizations that have used them for several years report that they pay off. EAPs salvage skilled and experienced workers who, without help, may leave a company.

The Least You Need to Know

- ◆ Chronic complainers may just be seeking attention. To ward off some of their complaints, speak to them, ask for their opinions, and listen to them regularly.

- ◆ Even if a complaint seems unfounded, you may not be familiar with certain facets of the situation. Investigate, report back, and, if justified, correct the situation.

- ◆ If you can't resolve a complaint, refer it to someone who can. Keep the complainant advised of what's going on.

- ◆ By resolving problems as soon as possible, you avoid having to file time-consuming formal grievances.

- ◆ In mediating conflicts among your team members, make sure that each party fully understands the other's viewpoint.

- ◆ When personal dislikes inhibit team harmony, make every effort to resolve differences. If you can't, take a firm stand. Insist that if they can't put aside their personal feelings and work together, you'll take disciplinary action.

◆ When you counsel an employee, be an empathetic listener. Let the other person do most of the talking. Help put the problem into focus, but don't give advice about serious personal matters.

◆ When your employees' work performance suffers because of personal problems, refer them to your company's employee assistance program. If your company doesn't have one, refer them to an appropriate professional.

Part 7

The End of the Line

When you hear or see the word discipline, the first thing that usually pops into your mind is punishment. Look at that word again. Notice that by dropping just two letters, it turns into *disciple*, a synonym for "student." Both words are derived from the Latin word meaning "to learn." If you look at discipline, not as punishment, but as a means of learning, both you and your associates get much more out of it. You are the *coach*, and your associates are the *learners*.

Unfortunately, people don't always learn what they are taught. Despite your best efforts, some of your employees may not perform satisfactorily. If infractions still occur, even after you've clearly explained the rules, you must take steps to get things back on track.

Discipline may lead to termination, but firing people isn't the only reason people are separated from the company. Some people voluntarily resign, others are laid off because of company cutbacks. In this final section of the book, We'll explore all of these.

Chapter 23

Doling Out Discipline

In This Chapter

- The steps of progressive discipline
- How and when to reprimand
- Written warnings
- Probation and suspension
- Documenting the action

Some companies have workers who have always met all the requirements of their jobs, followed all the company rules and regulations, and never had to be disciplined. They are robots, but even in technocrats' wildest dreams, robots will never totally replace humans. All except the most routine and highly structured work must be done by people, who from time to time don't meet expectations, are absent or come to work late, and violate company rules and must be corrected.

This chapter looks at the system of progressive discipline used by most organizations today and examines how it can be used effectively by supervisors and team leaders. You'll learn when a reprimand is appropriate and how to reprimand a team member without causing resentment.

You'll learn when and how to "write up" an employee and when he should be placed on probation or suspended. Keep in mind that the contents of this chapter are based on general practices that are used in many organizations. Your company's policies may differ. You may get some good ideas from this chapter that you can't use now, but you can suggest them to your company's management. *Until your company incorporates these ideas into its policies, however, follow your company's current practices.*

Words to Work By

Progressive discipline is a systematic approach to correcting rule infractions. A typical program has six steps, beginning with an informal warning. If the warning doesn't succeed, the following steps are taken, in order: disciplinary interview, written warning, probation, suspension, and termination (if necessary).

Progressive Discipline

In most organizations, it's important for every member of a team to be at his or her workstation at starting time. If one person comes to work late, it can hold up an entire team.

Suppose an employee was late three times in his first month on the job. You spoke to him about it, and for several months he kept his promise to be on time. He was late one day last week, and this morning he was late again. His reason for the tardiness is vague. Your informal chats with him about the matter haven't done any good, so now you're ready to apply *progressive discipline*.

The Reprimand: An Informal Warning

The chats you've had with the employee weren't part of the progressive discipline system; instead, they were friendly reminders of his responsibility to your group.

The first official step in the progressive discipline system is often called the "oral," or "verbal," warning: You take the associate aside and remind him that the two of you have discussed his lateness and that, because he continues to come to work late, you must put him on notice. Inform him of the next steps you'll take if the behavior continues.

You may be exasperated about his failure to keep a promise to be on time. It's normal to be annoyed if your group's work is delayed, but don't lose your cool. A typical conversation shows you what *not* to do:

> **You** (angrily): How many times do I have to tell you that we need you here at 8 A.M.? You know that we have a deadline to meet today. Haven't you any sense of responsibility?

Employee (annoyed): I was only 10 minutes late. It's not my fault—I ran into a traffic problem.

You: If you had left home early enough, you wouldn't have had a traffic problem. The rest of us were here on time. You just don't have a sense of responsibility.

Employee: I have as much of a sense of responsibility as anyone.

You: If you're late again, I'll write you up.

Did this conversation solve anything? The objective of an informal warning is to alert staff members that a problem needs correction. By using an angry tone and antagonistic attitude, you only rile the person and avoid solving the problem.

Let's replay that reprimand as it should be done:

You: You know how important it is for you to be here when the workday begins. It's very important for all of us to be on time.

Employee: I'm sorry. I ran into unusual traffic this morning.

You: We all face traffic in the morning. What can you do to make sure that you'll be on time in the future?

Employee: I've tried alternative routes, but it doesn't help. I guess I'll have to leave earlier every day so that, if I do run into traffic, I'll at least have a head start.

You: That sounds good to me. You're a valuable member of our group, and being on time will help all of us.

Guidelines for Reprimanding

When you're preparing to reprimand someone, to ensure that you conduct the reprimand in the most effective manner, reread the following guidelines for reprimanding.

◆ Time the reprimand properly. As soon as possible after the offense has been committed, call the offender aside and discuss the matter in private.

◆ Never reprimand when you're angry. Wait until you've calmed down before talking to the employee.

◆ Emphasize the *what*, not the *who*. Base the reprimand on the action that was wrong, not on the person.

- Begin by stating the problem and then ask a question. Don't begin with an accusation: "You're always late!" Say instead, "You know how important it is for all of us to be on the job promptly. What can you do to get here on time from now on?"

- Listen! Attentive, open-minded listening is one of the most important factors of true leadership. Ask questions to elicit as much information about the situation as you can. Respond to the offender's comments, but don't let the interview deteriorate into a confrontation.

- Encourage the employee to make suggestions for solving the problem. When a person participates in solving a problem, there's a much greater chance that it will be accepted and accomplished.

- Provide constructive criticism. Give him or her specific suggestions, when possible, about how to correct a situation.

> **CAUTION**
> **Stop! Look! Listen!**
>
> Never reprimand people when you're angry, when they're angry, or in the presence of other people. Reprimands should be a private matter between two calm people working together to solve a problem.

- Never use sarcasm. Sarcasm never corrects a situation; it only makes the other person feel inadequate and put upon.

- End your reprimand on a positive note. Comment on some of the good things the person has accomplished so that he or she knows that you're not focusing only on the reason for this reprimand, but instead on total performance. Reassure the person that you look on him or her as a valuable member of the team.

They Always Have an Excuse

If you've been in management for any length of time, you've probably heard some wild excuses. No matter how silly, ridiculous, or improbable the excuse may be, listen—and listen carefully—for these reasons:

- Until you listen to the entire story, you cannot know whether it's valid. In most companies, there are acceptable reasons for not following a company rule or procedure. Under extenuating circumstances, it's sensible to be flexible when you enforce the rules.

- Even if an excuse is unacceptable, let your associate get it out of her system (psychologists call this catharsis). When people have something on their minds, they won't listen to a word you say until they get their story out. Whether it's a person's tardiness or a customer's complaint, let the person talk. Only after his mind is clear will he listen to you. Afterward, you can say, "I understand what you're saying, but the important thing is to be here on time."

> **Tactical Tools**
>
> If during the discussion the employee raises his or her voice, lower yours. Most people respond to a raised voice by raising their own. By responding in a soft voice, you disarm the other person. It has a calming effect.

Ask for a Plan of Action

When you deliver a verbal warning, throw the problem back to your associate. Rather than say, "This is what you should do," ask "What do you think you can do to correct this situation?" Get people to come up with their own plans of action.

In a simple situation such as tardiness, a plan of action is relatively easy to develop: "I'll leave my house 15 minutes earlier every day." In more complex situations, a plan may take longer to develop. You may suggest that the person think about the problem for a day or so and arrange a second meeting in which to present and discuss it.

Document All Reprimands

Even informal reprimands shouldn't be strictly oral. You should keep a record of it. Legal implications mandate that you document any action that could lead to serious disciplinary action.

Some team leaders document an informal warning by simply noting it on their calendars or entering it in a departmental log. Others write a detailed memo for their files. You should use the technique your company prefers.

Conducting a Disciplinary Interview

If an employee repeats an offense after receiving a verbal warning, the next step is the disciplinary interview.

This interview differs from a reprimand in that it is more formal. A verbal warning is usually a relatively brief session, often conducted in a quiet corner of the room. A disciplinary interview is longer and is conducted in an office or conference room.

A disciplinary interview should always be carefully prepared and result in a mutually agreed upon plan of action. Whereas a plan of action after a verbal warning is usually oral, the resulting plan in a disciplinary interview should be put in writing. It not only reminds both the leader and the team member of what has been agreed on but also serves as documentation.

To ensure that a disciplinary interview is carried out systematically, use the following discipline worksheet.

Discipline Worksheet

Part I ((Complete before interview begins)

Team member: _____   Date: _____

Offense: _____

_____

_____

Policy and Procedures provision: _____

Date of occurrence: _____

Previous similar offenses: _____

_____

What I want to accomplish: _____

_____

Special considerations: _____

_____

_____

Questions to ask at beginning of interview: _____

_____

_____

Part II (Keep in front of you during interview)

- Keep calm and collected.
- Listen actively.
- Emphasize the *what*, not the *who*.
- Give *team member* an opportunity to solve the problem.
- Get the whole story.
- Don't interrupt.
- Avoid sarcasm.

Part III (Fill out near end of interview)

Suggestions made by team member: _____

_____

_____

Agreed-on solution: _____

_____

_____

Part IV (Action taken: Fill in when interview is finished)

Documentation completed: _____

_____

_____

Writing Up Warnings

The next step in progressive discipline is to give the offender a written warning—a letter or form that will be placed in his or her personnel file. Written warnings often are taken more seriously than the first two steps. Employees don't want negative reports in their personnel files, and even the possibility that they'll be "written up" serves as a deterrent to poor behavior.

If the written warning concerns poor performance, specify the performance standards and indicate in what way the employee's performance fell short of the standards. Also state what was done to help the employee meet the standards. This will protect you against potential claims that you made no effort to bring the performance up to standard.

If the warning concerns infraction of a company rule, specify the nature of the offense and what disciplinary steps were taken before writing the warning (see the following two sample memos).

To protect your company from potential legal problems, check any form letters concerning discipline with your legal advisors before sending them to be printed.

Memo for Poor Conduct

From (team leader): _____   Date: _____

To: _____

On (date): _____ , we had a discussion concerning _____

_____

_____

At that time, you agreed to: _____

_____

Because you have not complied with this agreement, you are being formally notified that if the above matter is not corrected by (date) _____ , additional disciplinary steps will be taken as specified in Section _____ of the Policies and Procedures manual.

Signed (team leader): _____

Team member's comments: _____

_____

_____

Signed (team member): _____

Memo for Poor Performance

From (team leader): _____   Date: _____

To: _____

The performance standard for (specify job) _____ is (specify standard in quantity, quality, or other terms) _____

_____

_____

Your performance has not met these standards (give details): _____

_____

_____

To help you, I gave you _____ hours of special coaching. The areas covered include: _____

_____

_____

Signed (team leader): _____

Team member's comments: _____

Signed (team member): _____

Although it's always advantageous from a legal standpoint to have employees sign *all* disciplinary documents, it becomes imperative when the warning itself is in writing.

You can't force anyone to sign anything. If an employee refuses to sign a disciplinary document, call in a witness—a person who isn't directly involved in the situation—and repeat your request. If he still refuses, have the witness attest to that response on the document.

One tough supervisor reported that he never had trouble getting employees to sign a document. If they refused to sign, he'd turn the paper over, slam it onto the desk, and order "Okay, then just write on the back 'I refuse to sign' and sign it." They always did.

To avoid misunderstandings, give copies of all disciplinary documents to the employee. In addition, you should send a copy to the human resources department to include in the person's personnel file.

Refer to the sample poor conduct and poor performance memos in this chapter for ideas about how to phrase a written warning.

Putting Employees on Probation

Until now all your attempts to correct an employee's performance or behavior have been positive, and you've provided advice and counsel. If nothing has worked, your next step is to put him or her on probation. Set a deadline for adjusting the situation.

What you're doing is giving your associate one more chance to shape up before you invoke some form of punishment. Most people take probation seriously—they know that you mean business.

The two primary reasons for progressive discipline are poor performance and poor conduct. If performance is a problem, probation is the last step before termination. If all the retraining, counseling, and coaching you give a team member fails, you can give the person one last chance to overcome the problem over a probationary period. If that doesn't help, additional disciplinary steps won't help. If you can transfer the person to a more suitable job, do so; if not, you have no other choice than to terminate him or her.

Company practices for administering probation vary considerably. They're governed by union contracts, company policy manuals, or sometimes unwritten (but previously followed) practices. Usually the notification of probation is in the form of a written statement, signed by the supervisor or team leader or, in some cases, a higher ranking manager and acknowledged by the employee. The employee keeps one copy; the supervisor or team leader gets another copy; and the human resources department keeps a copy in its files.

Probationary periods vary from as few as 10 days to the more customary 30 days and sometimes even longer. If the employee makes significant progress, lift the probation. If she repeats the offense after the probation is lifted, you can either reinstate the probation or invoke the next step.

When an offense violates company rules (tardiness, absenteeism, or other misconduct), the next step is usually suspension.

Suspension: The First Real Punishment

You're severely limited in the ways you can punish employees. Ever since flogging was abolished, only a few types of punishment can be legally administered. The most commonly used method, short of termination, is suspension without pay.

Although supervisors often have some leeway in determining the length of a suspension, most companies set specific suspension times depending on the seriousness of the offense.

The mechanics of issuing a suspension are similar to that of probation. Union contracts often mandate consultation with a union representative before suspending an employee. Companies that aren't unionized usually require approval for suspensions by both the manager to whom the supervisor or team leader reports and the human resources department. Appropriate documentation specifying the reason for the suspension and the exact period of time involved should be made, signed by the appropriate manager, and acknowledged by the suspended employee.

If an employee returns from a suspension and continues to break the rules, your next step may be a longer suspension or even termination.

> **Tactical Tools**
>
> The downside of suspending an associate is that you lose that person's contribution to the team effort during the suspension period. Make every effort to keep the person employed by training and counseling so that suspension isn't necessary.

Termination: The Final Step

The chief purpose of progressive discipline is to give the offending employee an opportunity to change his or her behavior and become a productive, cooperative team member. Take stricter steps only after less strict steps have failed to solve the problem. The objective is to help the person succeed so that termination isn't necessary. If the employee fails to improve, however, the termination should take place.

The practical and legal facets of terminating employees are discussed in detail in Chapter 24.

> **Stop! Look! Listen!**
>
> It's not a good idea to extend a probationary period. If the employee makes some progress by the end of the probationary period but his behavior still isn't up to par, you can extend the time period—but only once. Continuous probation is bad for morale and rarely solves the problem.

The Least You Need to Know

- ◆ Progressive discipline gives employees several opportunities to correct their behavior before any form of punishment is applied.

- ◆ When you reprimand an associate, stay cool, be constructive, and focus on the problem—not on the person.

- ◆ Disciplinary interviews should result in a mutually accepted plan of action to correct the situation.

- ◆ All disciplinary actions should be documented. ("If it ain't written down, it ain't never happened.")

- ◆ Probationary periods give employees another chance to improve performance or correct behavior.

Chapter 24

How to Fire an Employee Legally and Tactfully

In This Chapter

◆ Terminating someone after progressive discipline has failed

◆ Preparing for a termination meeting

◆ Terminating employees spontaneously

◆ Knowing what "employment at will" really means

It's never pleasant to fire people. Even if you're glad to get rid of someone, firing is a disagreeable task that most people do reluctantly. Yet sometimes your only course of action is to terminate an employee. A series of disciplinary steps usually leads to this final act, but occasionally circumstances warrant an unplanned discharge.

Terminating employees is a serious matter that always needs careful consideration. In most companies, before a supervisor or team leader can terminate anyone, approval must be obtained from both the person to whom the leader reports and the human resources department. This step is important to ensure that company policies and legal requirements are fully observed. This chapter examines the importance of this process.

The End of the Line in Progressive Discipline

Employees who have experienced the steps of progressive discipline (see Chapter 23) should never be surprised when they get fired. Presumably, at every step along the way they were told what the next step would be. When you suspend an employee—the next-to-the-last stage in the disciplinary process—you must make clear that, if he doesn't improve in the areas that are suggested, the next step is termination.

Careful: Watch Your Words!

Because the issue of firing employees is such a sensitive one, you must do it diplomatically and be fully aware of any legal implications. Ask your human resources department for advice about dealing with this situation.

Some supervisors get more upset about having to fire someone than the person who is being fired does. Here are some suggestions to help you prepare:

- ◆ Review all documents so that you're fully aware of all the reasons and implications involved in the decision to terminate the employee.

- ◆ Review all that you know about the associate's personality:

    What problems have you had with the person?

    How did she respond to the preceding disciplinary steps?

    How did you and the associate get along on the job?

    How did he relate to other people in the department?

    What personal problems does the person have that you're aware of?

- ◆ Review any problems you've had in firing other employees, and map out a plan to avoid those problems.

- ◆ Check your company's policy manual or discuss with the human resources department any company rules that apply.

- ◆ Relax before the meeting. Do whatever helps you clear your mind and calm your emotions. If you've done your job correctly, you've made

> **Stop! Look! Listen!**
>
> Some people will sue for any reason. When you fire someone, you may have to defend your actions in court. Keep complete records and appropriate documentation for all steps that led to the termination. Make sure that what you do is in accordance with your company's policies. Or, if there's no written policy, study how similar situations were handled in the past.

every effort to help the associate succeed. The progressive discipline system has given the person several chances to change, so you don't have to feel guilty about the firing.

It's Show Time!

You've stalled as long as you can. Now you're ready to sit down with the employee and make clear that this is the end of the line.

Find a private place to conduct the meeting. Your office is an obvious spot, but it may not be the best one. A conference room is better because, if the fired employee breaks down or becomes belligerent, you can walk out.

Most people who are fired expect it and don't cause problems. They may beg for another chance, but this isn't the time to change your mind. Progressive discipline has given people several "other chances" before they reach this point. Don't let the termination meeting degenerate into a confrontation.

If the employee gives you a hard time, keep cool. Don't lose your temper or get into an argument.

It's a good idea to have another person in the room at a termination meeting. A person being fired may say or do inappropriate things. Also, you may become upset and say something that's best left unsaid. The presence of a third person keeps both you and the employee from losing your temper and from saying or doing something that can lead to additional complications.

The best "third person" in a termination meeting is a representative from the human resources department. If this person isn't available, call in another manager or team leader. If the employee belongs to a union, the union contract usually stipulates the presence of a union delegate.

Having a third person in the room when you terminate an employee also provides a witness if an employee later sues your company. Suppose that a former employee files an age discrimination suit several weeks after being fired for poor performance. She claims that during the termination meeting, you stated that the company needs younger people in order to meet production standards. Although the claim is false, you'll

Now Hear This

Most people are fired at the end of the workday on Friday afternoon. Some companies prefer to terminate employees in the middle of the week, however, so that people have a chance to begin looking for a new job the next day and not brood about the firing over the weekend.

have to spend time, energy, and money to defend against it—and it's your word against the other person's.

If a third person attends the termination meeting, the terminated employee will be less likely to file a false claim because he or she knows that it will be refuted by the witness.

Tactical Tools

To avoid legal problems, be sure to have all the facts before you fire someone. Investigate: Get witnesses, and get legal advice. Don't discuss the case with people who don't need to know about it.

In most organizations, when a termination meeting ends, the employee is sent to the human resources department for out-processing or handling the administrative details for completing the separation procedure. If your company assigns you to handle this chore, follow the company's procedures carefully.

Use the following termination checklist to ensure that you take the necessary steps in terminating an employee.

Termination Checklist

Name of employee: _____ Date: _____

Part I

If discharged for poor performance, steps taken to improve performance:

Date   Action

_____

_____

_____

Comments: _____

_____

_____

If discharged for poor conduct, list progressive disciplinary steps taken:

Date   Action

_____   Informational warning

_____   Written warning

_____   Disciplinary interview
_____   Suspension
_____   Other (specify): _____
_____

Comments: _____
_____
_____

Part II

Have you reviewed all pertinent documents?   _____

Have you treated this case in the same way as similar cases in
the past?   _____

Has this action been reviewed by your immediate superior?   _____

By human resources?   _____

By legal department?   _____

Does employee have any claim pending against company?   _____

Any workers' compensation claims?   _____

Other (specify): _____
_____

Part III

Conducted by: _____

Date: _____   Place: _____

Witness: _____

Comments: _____
_____
_____

Final actions: _____
_____
_____

continues

continued

ID and keys returned? _____

Company property returned? _____

Final paycheck issued? _____

Additional comments: _____

_____

_____

Spontaneous Termination: When You Fire Someone Without Progressive Discipline

Are there times when you're so annoyed with people that you wish you could just be the old-school boss and tell them to get out? Of course, there are. That's why progressive discipline was instituted—so that supervisors don't let their emotions of the moment dictate their actions.

Occasionally, termination without warning is permitted. These occasions are rare and usually limited to a few serious infractions that are clearly delineated in company policies. Serious offenses include drinking on the job, fighting, stealing, and insubordination. Because these charges aren't always easy to prove, be very careful before you make the decision to fire someone without progressive discipline. You must have solid evidence that can stand up in court. Law books are loaded with cases in which people who, because of a rash firing decision, have sued former employers for unlawful discharge, defamation of character, false imprisonment, and whatever else their lawyers can dream up.

Insubordination, which is one of the most frequent causes of spontaneous termination, isn't always easy to prove. If an employee simply fails to carry out an order, it may not be grounds for termination. Unless a failure to obey instructions can lead to serious consequences, it's better to use progressive discipline. On the other hand, if a team member becomes unruly in his refusal (if he hollers and screams or spits in your face, for example), spontaneous discharge may be appropriate.

Documenting a Spontaneous Discharge

When you fire someone after progressive discipline procedures fail, you have an entire series of documents to back you up. In spontaneous termination, however, you have no documents.

Immediately after a termination, write a detailed report describing the circumstances that led up to it. Get written statements from witnesses. If you can, get the employee to sign a statement presenting his or her side of the story. In the event that this discharge is challenged, having the terminated employee's immediate comments will protect you in case of a lawsuit.

You Can't Fire Me—I Quit!

Suppose, after all your efforts to help someone improve his performance, you tell him that you have to let him go. You explain that if he quits voluntarily, it will look better when he applies for another job. This option may sound sensible, but what happens if he applies for unemployment insurance and is told that he's not eligible because he quit?

If you give someone the option of resigning, be sure to inform the person about the probable loss of unemployment insurance and any other negative factors.

Now suppose that you think you'll be shrewd in getting rid of the person: "If I fire him, he'll give me problems. I'll just make his life so miserable that he'll quit." Over the next few weeks, you give him as many unpleasant assignments as you can. You time his returns from breaks and even how long he spends in the restroom. You chastise him for every minor violation of company rules, and, after a few weeks, he quits.

Don't be shocked when the person sues your company for unlawful discharge! When you tell the court, "I didn't fire him—he quit," the judge will respond "Not so. This is a *constructive discharge*—your treatment forced him to quit." You may be ordered to pay the person back wages, rehire him, or make a satisfactory financial settlement.

> **Tactical Tools**
>
> As angry as you may be about the trouble an employee has caused or how nasty he may be, don't use the termination meeting to tell the person off. A termination is a business decision, not a personal one.

> **Words to Work By**
>
> Rather than fire employees, some managers make life so miserable for them that they quit. When an employee quits because of intentional unfair treatment on the job, it is "constructed" by the courts to be equivalent to being fired and is referred to as **constructive discharge**.

Employment at Will

Unless you have a personal contract with your employees or they are covered by a union contract, they are "employees at will."

This concept has governed employment since colonial times. Bosses always had the right to fire employees, and employees could always quit. Only recently has this concept been challenged.

To understand *employment at will*, you first have to know a little about our legal system. Americans are subject to two kinds of law: legislated acts and common law. The former are the laws passed by Congress, the states, and local governments. Common law is based on accepted practices as interpreted by court decisions over the years.

The primary difference between the two types of law is that common law can be superseded or modified by legislation and can be changed in individual cases by mutual agreement between the parties involved. A violation of common law is not a criminal offense and is handled in a lawsuit as a civil action. Legislated statutes can be changed only by amendment, repeal, or court interpretation.

Employment at will, a common law principle, has been modified over the years by various statutes. For example, there are laws that prohibit a company from firing or refusing to hire someone for union activity, race, religion, national origin, gender, disability, and age. Your right under common law to hire or fire at will is, therefore, restricted in these circumstances.

> **Words to Work By**
>
> **Employment at will** is a legal concept under which an employee is hired and can be fired at the will of the employer. The employer has the right, unless restricted by law or contract, to refuse to hire an applicant or to terminate an employee for any reason or for no reason.

This principle also means that employment at will can be waived by mutual consent. For instance, the company and employee can sign a contract in which the employee agrees not to quit and the company agrees not to fire him or her for the duration of the contract. Or a company and a union can agree that no union member will be fired except under the terms of the contract. In both cases, the company has given up its right to employment at will.

Employment Rights When No Contract Exists

During the past several years, a number of cases have extended employees' rights that are not covered by specific legislation. Courts in several states have ruled that, although a company's policies and procedures manual isn't a formal contract, it can be considered to have the same effect as a contract.

In one case, a supervisor at a New York publishing firm was fired without having the benefit of progressive discipline measures. He sued on grounds that the policy manual called for progressive discipline before terminating an employee. In his supervisory capacity, he was required to follow the manual when he had to discharge one of his staff members. When he was fired, however, the company didn't follow the procedure. The company's contention was that the manual was intended only as a guide and not as a rigid procedure. The court ruled in favor of the employee. It said that, if a policy is published in a manual, employees can expect that it will be followed.

Stop! Look! Listen!

You cannot waive a legislated right by signing a contract. For example, an employee cannot agree to work for less than the minimum wage.

To avoid this type of problem, attorneys advise their clients to specify clearly in their company policy manuals that they are "at will" employers and to include a statement to that effect on their employment-application forms.

> **Tactical Tools**
>
> The following clause or one similar to it should be printed on all applications for employment and in employee handbooks: "This company follows an employment-at-will policy and employment may be terminated for any reason consistent with applicable federal and state laws. This policy cannot be changed verbally or in writing unless authorized specifically by the president or executive vice president of the company."

Oral Commitments

Suppose, during an interview, you told Stella that her job would be permanent after a six-month probationary period. A year later, your company downsizes, and Stella is laid off. She sues. She says, "I left my former job to take this one because the team leader assured me that it was a permanent job." You respond, "I made that comment in good faith. Our company had never had a layoff." Your reply won't be good enough—the court may award Stella a large settlement.

Preventative Maintenance

To avoid these types of these complications, follow these guidelines:

- ◆ All managers and team leaders should be trained in procedures concerning termination and adhere to them.

- Team leaders or anyone who represents management should never make commitments concerning tenure or other employment conditions orally or in writing.

- Make written job offers only after consulting with legal specialists.

- Never use the term "permanent employee." *No one* is a permanent employee. If your company must differentiate between temporary and part-time staff members, refer to the full-time people as "regular employees."

- On all documents and records relating to employment conditions, state that the company has a policy of employment at will.

The Least You Need to Know

- Prepare for a termination meeting by studying all the pertinent documents, reviewing the employee's personal characteristics, and psyching yourself up for the meeting.

- Check with your human resources department to ensure that all policies are followed and laws complied with.

- Invite a third party to participate in and witness termination meetings.

- Use spontaneous termination only for extreme infractions.

- Other than for reasons prohibited by law or waived by contract, an employer can fire any employee for any reason or for no reason ("employment at will").

- Oral commitments to an employee about tenure or conditions of employment are as binding as written agreements.

Chapter 25

Separations, Layoffs, and Downsizing

In This Chapter

- ◆ How to handle employee resignations
- ◆ Keeping temporarily laid-off workers from seeking new jobs
- ◆ Downsizing dos and don'ts

The days when a person joined a company after graduating from high school or college and stayed until retirement have long since passed. Most people now have several jobs during their working years. Sometimes it's a personal decision to leave a company, and sometimes it's involuntary—a company reduces its workforce, or an individual is discharged.

Chapter 19 listed many of the reasons that good employees leave their jobs. Although managers must make every effort to keep turnover down, sometimes people will quit no matter what you do. At other times, due to downsizing, managers are forced to let even some of their best people go. This chapter explores how to make the best of these types of situations.

What to Do When Employees Give Notice

Some supervisors and team leaders take an employee's resignation as a personal affront. "How could she do this to me?" Be aware that other team members are carefully monitoring the way you handle this situation. Take care to make the transition smooth.

The following suggestions help reduce the confusion that often results when a staff member leaves your company:

◆ Don't blow up. I once worked for a manager who considered anyone who quit to be disloyal. If someone gave him the courtesy of two weeks' notice, he ordered the person to leave immediately. He then bad-mouthed the employee to everyone in the company. The result was that employees quit without giving notice, which caused serious production problems.

Now Hear This _____

No law requires employees to give notice when they leave a company. The customary two-week notice is a courtesy that gives managers the opportunity to plan for a smooth transition. If you feel that the continued presence of this person may be disruptive to the team, you don't have to accept the notice, and you can then arrange for immediate separation.

◆ Agree on a mutually satisfactory departure date. You may need time to readjust your plans.

◆ Request a status report on the team member's projects so that you can arrange for others to handle them. Develop a list of vendors, customers, or other people outside your department that he or she interacts with so that you can notify them of the change.

◆ Contact your human resources department to arrange for either an internal transfer or hiring from outside.

◆ Let all of the associates in your group know as soon as you're notified. Tell them how it will affect their work until someone else is hired.

Furloughs: Short-Term Layoffs

If you work in an industry in which work is done seasonally (construction, certain clothing manufacturing, landscaping, and the automobile industry, for example), you're accustomed to temporary *layoffs* or *furloughs*. Workers in these fields expect to be laid off at certain times of the year and plan their lives accordingly. They're usually covered by unemployment insurance or, in some union contracts, additional payments. When the new season begins, most of them are rehired.

Some layoffs are unexpected, however, even though they're temporary. Business may slow down or a company may cut its payroll, for example. Laid-off workers have a reasonable chance of being rehired when business picks up, but they have no guarantee.

Although some people will wait for a recall, many choose to look for other jobs. This situation poses a problem for the company because many experienced workers won't be available when they're needed.

Words to Work By

When companies don't have enough work to keep their work force busy or when they want to reduce payroll to increase profits, workers are dismissed. These **layoffs** are sometimes temporary (until the workers are needed) and sometimes permanent.

Alternatives to Layoffs

When team members know that a layoff is for a specified period and that the company has a history of calling back the entire team after a furlough, they're less likely to seek other jobs. If a layoff is indefinite but you know that you will be rehiring sooner or later, take steps to keep available as many people as you can so that, when the recall comes, your team will be intact and ready to function.

When you're part of a smooth running, highly productive team, a layoff can be devastating. The loss of some workers means that the surviving associates will have to do more work to pick up the slack. Team interaction that had been developed over time is lost and must be rebuilt. Morale suffers, and productivity is most likely reduced. The best way to rebuild morale is to find alternatives to a layoff.

This list describes some ways companies have avoided layoffs:

♦ **Pay cuts.** The main reason for most layoffs is to reduce payroll. When companies institute a general pay reduction for all employees (including management), the entire workforce shares the burden.

When a company has a union contract, any reduction in pay must be negotiated. Point out to the union that reducing pay of all workers is a means of saving its members' jobs.

Where no union exists, a company can arbitrarily cut its payroll. No one wants to take a pay cut, of course, and some people aren't willing to suffer even a small personal loss to save somebody else's job. Unless management can "sell" it to employees by appealing to their nobler motives, a pay cut may cause more problems than it solves.

◆ **Work sharing.** All team members share the work that remains after jobs are eliminated. The standard work week is reduced by working fewer hours each day or fewer days each week. Another alternative involves working full weeks, but fewer weeks each month. With this strategy, hourly pay remains the same, but reduced hours decrease the payroll.

Work sharing enables companies to keep skilled employees during slow periods and enables teams to stay together. Employees earn less total pay but retain their benefits. Some states have amended their unemployment-insurance laws so that employees can collect some unemployment benefits during work-sharing periods.

◆ **Early retirement.** One way to minimize the number of employees who are laid off during an indefinite layoff is by encouraging older workers to retire earlier than they had planned. Under the Age Discrimination in Employment Act (see Chapter 7), companies cannot compel employees to retire. They can offer incentives, however, to make it worth their while. When more highly paid senior employees leave a company, the payroll is reduced significantly.

Stop! Look! Listen!

As much as you may want to keep laid-off associates available for recall, don't mislead them with false hopes. It isn't fair to someone who may turn down another job, and it can also have legal repercussions. Former employees have sued companies because of implied promises to rehire that didn't materialize.

Usually, an entire work group or team isn't laid off. Unless you have a union contract or rigid policy which mandates that layoffs happen on a seniority basis, keep your best people—those who can form the cadre of a new team if some of the laid-off members don't return when they're recalled.

Keep in touch with laid-off associates. Phone them, and send them the company newsletter. Let them know that you still consider them part of your team and that you're looking forward to the recall so that you can work together again.

Rehiring Furloughed Workers

Seniority in most companies is the basis of both layoffs and recalls. The most senior employees are the last to be let go and the first to be rehired. However, this approach isn't always the most desirable one. If you have no contractual obligation to do so, it may be more advantageous to rehire people according to the skills you need as the work expands. Your immediate need might be for a specialist in one area, but the most senior furloughed member may have a different skill. In this way, you can rebuild your staff most effectively.

Downsizing: The Permanent Layoff

As defined earlier, downsizing involves the elimination of a job. An entire facility may be closed, an entire unit or department eliminated, or an organization restructured by doing away with certain jobs or entire job categories.

The downsizing of major corporations which started in the mid 1990s has continued and even accelerated into the 2000s. This has resulted in the elimination of tens of thousands of jobs, causing disruptions not only in the lives of laid-off workers but also often to entire communities. This section explains how to cope with the fallout from downsizing cuts.

Tactical Tools
Even if you know that a laid-off associate has accepted another job, offer the person the opportunity to return to his old job. He may not be satisfied with the new job and may prefer to rejoin your staff.

WARN—the Law on Downsizing

To ease the burden on laid-off workers, Congress passed the Worker Adjustment and Retraining Notification Act (WARN). This law applies to companies that have 100 or more employees when they have mass layoffs or plant closings. A *mass layoff* is a layoff or reduction in hours at a single site that affects 500 or more full-time employees or 50 or more if they constitute at least 33 percent of an active, full-time workforce. A *reduction in hours* means to cut hours worked by 50 percent or more each month for a six-month period or longer. A company must give notice to employees who will be laid off at least 60 days before their final day of work.

There are some exceptions to this law. It exempts companies with fewer than 100 employees. Companies that are covered aren't required to comply with the law when they lay off small numbers of workers. Other exemptions also apply, so check with your legal department to determine how it affects you.

Dealing With Downsizing and the EEO Laws

Until relatively recently, members of some minority groups and women weren't usually hired or promoted to certain positions because of past company policies or community practices. During the past few years, many companies have made significant strides in bringing minorities and women into the workforce.

If seniority is the policy followed during downsizing, minorities and women—who often have relatively low seniority—are often the first to have to leave. This practice can have an adverse effect on a company's affirmative action endeavors.

The Civil Rights Act of 1964 specifically exempts companies that have established a seniority system for layoffs and rehiring from being charged with discrimination if seniority is the basis for their actions. There is, however, an exception: If a member of a protected group can show that she personally experienced discrimination that resulted in lower seniority than if there had been no discrimination, that person may claim protection.

Suppose a woman was rejected for a job as a traveling auditor in 1980 because that company didn't hire women in that category and that she applied again in 1985 and was hired. If she is laid off later because of her lack of seniority, she can sue, claiming that, if not for that discriminatory policy, she would have had higher seniority. Each case is decided on its own merits.

> **Tactical Tools**
>
> When an employee leaves, reexamine the job description and specifications. A person performing a job often molds it to conform to his special interests or talents. You may not have the same view of the job, however, and this is your chance to readjust the job description.

Providing Continuing Benefits

Under the federal law known as COBRA (Consolidated Omnibus Budget Reconciliation Act), employees of companies with 20 or more employees are entitled to maintain their health insurance coverage for 18 months after they leave a company (disabled people can maintain it for 29 months). The company isn't expected to pay their premiums, however. Former employees who enroll in COBRA must pay the full premium at the same rate the company had been paying (usually considerably less than if they had to purchase individual insurance) plus a small administrative charge. COBRA also provides for continuing health insurance coverage for survivors of employees who die.

Processing Out Laid-Off Employees

The human resources department usually handles the administrative details of the separation processing. In smaller companies or at branch facilities that have no HR department, a supervisor or team leader usually handles the process.

Inform the people who are to be laid off at an appropriate time. If your company is covered by WARN, you must provide written notice 60 days in advance. If it's not covered by WARN, there's no required time, but it's only fair to give adequate notice about when they will be laid off. For temporary layoffs, two weeks is typical; for permanent layoffs, 30 days.

Helping the Laid-Off Worker Adjust

The loss of a job can be traumatic for many people. In particular, employees who have been with the company for many years may have no idea about how to go about seeking another job. Even when severance pay is given, employees are usually very concerned about personal finances and finding new employment.

To alleviate this to some degree, many companies have instituted *outplacement* programs to assist laid-off associates cope. Here are some of the areas in which help may be offered:

- At a minimum, provide use of company facilities to photocopy resumés, make phone calls, and use computers for a limited period of time.

- Provide employment counseling. This may include workshops or individual counseling on how to write a resumé, how to institute a job search, improving interviewing skills, and sometimes making a career change.

Words to Work By

Outplacement: Services provided to laid-off personnel to assist them in locating a new job and adjust to the period of transition between jobs.

- Take active steps to help find them new jobs. For example, contact companies that employ people with the skills your laid-off associates have; let the companies know that these people are available.

- Provide financial counseling.

- Provide psychological counseling.

Guidelines for Separation

At the time of the separation, follow these guidelines. Using a checklist will ensure that everything is covered:

- ❏ Discuss the continuation of benefits under COBRA, as mentioned earlier in this chapter.

- ❏ Discuss severance pay. No law requires severance pay, but some union contracts mandate it. Many companies voluntarily give severance pay to laid-off workers. The amount varies from company to company and often within a company by job category. Check your company policy.

❏ If appropriate, discuss the callback procedure.

❏ If an employee isn't receiving a final paycheck at the same time he is leaving the company, specify when it's expected.

❏ If provisions have been made to help laid-off employees seek other jobs, refer the person to whomever is responsible for that function.

❏ Retrieve company property: keys, credit cards, ID cards, tools, company computers used at home, computer log-on IDs, or computer passwords, for example.

❏ Change passwords that provide access to sensitive information.

❏ If an employee has incurred expenses for the company, such as travel and entertainment expenses that haven't yet been reimbursed, arrange for prompt attention to this matter.

❏ Answer any questions the employee has.

❏ Arrange for the employee to clean out her desk, office, or locker.

❏ Arrange for forwarding of any mail and messages that are received at the company after the employee leaves.

❏ Express your good wishes.

When Laid-Off or Terminated Employees Have Access to Sensitive Information

Most employees, although not happy about being laid off, will accept it and seek and find another job. However, there have been situations in which the employee was resentful and took actions that were, minimally, annoying or disruptive and in some cases caused serious problems. For instance, disgruntled laid-off workers have sabotaged computers or equipment, deleted key information from computer files, or downloaded data that could be of value to a competitor.

Quite often, a supervisor or team leader can identify unstable workers from their past behavior and can take steps to prevent such problems by removing the worker from access to sensitive areas before notifying him or her of the layoff. Some companies require that a security guard or a supervisor stay with the employee when they clear out their desks to ensure that only personal belongings are removed.

In any case, to minimize risk, change all passwords whenever a person who works with sensitive data voluntarily or involuntarily leaves the organization.

The Least You Need to Know

- When a team member resigns, ease the transition by getting a status report about what she has been working on. Reassign that work until a successor is in place.

- Try to find alternatives to layoffs, such as work sharing, shorter hours, or general pay cuts.

- Keep in touch with temporarily laid-off team members to ensure the likelihood that they'll return when needed.

- If your company is covered by the WARN law, it must give 60 days' notice when it closes a facility or lays off a large number of employees.

- COBRA mandates that laid-off employees be allowed to continue their medical insurance coverage for a specified period if they pay their own premiums.

Words to Work By: A Glossary

affirmative action　A written plan to commit to hiring women and minorities in proportion to their representation in the community where the firm is located. Required of companies that have government contracts in excess of $50,000 and more than 50 employees.

Age Discrimination in Employment Act (ADEA)　As amended, prohibits discrimination against individuals 40 years of age or older. Some state laws cover all persons over the age of 18.

Americans with Disabilities Act (ADA)　Prohibits discrimination against people who are physically or mentally challenged.

aptitude test　A test designed to determine the potential of candidates in specific areas, such as mechanical ability, clerical skills, or sales potential. The tests are helpful for screening inexperienced people to determine whether they have an aptitude for the type of work in which a company plans to train them. Most aptitude tests can be administered and scored by following a simple instruction sheet.

arbitration　A process in which two parties present their sides of a problem and an arbitrator decides how the problem should be resolved. *See also* mediation.

behavioral science   The study of how and why people behave the way they do.

benchmarking   A process of seeking organizations that have achieved success in an area and learning about their techniques and methods.

body language   A method people use to communicate—not only by what they say but also by their gestures, facial expressions, and movements.

bona fide occupational qualifications (BFOQ)   Positions for which a company is permitted to specify only a man or only a woman for a job. There must be clear-cut reasons, however, for why a person of only that gender can perform the job.

brainstorming   A technique for generating ideas in which participants are encouraged to voice any idea, no matter how "dumb" or useless it may be. By allowing participants to think freely and express ideas without fear of criticism, they can stretch their minds and make suggestions that may seem worthless but that may trigger an idea that has value in the mind of another participant.

buzzword   A bit of jargon—a phrase or term—that gains widespread, yet temporary, popularity.

case study   A description of a real or simulated situation presented to trainees for analysis, discussion, and solution; used in graduate schools, seminars, and training programs to enable trainees to work on the types of problems they're most likely to meet on the job. Case studies are often drawn from the experiences of real companies.

channel of communication   The path information takes through the organization. If you want to give information to (or get it from) a person in another department, you first go to your boss, who goes to the supervisor of the other department, who, in turn, goes to the person with the information, who gets it and conveys it back through the same channels. By the time you get the information, it may have been distorted by a variety of interpretations.

charisma   The special charm some people have that secures for them the support and allegiance of other people.

Civil Rights Act of 1964   Title VII, as amended, prohibits discrimination in employment on the basis of race, color, sex, religion, and national origin.

coasters   Long-term employees (not likely to be fired because of their tenure) who have gone as far as they can and "coast along" until their retirement.

COBRA   An acronym for the Consolidated Omnibus Budget Reconciliation Act, in which employees of companies with 20 or more employees are entitled to maintain their health insurance coverage for 18 months after they leave the company (29 months for people who are disabled at the time they leave). The company isn't expected to pay their premiums. Former employees must pay the full premium at the same rate the company had been paying (usually considerably less than if they had to purchase individual insurance) plus a small administrative charge.

collaborative performance evaluations   *See* joint supervisor/associate evaluations.

communication   The process by which information, ideas, and concepts are transmitted between persons and groups.

constructive discharge   When an employee quits because of purposeful unfair treatment on the job, it is "constructed" by the courts to be an involuntary termination.

control point   A point in a project at which you stop, examine what has been completed, and correct any errors that have been made (before they blow up into catastrophes).

counseling   A means of helping troubled associates overcome barriers to good performance. With careful listening, open discussion, and sound advice, a counselor helps identify problems, clarify misunderstandings, and plan solutions.

cross training   A method of training team members to perform the jobs of other people on the team so that every member is capable of doing all aspects of the team's work.

decentralization   When the focus of a business is shifted from one central facility where all decisions are made and most of the work is done to localized facilities where, within guidelines, decisions are made and work is performed autonomously.

delegation   A process that enables you to position the right work at the right responsibility level, helping both you and the team members you delegate to expand your skills and contributions, while ensuring that all work gets done in a timely manner by the right person with the right experience or interest in the right topic.

documentation   A written description of all disciplinary actions taken by a company to protect it in case of legal actions. ("If it ain't written down, it ain't never happened.")

downsize   To lay off employees, primarily when business is slow, so that a company can reduce costs. Downsizing differs from traditional layoffs in that total job categories are eliminated—people who held these jobs have little chance of being rehired. *See also* layoff.

employee assistance program (EAP)   A company-sponsored counseling service. Many companies have instituted these types of programs to help their employees deal with personal problems that interfere with productivity. The counselors aren't company employees; they're outside experts who are retained on an as-needed basis.

employee stock ownership program (ESOP)   A program in which a major portion of a company's stock is given or sold to employees so that they actually own the company.

employment at will   A legal concept under which an employee is hired and can be fired at the will of the employer. Unless restricted by law or contract, the employer has the right to refuse to hire an applicant or to terminate an employee for any reason or for no reason at all.

empowerment   Sharing your managerial power with the people over whom you have that power.

Equal Pay Act of 1963   An act which requires that the gender of an employee not be considered in determining salary (equal pay for equal work).

exit interview   *See* separation interview.

goals/objectives   Interchangeable terms to describe an organization's or individual's desired long-run results.

going rate   An amount paid to employees to keep them from leaving a company.

grievance   A formal complaint, usually based on the violation of a union contract or formal company policy.

gripe   An informal complaint about working conditions or other aspects of an employee/company relationship.

halo effect   The assumption that, because of one outstanding characteristic, all of an applicant's characteristics are outstanding (that person then "wears a halo"). The opposite is the *pitchfork effect,* or the symbol of the devil: You assume that, because one trait is so poor, the person is entirely bad.

hot button   The one thing in a person's makeup that really gets him excited—positively or negatively. (To really reach someone, find that person's hot button.)

"I" meeting   An idea-generating meeting at which each participant presents at least one idea for solving the problem being considered.

intelligence test   Like the IQ test administered in schools, this test measures the ability to learn. It varies from brief, simple exercises that can be administered by people with little training to highly sophisticated tests that must be administered by a person with a Ph.D. in psychology.

job analysis   The process of determining the duties, functions, and responsibilities of a job (the *job description)* and the requirements for the successful performance of a job (the *job specifications*).

job bank   A computerized list of the capabilities of all employees in an organization.

job description   A listing of the duties, responsibilities, and results a job requires.

job enrichment   Redesigning jobs to provide diversity, challenge, and commitment (and to alleviate boredom).

job-instruction training (JIT)   A systematic approach to training that has four steps: preparation, presentation, performance, and follow-up.

job posting   A listing on company bulletin boards of the specifications for an available position. Any employee who is interested can apply. After preliminary screening by the human resources department, employees who meet the basic requirements are interviewed.

job specifications   The requirements an applicant should possess to successfully perform a job.

joint supervisor/associate evaluations   Using the same evaluation format, associates evaluate their own performance. The supervisor or leader also evaluates the performance. The final report results from a collaborative discussion between leader and associate.

just-in-time delivery   Rather than store large inventories of supplies, companies today arrange with suppliers to deliver supplies as needed. The project manager or team leader must interface with the suppliers to schedule and ensure that supplies are delivered at the exact time they're needed.

KITA   A *kick in the* you-know-what.

KRA (key results area)   An aspect of a job in which employees must concentrate time and attention to ensure that they achieve the goals for that job.

lateral thinking   Looking at a problem from different angles that may give new insights into its solutions (instead of approaching it by logical thinking).

layoff   Termination of employees permanently or for a specific period of time due to lack of work or restructuring of an organization.

leadership   The art of guiding people in a manner that commands their respect, confidence, and wholehearted cooperation.

lookism   Overemphasizing appearance in making decisions about a person.

M.O. (method, or mode, of operation)   The patterns of behavior a person habitually follows in performing work.

management   The process of achieving specific results by effectively using an organization's available resources (money, materials, equipment, information, and employees).

mediation   A process in which two parties present their sides and a mediator works with them to reach a mutually satisfactory solution. *See also* arbitration.

mentor   A team member assigned to act as counselor, trainer, and "big brother" or "big sister" to a new member.

motivators   Factors that stimulate a person to expend more energy, effort, and enthusiasm in a job. *See also* satisfiers.

negative personality   A person's outlook in which any suggestion is taken as a personal affront, any new assignment is accepted with reluctance, and relations with coworkers and leaders are usually considered confrontational.

network   To make contacts with managers in other companies to whom you can turn for suggestions and ideas.

objective   *See* goals/objectives.

on-boarding   A systematized approach to orienting a new employee to the company, the department or team, and the job.

opportunity   The combination of being in the right place at the right time and having the ability and desire to take advantage of it.

outplacement   Services provided to laid-off personnel to assist them in locating a new job and adjusting to the period of transition between jobs.

outsourcing   Contracting to outside sources any work that previously had been done in-house. As companies become "leaner and meaner," they outsource activities that can be done more effectively by outside specialists. Some examples are payroll, traffic, training, computer programming, advertising, and certain manufacturing activities.

ownership   A feeling that you're a full partner in the development and implementation of a project, committed to its successful achievement.

performance standards   The results expected from persons performing a job. For performance standards to be meaningful, every person doing that job should know and accept these standards.

performance test   A test that measures how well candidates can do the job for which they apply (for example, operating a lathe, entering data into a computer, writing advertising copy, or proofreading manuscripts). When job performance cannot be tested directly, a company may use written or oral tests about job knowledge.

personality test   A test designed to identify personality characteristics that varies from *Readers Digest*-type quickie questionnaires to highly sophisticated psychological evaluations.

piece work   A system of compensation in which earnings are based solely on the number of units produced.

pitchfork effect   *See* halo effect.

platinum rule   "Do unto others as they would have you do unto them."

prioritize   To rank tasks, by determining their degree of importance, to accomplish your goals on the job or in your life and in taking action accordingly—putting first things first.

profession   An occupation requiring special training or advanced study in a specialized field. Physicians, lawyers, psychologists, and engineers all have to take advanced education and pass examinations to qualify for certification in their professions.

progressive discipline   A systematic approach to correcting infractions of rules. A typical program has six steps, the first of which is an informal warning. If this step isn't successful, it's followed by (as necessary) a disciplinary interview, a written warning, probation, suspension, and, possibly, termination.

project manager   A team leader assigned to head up a specific project, such as the design and manufacture of an electronic system or the development and marketing of a new product.

quality circles   Groups of workers who voluntarily meet on a regular basis to discuss ideas about improving the quality of a product or service they produce.

real time   What's going on here and now. The actual time in which a process occurs (for example, a computer can report real-time data or information about the status of a situation as of the time it's provided).

recruit   To seek candidates to be considered for employment, usually done by personnel or human resources departments.

reengineer   To radically restructure the design of business processes (not just tinker with methods and procedures). When companies reengineer their processes, its managers must rethink everything they're doing in order to take advantage of the changes that will be made.

religious practices   Practices that include, according to the EEOC, not only traditional religious beliefs but also moral and ethical beliefs and any beliefs an individual holds "with the strength of a traditional religious view."

results-oriented evaluation system   A system in which performance expectations are agreed on at the beginning of a period and measured at the end of that period. At that time, new goals are developed, which are to be measured at the end of the next period.

role playing   A variation of case studies in which participants act out the parts of the characters involved. Used chiefly in studying problems in which interaction between characters is a major aspect.

satisfiers   Also called maintenance factors; the factors—including working conditions, money, and benefits—employees must get from a job in order to expend even minimum effort in performing their work. After employees are satisfied with these factors, however, just giving them more of the same factor doesn't motivate them to work harder. *See* motivators.

selection   A process of screening applicants to determine their suitability for a position. Preliminary screening is usually done by the human resources department; subsequent screening is done by supervisors or team leaders.

self-esteem   The way you feel about yourself. If you think of yourself as a success, you will be a success; if you think of yourself as second-rate, you will always be second-rate—unless you change your self-perception. And it *can* be done.

separation interview   Also called *exit interview*, it is designed to probe for the real reasons people leave jobs and to obtain from them information about the job or the company that may cause discontent.

sexual harassment   Any unwelcome sexual advances or requests for sexual favors, or any conduct of a sexual nature when an employer makes submission to sexual advances a term or condition of employment, either initially or later on; or when submission or rejection is used as a basis of working conditions, including promotion, salary adjustment, assignment of work, and termination, or has the effect of interfering with an individual's work or creating a hostile or intimidating work environment.

single use plan   A plan developed for a specific nonrecurring situation; for example, introducing a new product, moving to a new location, or opening a new facility.

SOP (standard operating procedure)   A set of standard practices in which company plans and policies are detailed (sometimes called "the company bible").

spontaneous termination   A situation in which an employee is discharged without progressive discipline, usually precipitated by an egregious violation of company rules such as fighting, drunkenness, or gross insubordination. *See* progressive discipline.

stress or **distress**   A chronic state of anxiety caused by unremitting pressures of job, personal, or societal problems.

synergy   Two or more people or units working together so that the contributions of each enhances the results by more than the individual contribution by itself. "The whole is greater than the sum of its parts," or 2 + 2 may equal more than 4.

team   A group of people who collaborate and interact synergistically in working toward a common goal.

telecommuting   Technology that enables a person to perform work at home or at a location remote from a central office by receiving assignments and submitting completed work via computer.

training manuals   Handbooks for teaching routine tasks; they make the training process easy for both trainer and trainees and can always be referred to when an employee is in doubt about what to do.

trait system of performance evaluation   A system in which employees are rated on a series of traits, such as quantity and quality of work, attendance, and initiative. Ratings are usually measured on a scale from poor to superior.

upward communication   The flow of ideas, suggestions, and comments from people in lower echelons of the organization to those in decision-making positions.

work sharing   An alternative to layoffs in which all team members share the work that remains after some jobs are eliminated. The standard work week is reduced by working fewer hours each day or fewer days each week. Another alternative is working full weeks, but fewer weeks each month. The hourly pay remains the same, but because of reduced hours, the payroll is decreased.

WARN (Worker Adjustment and Retraining Notification Act)   A law that applies to companies that have 100 or more employees when a mass layoff or plant closing occurs. Notice must be given to those employees at least 60 days before their final day of work. There are some exceptions to this rule, so check with your legal department to determine how it affects you.

Pertinent Publications and Professional Associations

The field of management is dynamic. Companies experiment with new approaches. New laws and new interpretations of old laws are promulgated by state and federal government agencies. The ups and downs of the economy change the ways organizations deal with their employees.

Managers, team leaders, and others who deal with people must keep up with what is going on. The best way to be on the cutting edge of change is to read regularly several of the magazines that cover these matters and to belong to a professional association that deals with management matters.

Publications Dealing with Managing People

Nearly every industry and profession has periodicals devoted to its field— and most of these magazines have occasional articles on management techniques and interpersonal relations. Such periodicals are excellent sources of information.

Here is a list of some of the better publications that either specialize in the art of management or have significant coverage of it.

Across the Board
The Conference Board
845 Third Avenue
New York, NY 10022
Phone: 212-339-0345
Website: www.conference-board.org

Business Week
1221 Avenue of the Americas
New York, NY 10020
Phone: 1-800-635-1200
Website: www.businessweek.com

Forbes
60 Fifth Avenue
New York, NY 10011
Phone: 212-620-2200
Website: www.forbes.com

Fortune
Time & Life Building
Rockefeller Center
New York, NY 10020
Phone: 1-800-621-8000
Website: www.fortune.com

Harvard Business Review
60 Harvard Way
Boston, MA 02163
Phone: 1-800-274-3214
Website: www.hbsp.harvard.edu

HR Magazine
Society for Human Resources Management
1800 Duke Street
Alexandria, VA 22314
Phone: 1-800-283-SHRM
Website: www.shrm.org

Management Review
American Management Association
Box 319
Saranac Lake, NY 12983
Phone: 1-800-262-9699
Website: www.amanet.org

Training
50 S. 9th Street
Minneapolis, MN 55402
Phone: 1-800-328-4329
Website: www.trainingsupersite.com

Training and Development
American Society for Training
and Development
1640 King Street
Alexandria, VA 22314
Phone: 703-683-8100
Website: www.astd.org

Workforce
245 Fischer Avenue
Costa Mesa, CA 92626
Phone: 714-751-1883
Website: www.workforce.com

Associations Dealing with Human Resources Matters

Professional societies in your industry are excellent sources of information. Membership in one or more of these groups can give you access to the latest developments in your field, experiences of other members in dealing with problems similar to yours, opportunities at meetings and conventions to meet your peers in other organizations, and often, resource material from other companies' libraries or archives.

Here is a list of associations that may be of value to you.

American Management Association (AMA)
1601 Broadway
New York, NY 10019
Phone: 1-800-262-9699
Website: www.amanet.org

Membership is by company. Provides seminars, publications, and library facilities on all aspects of management.

American Society for Training & Development (ASTD)
1640 King Street
Alexandria, VA 22313
Phone: 703-683-8100
Website: www.astd.org

Dedicated to professionalism in training and development of personnel. Local chapters throughout United States. Annual national convention. Publications include magazine, special reports, and books.

American Staffing Association (ASA)
277 South Washington Street
Alexandria, VA 22314
Phone: 703-253-2020
Website: www.staffingtoday

Provides information on temporary employment services.

Employee Assistance Society of North America (EASNA)
230 Ohio Street
Chicago, IL 60611
Phone: 312-644-0828
Website: www.easna.org

Source to locate individuals and organizations that provide various types of employee assistance programs.

International Foundation of Employee Benefit Plans (IFEBP)
18700 West Bluemound Road
Bloomfield, WI 53008
Phone: 414-786-6700
Website: www.ifebp.org

Excellent source of information on employee benefits. Accredits benefits specialists.

National Association of Personnel Services (NAPS)
10905 Fort Washington Road
Fort Washington, MD 20744
Phone: 301-203-6700

Source of information about private employment agencies.

Society for Advancement of Management (SAM)
630 Ocean Drive
Corpus Christi, TX 78412
Phone: 1-888-827-8077
Website: www.cob.tamucc.edu/sam

Provides publications and conferences on various aspects of management.

Society for Human Resources Management (SHRM)
1800 Duke Street
Alexandria, VA 22314
Phone: 703-548-3440
Website: www.shrm.org

Members are human resource specialists in all types of companies and organizations. Provides publications, special reports, and books. Local chapters throughout the United States conduct monthly meetings. National convention annually.

Index

N

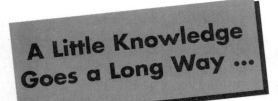
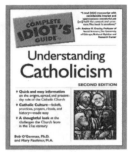

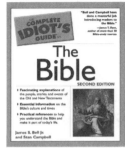

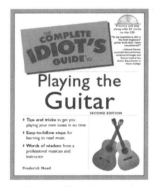